The Frontiers of
Sex Research

Edited by
Vern L. Bullough

PB *Prometheus Books*
Buffalo, New York 14215

Published by Prometheus Books
1203 Kensington Avenue, Buffalo, New York 14215

Library of Congress Catalog Card Number 79-2462
ISBN 0-87975-110-X

Printed in the United States of America

This book owes its origin to Paul Kurtz, who as editor of *The Humanist* encouraged me to edit a special issue on human sexuality. The book could not have been completed, however, without the yeoman service of Victor Gulotta, who saw it through the press, edited the copy, and did all the things necessary to bring about publication. I would also like to thank my colleagues at the Center for Sex Research, California State University, Northridge, for their assistance.

Contents

Introduction

The discussion of sex has come out of the closet, and in the process it has become a media event. Television, radio, movies, newspapers, and magazines seemingly trumpet the existence of sex at every opportunity. The nonorgasmic woman receives advice from Dear Abby while the impotent male gets help from a plethora of books on the newsstand at the corner supermarket. Candidates campaign for or against homosexuality or for or against abortion. Contraceptives once sold under the counter, if sold at all, are openly displayed. Clergymen who still oppose the use of contraceptives find their congregations ignoring them on this issue. Male go–go dancers have proved an attraction for women only audiences in the Bible and Burlesque Belt of the Midwest, which just a few years ago believed that only "bad" women had sexual curiosity. Movies often include a pro forma sexual scene even when it has no correlation to the story line, while television, not quite so open, has found that hints of sexual activity raise their ratings.

All this emphasis on sex has been labeled the Sex Revolution by the very media that are trying to exploit it. How much of the alleged changes in sexuality constitute a genuine revolution and how much is due to the media's discovery that sex sells? In reality, what has taken place is not so much a *sex* revolution as a *contraceptive* one. The chief effect of this has been to give women the same kind of freedom to engage in sexual activities that men traditionally have had. In the process women have become freer to look at their own sexuality and to demand more from their partners. Even if there is a contraceptive failure, the woman has the fallback of abortion instead of carrying an unwanted child to term.

The contraceptive revolution is also tied in with the public acceptance of the dangers of overpopulation, an acceptance that has led large segments of the American population to cut down on family size. Young people are also putting off marriage to a later age, and women increasingly are seeking some sort of economic independence for themselves. Since sexual drives continue to exist and in fact exist most strongly in the young, society has become more tolerant of young people who are not married but who live together. The lack of a hymen is no longer regarded as the barrier to marriage that past generations claimed it was.

Once society accepts not only the desirability of contraceptives, but recognizes a need to limit family size, the nonprocreative aspects of human sexuality can be explored. During the past few years sex manuals telling us how to achieve a more effective orgasm have become best sellers, and a new occupational speciality, that of sex counselor or sex therapist, has appeared. Inevitably, society has also become more tolerant of those persons whose sex activities have always been nonprocreative—such as homosexuals. Some indication of the change in public attitudes is indicated by the fact that only two decades ago a woman tennis player achieved widespread notoriety for playing in a tennis match with lace trimmed panties, but by 1977 a male–to–female transexual could become a woman tennis star with less public disapproval.

Not all the changes in sexual attitudes are due to the media, nor is the growing acceptance of sex for pleasure merely the result of the contraceptive revolution or the population explosion. Equally important has been the growing understanding of the nature of sex and the inherently wide variations in sexual conduct. This last, as was the contraceptive revolution itself, is the result of increasing research in the nature of sexuality and sexual conduct. Though the roots of this research can be traced back to the nineteenth century, it has only been in the post–World War II period that sex research came to be looked upon as in any way academically respectable.

In fact, up to the end of World War II most sex research was dominated by those who followed the medical model of sexuality and looked upon variations from the norm as pathological. Though some of these medical researchers such as Richard von Krafft-Ebing helped make sex research respectable, in the long run they caused millions of people to suffer from being labeled pathological when their only deviation from the publicly stated norm was that they had masturbated as young people. More influential in changing attitudes was Havelock Ellis, who spent much of his lifetime undoing the harm that had been done by von Krafft-Ebing. Ellis' studies in the *Psychology of Sex* put many of the variations of sexuality into their historical perspective, and tended to emphasize the cultural influences in forming sex attitudes. Magnus Hirschfeld, his German contemporary, collected hundreds if not thousands of sex histories, inventing terms such as *transvestism* to describe the kind of sexual behavior he observed. He also popularized the term *homosexuality*. Both of these men operated independently of the university and the research establishment of the time. Most "respectable" institutions steered clear of sex research and would only deal with sex in a tangential way. Gregory Pincus, the man most responsible for the development of the oral contraceptive, did not hold a regular academic position for most of his career.

One of the keys to effective research has always been money, but few foundations or individuals were willing to be associated with the subject. Eventually the Rockefeller Foundation entered the field, as did individuals such as Clarence Gamble and Reed Erickson. Alfred Kinsey, for example, not only had a university affiliation, but was supported by the Rockefeller Foundation. When his studies came under attack, however, the Rockefeller Foundation decided to withdraw entirely from the sex field. If private foundations for the most part have been reluctant to support sex research, the federal government except in the field of population, has avoided the subject like the plague. Researchers seeking government grants now still have to disguise their topics under such terms as *alcoholism* and *lesbianism* or *narcotic addiction* and *prostitution,* since the government's interest is in alcoholism and drug addiction, not in advancing the frontiers of sexual knowledge.

Kinsey marks the watershed of contemporary sex research, and since his efforts, several universities have rather gingerly supported some form of sex research. John Money, whose paper is included in this book, and who is one of the leading sex researchers today, is at Johns Hopkins. Others, such as Milton Diamond, have found academic tolerance at the University of Hawaii. The State University of New York at Stony Brook has proved a gathering place for several researchers, as has the University of California at San Francisco, and California State University at Northridge. William Masters and Virginia Johnson have their center in St. Louis. Few individuals, however, receive training as sexologists, and Wardell Pomeroy, one of the coauthors of the Kinsey studies, joined with Ted McIlvenna to found the Institute for the Advanced Study of Human Sexuality in San Francisco. The Institute offers advanced degrees to those interested in achieving professional expertise in human sexuality.

The field of sexual studies is just beginning to emerge as a serious one. There is still much that is unknown. The youth of the field is indicated by the fact that almost all the significant researchers in the field are active today, although they are building on the foundations laid by Kinsey, Havelock Ellis, and Magnus Hirschfeld. Predictably, their findings will help change societal attitudes even more radically than they have over the past half century. One of the marks of a new field of expertise is the establishment of a professional society and the publication of scholarly journals. This has also begun to happen with the establishment of the Society for the Scientific Study of Sex and the *Journal of Sex Research* and the *Archives of Sexual Behavior.*

This book is an effort to have several of the authorities in this emerging field present the results of their research and observations and to try to draw some implications from these studies. Three decades after the publication of the Kinsey studies it is important to state what we know about human sexuality that we did not know before, and what the implications these findings hold for us today or in the forseeable future. Read on.

1

The Physiology of
Sexual Function

J. Robert Bragonier
Barbara J. Bragonier

The foundation for much of the ongoing
research into human sexuality derives from
research into the physiology of sexual
response. The findings in this area are
summarized by the Bragoniers. He holds both
the M.D. and Ph.D. degrees while she holds
an M.A. and is a licensed marriage, family,
and child counselor. Together they have
conducted workshops for educators and
those in the helping professions, and have
also led marriage and sexual enrichment
seminars for lay persons in a number of
religious and community settings. They have
been married for twenty years and are the
parents of three children.

The understanding of the physiology of human sexual response continues to rest heavily upon the work of William H. Masters and Virginia Johnson, published in 1966.[1] Although research into the physiology of sexual response was published as early as 1896 in the German literature,[2] research in the United States into human sexual functioning remained extremely limited until the past few decades, when the work of Kinsey[3] and Masters and Johnson appeared. Our knowledge is still limited, but an increasing number of publications on biologic aspects of human sexuality have appeared in medical and behavioral science journals over the past ten years. In fact, since 1966 more articles have been published on the biology of human sexual function than in all previous years combined.

Most of this research has tended to substantiate the findings of Masters and Johnson. Our efforts here will be devoted toward reviewing their findings, updating the conceptualization of the physiology of sexual response, and looking at some of the implications of these findings for the enjoyment of healthy and pleasurable sexual interaction.

Normal sexual function is primarily dependent upon an intact nervous system. The *primary* and *secondary* physiologic changes associated with sexual response, that is, *vasocongestion,* or dilatation and filling of blood vessels, and *myotonia,* or increase in muscle tone, are both under primary control of the central nervous system and peripheral nerves.

According to Masters and Johnson, human sexual response can be divided into four separate phases: (1) the excitement phase; (2) the plateau phase; (3) the orgasmic phase; and (4) the resolution phase.

The *excitement phase* in both men and women may occur as a result of physical stimulation or erotic psychological cues. Changes that occur are not limited to the genital area but affect the functioning of the entire body to some degree. Women may notice an increase in breast size, nipple erection, and swelling and darkening of the nipples and surrounding pigmented areolae; men may also notice nipple erection. Approximately 75 percent of females develop a sex flush on their cheeks, neck, stomach, and breasts, while only approximately 25 percent of males demonstrate this change. (This difference may well be related to the increased permission women in our culture receive to be emotionally demonstrative, rather than to a physiologic difference between the sexes, but this has not been proven.) Both men and women experience an increase in muscular tension throughout their bodies which increases as sexual tension increases. Heart rate and blood pressure may also increase with rising tension.

Genital reactions in women include enlargement of the clitoris, both in diameter and length, and expansion of the vaginal wall. A moistening of the vaginal membrane occurs, and the vagina takes on a darker hue due to dilatation of the underlying blood vessels. The blood supply increases to the inner lips and they thicken, deepening the vagina by approximately one centimeter. Muscle tension causes flattening and separation of the outer lips, together with elevation of the uterus and "tenting" of the vagina.

Genital reactions in men include rapid erection of the penis, tensing and thickening of the skin of the scrotum, and flattening and elevation of the scrotal sac. Partial elevation of the testes may occur, due to shortening of the muscles which suspend the testes in the scrotum.

During the *plateau phase,* turgidity of the nipples may be marked in both men and women, and women may demonstrate a further increase in breast size with more areolar engorgement. The sex flush may become more widespread throughout the body. Muscle tension, blood pressure, heart rate, and respiratory rate may all increase with rising tension. In women, the clitoris retracts beneath its hood and pulls up against the pubic bone. The vagina increases in width and depth, and engorgement of its outer third forms an orgasmic platform. Full uterine elevation increases the tenting effect within the vagina, and further swelling of the major and minor lips occur, the latter becoming deep wine in color. The Bartholin's glands may secrete a drop or two of mucoid material, which aids in lubrication.

In men, the penis completes its erection and may become darker in color. The testes increase in size due to engorgement and continue to elevate toward the perineum. The Cowper's gland in men, like the Bartholin's gland in women, may secrete several drops of mucoid fluid at this time, which moisten the head of the penis.

During the *orgasmic phase*, the sexual flush achieves its maximum intensity. Heart rate, blood pressure, and respiratory rate characteristically reach their maximum elevations. Both men and women lose control of their muscles and experience involuntary contractions of muscle groups throughout their body, including those of the arms, legs, back, the floor of the pelvis, and the anal sphincter. In women, uterine contractions occur, and the vagina begins to contract in the area of the orgasmic platform at 0.8 second intervals. In men, expulsive contractions occur along the entire length of the penis, also at 0.8 second intervals, although generally fewer in number than those experienced by women.

The *resolution phase* is characterized by the dissipation of changes throughout the body, as organs return to their normal unexcited state. Vascular congestion fades earliest and most quickly, while muscle tension fades more slowly over a period of five to ten minutes. Masters and Johnson reported that women may go on to further orgasms without resolution, while men experience a refractory period during which orgasmic response to further stimulation will not occur.

As we can see, a number of differences exist between men and women as they respond to erotic stimuli, but the similarities far outweigh the differences. Other investigators have noted that even Masters and Johnson may not have fully appreciated the degree to which sexual response in the male and female is similar. For example, Kinsey reported nearly thirty years ago that at age twenty-five, 10 percent of males were capable of multiple orgasms. It may be that the refractory period reported by Masters and Johnson simply signifies that ejaculation cannot recur until fluid within the prostate gland and seminal vesicles is reelaborated. In other words, some males may experience multiple orgasms when they accept continued stimulation, although semen may not be ejaculated with the subsequent orgasms. Since only a minority of women regularly experience multiple orgasms, the significance of the refractory period as a major difference between men and women may have diminished since it was first reported.

Masters and Johnson reported more variation in intensity and duration of orgasmic response in women than in men. It seems likely, however, that this difference may also be due to the different patterns of learning that men receive. Men in our culture are allowed less latitude in expression of emotions ("Big boys don't cry"), and this may to some degree inhibit their recognition and expression of emotionality. It seems increasingly apparent that both men and women are capable of experiencing a wide range of intensity in orgasmic experience from episode to episode and from individual to individual.

Dr. Helen Singer Kaplan of Cornell University has found it useful to conceptualize sexual response as *biphasic* in nature.[4] Her writings draw further parallels between male and female sexual response. In her formulation, the sexual response cycle does not occur as a single entity with four stepwise parts. Rather, it consists of two separate components: the first is a genital vasocongestive reaction producing erection of the penis in men and vaginal lubrication and swelling in women; the second is a more generalized muscular reaction characterized by contractions occurring during orgasm in both men and women.

This formulation is based upon the fact that erection and lubrication are due to a preponderance of activity within the parasympathetic division of the autonomic nervous system, while ejaculation and orgasm are primarily functions of the sympathetic division. Thus, disturbances in the function of these two portions of the autonomic nervous system will be manifested by very different sexual dysfunctions, and this is exactly what occurs. Problems relating to achieving or maintaining an erection or vaginal lubrication and engorgement are different in a number of ways from those relating to orgasmic dysfunction, such as lack of orgasm in women, or retarded ejaculation and premature ejaculation in men.

Recognition of the biphasic nature of sexual response explains why in some instances a stepwise progression from excitement phase to resolution phase does not occur. It is well known, for example, that ejaculation in men may occur in the absence of erection. Likewise, some medicines interfere with one phase, while leaving the other unaffected. The animal studies of MacLean have demonstrated that stimulation of a portion of the brain near but not identical to those areas of the brain that cause erection will cause primates to ejaculate even without an erection.[5]

The writings of Dr. Kaplan have also helped us to understand the nature of female orgasm. Much controversy has centered on the distinction between clitoral and vaginal orgasms. Despite the finding of Masters and Johnson that orgasms in women are physiologically the same, regardless of whether they are precipitated by fantasy, breast manipulation, direct clitoral stimulation, or coitus, the Freudian notion that normal women experience "mature" orgasms through vaginal stimulation alone has continued to cause confusion, guilt, and despair in many women. Actually, the recently published Hite report confirms that no more than one-fourth of the women who answered the study questionnaire were capable of responding orgasmically to vaginal stimulation alone.[6] Three-quarters of the women respondents reported that some degree of direct clitoral stimulation was necessary for orgasmic response, and Dr. Kaplan has provided an explanation for this finding.

Anatomically, the clitoris is richly supplied with sensory nerve endings, and its stimulation is experienced as highly pleasurable by most women. On the other hand, the vagina has very few sensory nerve endings, especially in its deeper reaches. If one looks at orgasmic response as a reflex, and if one recognizes that a reflex requires a loop, or arc, with both incoming (sensory) and outgoing (motor) components, it is easy to understand how stimulation of the clitoris activates the sensory limb of a woman's orgasmic reflex arc, just as stimulation of the cornea, or surface, of the eye provides the sensory component of the blink reflex. When the cornea of the eye is irritated, by a gnat, for instance, a person reflexively blinks, with the muscles of the lid providing the motor component of the blink reflex arc. Similarly, muscles of the pelvic floor provide the motor limb of the orgasmic reflex arc, and it is easy to understand how the contraction of these muscles would be experienced within the vagina, since the muscles encircle the vagina and contract upon it. If a penis were occupying the vagina, both partners might be aware of the vaginal contractions. It is thus as absurd to talk about a "vaginal" or "clitoral" orgasm as it is to talk about a "corneal" or "lid" reflex. Both sensory and motor components are necessary to comprise a blink reflex, and both sensory and motor components are just as necessary to complete the orgasmic reflex. Subsequent studies designed to explore the role of hormones in sexual response have tended to support Dr. Kaplan's emphasis on autonomic nervous system function as essential and primary. While sex hormones appear to be important in preparing men and women both physically and psychologically to respond to erotic stimuli, pituitary, adrenal, ovarian, and testicular hormones do not appear to mediate sexual response, nor is it clear that they change predictably in response to sexual stimulation and orgasm. (So far, data regarding levels of adrenal and testicular hormones following ejaculation in men have proven contradictory.)[7]

What then are some of the implications of this physiological research? In our culture the level of misunderstanding of sexual physiology is such that most people are unaware of what changes take place during sexual arousal, when those changes take place, or what meaning they might have. For example, a man who loses a portion of his erection during the plateau phase may become anxious, not realizing that this occurrence commonly accompanies a decrease in stimulation during the plateau phase. His anxiety may then further decrease his ability to reachieve or maintain an erection (since erection is not under voluntary control, and anxiety overrides the involuntary control of his parasympathetic nervous system), and he becomes caught in a "vicious circle." Widespread confusion exists about such specifics as facial grimaces and back arching during orgasm, Cowper's gland secretions on the penis, vaginal lubrication and expansion, retraction of the clitoris beneath its hood, and so forth. A better understanding of sexual physiology can help to dispel this confusion. However, a number of points should be kept in mind:

First, not every sexually responsive person experiences every response that has ever been reported. (For example, a person may be regularly orgasmic and not experience a sex flush or nipple erection.) A whole new series of secondary sexual dysfunctions have arisen on the basis of performance pressures engendered by new sexual knowledge. Women who are regularly sexually responsive may seek help because their partners are concerned that they are not multiorgasmic. At a time when most sex therapists and counselors are emphasizing the communicational and relational aspects of sexual inter-action, this misplaced emphasis on performance is discouraging and pathetic.

Second, a person may experience different responses in different sexual settings. The capacity to experience and appreciate sexual arousal is not only individual, but variable, and the only true authority regarding a person's sexual satisfaction in any given episode is that individual, for himself or herself.

Third, sexual response occurs in essentially the same manner regard-less of whether the person is asleep or awake, or whether the source of stimulation is fantasy, the opposite sex, the same sex, or the self, that is, heterosexual, homosexual, or autosexual (masturbation). The major differ-ence may be that self-stimulation often leads to physiologic responses that are more intense.

Fourth, response patterns develop early in childhood and potentially remain throughout life. Orgasms were reported by Kinsey in infants four and five months of age, while Masters and Johnson studied sexually responsive persons as old as eighty-nine years. Although responses may slow down somewhat, men and women are physiologically capable, in the presence of reasonable general health, of responding sexually for as long as they live.

Bearing these points in mind, our knowledge of sexual physiology can help bring new insights into sexual interaction.[8]

1. Erection is an early response. Its presence does not necessarily indi-cate the need for intercourse, nor is it a signal for a man to "slow down" or for a woman to "catch up."

2. Erection need not necessarily lead to ejaculation. Erection occurs regularly in sleep and also comes and goes during waking hours. No ill effect comes to a man who experiences erections without subsequent ejaculation. While testicular aching can occur as a result of vascular congestion not relieved by ejaculation, it also occurs *after* ejaculation and appears to be more a function of the duration of stimulation, degree of arousal, and extent of vascular congestion than of presence or absence of ejaculation.

3. Many factors influence the physiologic sexual response, and men as well as women will, in some circumstances, be disinterested in sex. In other words, the "ever ready" syndrome, which states that men are always ready for sexual intercourse, is a myth.

4. During the excitement phase of sexual response, vaginal lubrication may remain entirely inside, and the vaginal opening may remain dry. In light of this, both partners may come to the erroneous conclusion that the woman is not aroused.

5. Sexual responses may vary from moment to moment within the same response cycle. Therefore, it is impossible for a partner to know how to

pleasure a person most effectively, unless that person communicates that information (usually nonverbally) on a moment to moment basis. This is especially true with regard to clitoral stimulation, since late in the plateau phase, the tip, or glans, of the clitoris may become exquisitely sensitive, and even painful, if directly stimulated.

6. Orgasm and ejaculation, although enjoyable, need not be the goal or end point of each sexual encounter. Exchange of pleasurable sexual feelings can be important in and of themselves, and excessive concentration on orgasmic release may diminish total pleasure. Likewise, mutual satisfaction and pleasurable exchange can occur even after ejaculation and orgasm. The presence or absence of orgasm, or the intensity of orgasm, do not necessarily correlate well with the level of sexual satisfaction.

7. Each person is responsible for his or her own sexual pleasure, and a person's stated satisfaction is more important in determining the quality of sexual interaction than is the number of orgasms obtained. The corollary of this statement is that the male partner need not shoulder entire responsibility for the "success" or "failure" of a sexual episode. Just because he "loves her" doesn't guarantee that he will know how to pleasure her, especially if she doesn't know, or keeps the information to herself.

8. Simultaneous orgasms by both partners are usually a matter of luck. On the negative side, they may deprive each partner of fully experiencing the other's orgasm. Since orgasm is one of the most intense and private of experiences, it is difficult to be fully "tuned into" a partner when one is experiencing an orgasm. On the positive side, simultaneous orgasms can certainly be enjoyable, but their attainment need not be the measure of a satisfactory sexual encounter.

9. Direct clitoral stimulation, if pleasurable for the female partner, may be continued before, during, and after penetration. There is nothing magic about a "Look, Mom, no hands!" orgasm that automatically makes it better, more appropriate, more proper, or more "mature."

10. After a period of abstinence, many men will ejaculate rapidly. After a brief pause, however, sexual stimulation can resume, be pleasurable, and lead to further sexual enjoyment. The fullness of erection will often recur, although a second orgasm may not. To avoid sexual interaction or pleasuring of the penis because of rapid ejaculation simply makes matters worse for most men.

11. Finally, every human being falls short of his or her expectations at some time or another, and an occasional difficulty with erection, lubrication, or orgasm does not constitute "impotence" or "frigidity." Most authorities today believe that these are poor terms, and that persons are not helped by wearing them as labels. When problems recur over a period of time, help should be sought before patterns of fear, anxiety, guilt, shame, and avoidance become fixed. Occasionally failing to meet his or her expectations should not be labelled dysfunction, however.

In summary, accumulating knowledge of the physiology of sexual function is giving us an important tool with which to better understand the larger area of human sexuality. Much remains to be learned. If our knowledge is used to erect new standards for sexual performance and thus to increase performance anxiety, greater sexual discomfort and dissatisfaction may result. If, however, the knowledge is used to dispel myths and misinformation, encourage communication,and redefine sexual interaction in terms of relationships and sharing, it holds the promise of providing the basis for a healthier and more satisfying sexuality for men and women alike.

Notes

1. W. H. Masters and V. E. Johnson, *Human Sexual Response* (Boston: Little, Brown, 1966).
2. M. Mendelsohn, "Ist das Radfahren also ein gesundheitsgemasse Uebung anzusehen und aus artzlichen Gesichtspunkt zu empfehlen," *Deut. Med. Wschr.* 24(1896): 381.
3. A. C. Kinsey et al., *Sexual Behavior in the Human Male* (Philadelphia: W. B. Saunders, 1948); and A. C. Kinsey et al., *Sexual Behavior in the Human Female* (Philadelphia: W. B. Saunders, 1953).
4. H. S. Kaplan, *The New Sex Therapy* (New York: Brunner/Mazel, 1974).
5. P. MacLean, "New Finding Relevant to the Evolution of Psychosexual Functions of the Brain," *J. Nerv. Ment. Dis.* 135 (1962): 289.
6. S. Hite, *The Hite Report* (New York: Macmillan, 1976).
7. C. A. Fox et al., "Studies on the Relationship Between Plasma Testosterone Levels and Human Sexual Activity," *J. Endocrinol.* 52 (1972): 51; see also P. A. Lee et al., "Lack of Alteration of Serum Gonadotropins in Men and Women Following Sexual Intercourse," *Am. J. Obstet. Gynec.* 120 (1974): 985; and K. Purvis et al., "Endocrine Effects of Masturbation in Men," *J. Endocrinol.* 70 (1976): 439.
8. P. M. Sarrel, "Sexual Physiology and Sexual Functioning," *Postgrad. Med.* 58 (1975): 67.

2

The Development of a Treatment Program for Sexual Dysfunction at the Center for Marital and Sexual Studies

William E. Hartman
Marilyn Fithian

Sex research is in large part applied research, that is its findings can be utilized by therapists to help patients with sexual dysfunction. Two of the leaders in this field are William E. Hartman and Marilyn A. Fithian, a pioneering team who describe the work of their Center for Marital and Sexual Studies in Long Beach. William E. Hartman, Ph.D., is also professor of sociology at California State University, Long Beach. Hartman and Fithian are coauthors of *Treatment of Sexual Dysfunction* (Long Beach, Center for Marital and Sexual Studies, 90804).

Sexual therapy, as we know it, came into prominence in this country with the publication of the classic Masters and Johnson book, *Human Sexual Inadequacy,* in 1970. Even before that time, there had been programs aimed at resolving sexual problems with action-oriented therapy if only because the traditional talk therapy usually provided by professionals did not seem to be adequate for the increasing number of serious problems of sexual dysfunction. Instead the underlying theme of these new action-oriented therapists was the proposition that sex is something that is done and not just talked about.

Not all cases of sexual dysfunction are the same and this fact complicates the therapy. Some cases of sexual dysfunction, for example, seem to be based on superb verbal skills which act either as a coverup or "copout" for the absence of nonverbal communication skills. Yet there appears to be a trend among those therapists using the action-oriented methods to apply the terminology "Masters and Johnson" as a legitimation of their own particular treatment approach even though it has little correlation. The variations on this theme appear to be numerous. Unfortunately, at present, there is no way of determining objectively which of the variations of the theme are more productive in terms of results in reversing the presenting symptoms, nor how the background, training, or personality of the therapists is related to the outcomes reported.

Our approach, which is described in detail in the following pages, began before the publication of *Human Sexual Inadequacy*, in 1970. It was an attempt to answer the cry for help from many dysfunctional people, where the theme of their cry seemed to be "put us in more intimate touch with each other." Much curiosity was aroused by the specific nature of the treatment techniques, the evolution and progress of the therapy from day to day. The term "process" refers to a series of related techniques, each of which is interrelated, and successive techniques are dependent upon the earlier ones for the success of the final outcome. The purpose of the process is to build and enrich a relationship. The end product is intimacy. Neither orgasm nor mechanistic movements designed to produce arousal and response are the goal of the process about to be reported.

The approach represents a dual-sex therapy team applying a tried and tested process based on research with the emphasis on building a relationship and helping couples feel closer and more intimate with each other. It is in this frame of reference that couples often report that in their opinion the treatment program was more than 100 percent successful. This refers to the fact that they didn't know how much was lacking in closeness or in intimacy in the relationship and typically have felt that if mechanistic perfection, with complete function of the genitalia, would produce physical satisfaction, they would be completely satisfied with the results. In our experience, biological intimacy enhanced psychological and sociological intimacy until it was not unusual for couples to report a deeper degree of spiritual intimacy. This new intimacy represented an increased degree of interaction between the couple which before had not existed, even though they may have had prior sexual experiences with each other and, on occasion, with others.

The Center for Marital and Sexual Studies opened in Long Beach, California, in the fall of 1968. This is a report on the Center's sex research and sex therapy activities. It covers the first ten years of operation at the Center.

Individuals and couples have participated in Center activities in one of several ways:

1. A corps of male and female volunteers have made themselves available for laboratory research studies. They have provided a baseline of understanding in what constitutes effective sexual functioning. Videotape recordings made of some of these volunteers have proved useful as data for analysis

and also as educational material; and the viewing of selected videotapes and films by couples in therapy has become an essential feature of the therapy program.

2. Couples have come to the Center for intensive, uninterrupted two-week courses of therapy. The bulk of this report is concerned with the content and sequence of these two-week programs.

3. A ten-day treatment program beginning on Friday and ending on Sunday which is a modification of the two-week program.

4. Couples have participated in group workshops, lasting from one to six days, which have been conducted in different parts of the country. This is a modification of the two-week program.

5. A program of six two-hour lecture, talk, film, and slide discussions has been helpful in sex education.

6. Ongoing men's and women's groups meeting on a weekly basis.

7. Hourly talk sessions on a time-limited basis.

8. Two-hour film, lecture and discussion programs conducted in groups on referral.

9. Biofeedback programs for dysfunctional females.

The overwhelming majority of all human sexual activity occurs within pair-bonds, marital or nonmarital. Our concern is primarily with improving sexual function within such pair-bonds. Accordingly, intensive therapy is provided only as a couple. Each couple meets through the two-week period with a team composed of a male and a female therapist. The primary emphasis of this therapeutic foursome is on improving nonverbal communication between the two partners in therapy, development of a better relationship, the ability to interrelate with someone on an intimate basis. The resolution of the presenting symptom is most often resolved in this atmosphere.

The initial programs and policies of the Center arose out of our research and numerous other sources. One was our five-year study of social nudism, completed in 1968, (Hartman and Fithian, 1970). One aspect of our research involved taking nonnudists into a nudist setting to see how they responded to the experience. We also interviewed a number of first-time visitors. This study taught us the paralyzing effects of body taboos and inhibitions, and the ease with which they can be discarded under appropriate auspices and circumstances. Our therapy program is in considerable part designed to establish a set of circumstances and attitudes which enable couples to discard their debilitating inhibitions within a nonthreatening therapeutic setting. We also learned during our nudist research to view the human being as a single organism rather than as an uneasy composite of a verbally stocked mind plus a body disguised in clothing. In our therapy we seek to deal with the organism as a whole rather than with minds and bodies separately.

Similarly useful as preparation was a study of eighty-three nonorgasmic females which we launched in 1966. Our findings were reported in 1968 to the counseling section of the National Council on Family Relations. These findings were: (1) A lowly self-concept or damaged self-image was considered by nonorgasmic females themselves to be the major single factor inhibiting their full sexual responses. ("I'm no good at anything, including sex," was a typical comment.) (2) When vaginal musculature was tested by means of the Kegel perineometer (pressure gauge), regularly orgasmic women showed significantly higher base-line vaginal readings and more intense contractions than nonresponsive or nonorgasmic women—raising the question whether vaginal exercises might affect sexual responsiveness. (3) Male partners were profoundly affected on the occasion of the female partner's first orgasm; in a few cases, indeed, the immediate result was impotence in the male at the time the partner had their first orgasm. It may not be an accident that a man marries a nonorgasmic woman. In therapy it has become obvious in numerous cases that the male evidences great anxiety at the thought of his partner having orgasm, fearing that once she became orgasmic, he could not satisfy her. Sex therapy, we thus learned, should concern itself with both partners together and should focus on their relationship.

Our preliminary training at Dr. Martin J. Haskell's California Institute for Socioanalysis alerted us to the possibility that action methods such as experienced in psychodrama, sociodrama, and role-training might prove useful in the therapy of sexual dysfunction. Experience since our Center opened demonstrated their invaluability. Indeed, from one point of view our entire therapy program might be deemed a role-training program, preparing a man and a woman to function together more effectively within the intimate personal relationship of their pair-bond.

Masters and Johnson (1970) had not yet published their second book when the Center for Marital and Sexual Studies opened in 1968; but the broad outline of their therapeutic approach was known from their published preliminary papers and personal appearances. The extent of our indebtedness to their pioneering efforts will be clearly visible in our description of the methods we have evolved.

The couples who come to a Southern California center today, however, appear to differ in significant respects from those who came to the Masters-Johnson Foundation in St. Louis in the 1960s. In particular, our couples in therapy are quite willing to engage in a variety of therapeutic procedures which might have proved threatening to couples a decade ago. Since twenty-one teams around the country have now been trained in the methods utilized at our Center, and over 100,000 professionals have attended professional workshops in the U.S. and overseas, these methods are now widely known and used. Our methods have been adapted to our population and to their willingness to "try things out."

We also reviewed a substantial body of prior research and therapy reports before launching our own program, looking particularly for promising therapeutic procedures. Thus we had ready in advance a quite extensive and eclectic list of techniques which might be worth working with, plus ideas and suggestions we evolved from experience with our early research subjects.

Our Center's initial policies were set in consultation with a professional advisory board composed of ten men and women from the specialities of law, medicine, psychology, sociology, and religion, all colleagues or former colleagues of ours at the California State University, Long Beach. Drawing on their experience counseling with students and with others, they were able to predict both the scope and the nature of the sexual problems likely to be brought to a new center in our area. They reported that the region had an abundance of verbal therapies available, but an unmet need for nonverbal approaches to therapy. Above all, they urged us to get started right away; the need, they informed us, was urgent. It was two years from the time of the inception of this group until the Center was opened.

Once the Center was opened, our experience with our first couples in therapy taught us much. We learned, for example, that the end-of-the-rainbow which most of them were seeking could be summed up in a single word: INTIMACY. Their cry for help was essentially a plea that they be put in warm and meaningful touch with each other, literally as well as figuratively. Helping a man learn to achieve and maintain an erection, we found, may be a worthwhile intermediate goal; but unless he also learns to bring pleasure, satisfaction, and happiness to a partner—and to himself—therapeutic benefits were likely to be shallow and elusive. Precisely the same proved true of women whose presenting symptom was lack of orgasm but whose underlying goal was intimacy and satisfaction within the pair-bond. Very early, accordingly, communication, especially nonverbal communication, became the keystone of our therapeutic approach.

Where we had done considerable research prior to opening the Center, our first laboratory instrumentation and research was launched simultaneously with our first ventures into therapy. The two have reinforced each other ever since. Our experience with therapy pointed out areas where additional laboratory research was urgently needed; and even our earliest research findings proved helpful when applied in therapy. For convenience, our laboratory program is briefly described later.

Some of our early couples came for therapy on weekends; some came for a week, went home, and returned for a second week; others came once a week or in other time patterns. Our experience with our first fifty-eight couples confirmed the Masters-Johnson view that an intensive, uninterrupted, two-week program, preferably with the couple housed in a nearby motel or hotel, released from all other activities and preoccupations, produces better results. That is accordingly the pattern we now follow with approximately 95 percent of our cases. Our experience with alternative patterns—intensive group therapy for a shorter period—is detailed separately.

The structure of our intensive two-week therapy program as it evolved to date can conveniently be summarized as a series of thirty-four steps shown in

Table 1. (The steps are varied, of course, to meet the needs of individual couples.)

1. *Initial referral.* Our main program takes two weeks, with a two-year follow-up, and costs $2,700.00; it should, therefore, not be entered into without serious consideration, or offered to couples who can be more economically benefited by short-term counseling programs. The prognosis should be favorable. Referral is one good way to weed out inappropriate candidates for our particular mode of therapy. We accept referrals from physicians—general practitioners as well as psychiatrists, obstetricians, gynecologists, and urologists—and also from psychologists, marriage counselors, social workers, ministers, and lawyers. Sometimes the referring authorities are themselves the applicants for therapy; indeed, approximately 20 percent of the couples coming to us for therapy include a professional from one of the above occupations who has referred himself and his partner (or herself and her partner). We have only refused to treat two clients who came in for therapy. Both needed other kinds of therapy.

Thirty-four films are available to show clients, and selections are based on what film would be of most value to the client.

2. *Sociopsychological testing.* We routinely administer a battery of tests.

The Minnesota Multiphasic Personality Inventory (MMPI) provides an indication of the degree of emotional imbalance or psychopathology present. This helps determine the degree of supervision needed.

For purpose of diagnostic evaluation, the Taylor-Johnson Temperament Analysis (T-JTA) is employed. The T-JTA is a personality test designed for diagnostic, counseling and research purposes. It measures nine important personality traits and their opposites and serves as a quick, convenient and effective method of measuring those characteristics that may significantly influence personal, social or marital adjustment. In addition to its other applications, the T-JTA was especially designed for use in marital and premarital counseling. We have found it to be uniquely appropriate for use in our work with couples because it may be taken by the couple, each on themselves, and also on one another, thus providing a measure of interpersonal perception of the individuals involved.

The T-JTA is therefore completed twice by each member of the couple. The first time, each answers the questions as they apply to themselves; the second time they answer the questions as they apply to their partner. The four completed answer sheets are then scored and charted on two T-JTA profiles, one for the male partner and one for the female partner. The self-image is plotted in a solid line. On each profile the difference between the self-image and the image that is perceived by the partner is graphically portrayed (Figures 1 & 2). When these profiles are examined, meaningful insight into possible areas of misunderstanding between the couple become evident.

For example, in Figure 1, the wife sees herself as nervous, depressive, quiet, inhibited, subjective, submissive, hostile, and impulsive, but also somewhat sympathetic. In contrast, her husband sees her as inhibited, indifferent, impulsive, but also as being composed, lighthearted, active, social, objective, dominant (i.e., confident), and tolerant. We find agreement only in the inhibited and impulsive tendencies. The husband tends to see his wife in a much more favorable light than she sees herself. The wife's self-rating suggests a very poor self-concept with considerable evidence of severe concern

Table 1.   Thirty-four Steps in Two-Week Therapy Program*

1. Initial referral
2. Sociopsychological testing
3. First sexual history
4. Second sexual history
5. Physical examination
6. Roundtable discussion
7. Developing sensuality
8. Sexological examination
9. Kegel film
10. Body imagery
11. Touching and relating (sensitivity)
12. Assignment: Combing the partner's hair†
13. Hand caress—foot caress
14. Film: Foot, face, body caress, and breathing together
15. Mutual bathing assignment
16. Face caress
17. Assignment: Wash partner's hair
18. Color film of body caress—body caress
19. Breathing together
20. Sexual caress
21. Film: Nondemand techniques— pleasuring/squeeze technique, etc.
22. Assignment: Male active/non-demand technique, female back against male's chest
23. Assignment: Female active/non-demand technique, squeeze technique
24. Assignment: Male active/non-demand technique, female supine, male pleasuring vagina
25. Assignment: The "quiet vagina"
26. Films of coital positions
27. Audiotape: "How to become orgasmic"
28. Film of coitus
29. Hypnosis when indicated
30. Film of coitus—romantic
31. Film of coitus—playful
32. Assignment: Spontaneity—How do you do your own thing? Write up a contract
33. Saying goodbye nonverbally
34. Follow-up

*A more complete description with illustrations is available in our book *Treatment of Sexual Dysfunction* (Long Beach, CA: Center for Marital and Sexual Studies, 1974; or New York: Jason Aaronson).

†All assignments are carried out in the privacy of the motel room.

Figure 1.   T-JTA Profile of Wife as Seen By Self and as Seen By Her Husband

G.P.C.C. Norm(s):	A	B	C	D	E	F	G	H	I	Attitude Score/Sten.
Mids		1	1 1	3 8	3 7	3	1 6	3 3	1 4	Total Mids: 15 30
Raw score	28 6	36 5	19 39	17 20	35 23	29 0	7 34	15 7	15 16	Raw score
Percentile	94 20	99 28	18 99	7 23	60 31	96 1	4 92	78 30	15 26	Percentile
TRAIT	Nervous	Depressive	Active-Social	Expressive-Responsive	Sympathetic	Subjective	Dominant	Hostile	Self-disciplined	TRAIT
TRAIT OPPOSITE	Composed	Light-hearted	Quiet	Inhibited	Indifferent	Objective	Submissive	Tolerant	Impulsive	TRAIT OPPOSITE

Excellent   Acceptable   Improvement desirable   Improvement urgent

━━━ Wife by self   ------ Wife by husband

about herself. On the other hand, the disparity between these two evaluations may also indicate little understanding of the wife by the husband, or it may be that he is simply oblivious of her emotional problems.

The husband's profile (Figure 2) is equally significant because there is also a wide difference in the way he sees himself and the way in which he is perceived by his wife. There is a remarkably vast disparity in the T-JTA traits of nervous/composed, depressive/lighthearted, active-social/quiet, and expressive-responsive/inhibited, as well as in subjective/objective and dominant/submissive, and to some degree in hostile/tolerant. While this example is rather atypical, it is one which clearly shows a marked divergence in "self" and "other" perception. A more typical profile (Figure 3) illustrates fewer disparities in perception, with a marked degree of difference indicated only in the sympathetic/indifferent traits.

Figure 2.   T-JTA Profile of Husband as Seen By Self and as Seen By His Wife

Norm(s): G.P.C.C.	A		B		C		D		E		F		G		H		I		Attitude (Step) Score: 8 2
Mids				1		1		1		1		1		1					Total 0 6 Mids:
Raw score	2	32	2	38	38	11	32	15	32	31	2	29	34	15	0	13	14	18	Raw score
Percentile	11	96	18	99	97	11	65	12	52	59	8	93	93	20	2	52	10	30	Percentile
TRAIT	Nervous		Depressive		Active-Social		Expressive-Responsive		Sympathetic		Subjective		Dominant		Hostile		Self-disciplined		TRAIT

| TRAIT OPPOSITE | Composed | Light-hearted | Quiet | Inhibited | Indifferent | Objective | Submissive | Tolerant | Impulsive | TRAIT OPPOSITE |

Excellent   Acceptable   Improvement desirable   Improvement urgent

——— Husband by self   - - - - - Husband by wife

Illustrated in these T-JTA profiles are the traits most frequently observed in couples with primary sexual dysfunction. The profiles of such individuals consistently reflect the T-JTA traits of quiet, inhibited, and indifferent, with inhibited being the most common characteristic encountered among those sexually dysfunctional individuals with whom we work. This pattern may be manifest either on the self-image, or the self as perceived by the other, or may appear in both evaluations.

The T-JTA is a valuable and effective diagnostic tool. While it does not provide all the answers any more than the other tests we utilize, it does provide clues, insight and direction which we might otherwise overlook in short-term therapy.

The Draw-a-Person Test is similarly administered in duplicate. Each member of the couple is asked to draw a nude front view of himself on a

Figure 3.   Typical T-JTA Profile

Norm(s): G.P.C.C.	A		B		C		D		E		F		G		H		I		Attitude (Sten) Score: 3 7
Mids	1		1		1	1	1	1	1	1		2		1	1				Total Mids: 5 7
Raw score	7	14	11	6	9	17	11	21	23	35	12	16	26	27	14	7	40	40	Raw score
Percentile	35	51	64	32	2	25	4	26	13	79	61	60	55	66	66	30	99	99	Percentile
TRAIT	Nervous		Depressive		Active-Social		Expressive-Responsive		Sympathetic		Subjective		Dominant		Hostile		Self-disciplined		TRAIT

| TRAIT OPPOSITE | Composed | Light-hearted | Quiet | Inhibited | Indifferent | Objective | Submissive | Tolerant | Impulsive | TRAIT OPPOSITE |

Excellent   Acceptable   Improvement desirable   Improvement urgent

———— Husband by self   ----- Husband by wife

8½″ x 11″ sheet of colored paper and a similar view of his partner on another sheet. Twenty-one paper colors are available. Each person is asked to select the color befitting himself and the color befitting his partner, and to note on the drawings the personality characteristics of the person drawn which led him to select these particular colors. We have found that the way the feet, face and hands are drawn is particularly revealing; the feet portray a firm foundation (or lack of it) while the face provides clues to identity. The hands indicate openness or lack thereof.

A See-Through Drawing is made—on a piece of typing paper—of self on one side, partner on the other. This is interpreted by holding the paper up to the light seeing the juxtaposition of the couple, one to the other or their relationship in size. We note how one draws the self as opposed to how one has drawn the other. Size variations, clothing differences, one or the other juxtaposed with one sitting on the other's lap or hands on genitalia are a few of the clues that may be seen.

The Luscher Color Test (N.Y.: Random House, 1969) is a simple test which involves the selection of eight colors in order of preference. Each pair of colors chosen gives an interpretation contained in the book. The client may be asked about percent of agreement with each interpretation. Extreme degrees of perception or lack thereof are noted by the therapist as the client gives a figure from 0–100 on the extent to which the test interpretation is accurate.

The Sexual Compatibility Test is a new test we are using which shows some promise in that it asks about the couple's sexual behavior over the last year—including frequency, interest, desire for, and projected interest. We have found it to be useful in suggesting behaviors not engaged in by the couple but which have been indicated to be of interest to both. (This test is available from Arthur Lee Foster, 248 Blossom Hill Road, Los Gatos, California, 95030.)

3. *First sexual history.* Our concern is with heterosexual functioning, and we seek to establish this heterosexual orientation from the very beginning. Accordingly, the female therapist takes the male's history while the male therapist is taking the female's history. This usually takes two or two and one-half hours, up to five hours in a few cases. The history follows the general lines laid down by Kinsey (1948), ourselves (1974), and by Masters and Johnson (1970), but has been developed overall to fit our needs. Histories are recorded and transcribed, and can be subsequently referred to as necessary.

4. *Second sexual history.* It is essential that lines of communication be opened among all four participants in the therapy and that both therapists receive information directly from each member of the couple. Accordingly, the male therapist next confers with the male while the female therapist is conferring with the female. In these sessions the highlights of the earlier history are more briefly reviewed, and rapport is established.

5. *Physical examination.* The male partner is examined by a physician in the Center offices, with both therapists present; and the female partner is similarly but separately examined. The physician explains as he goes along what he is examining and why; in addition to reporting out loud any variations from normal, he specifically announces each normal structure and function. One of the therapists writes down each finding on a form. We have found that this procedure minimizes the likelihood of misconceptions and of faulty communication among physician, therapists, and the person being examined. Laboratory tests and X-rays are taken where indicated. While the examination and lab tests provide significant clues in a few cases, the overwhelming majority of cases (perhaps 98 percent) show no ascertainable

physical basis for sexual dysfunction. Even where there is a physical basis for the problem, the psychological factors are a critical part of the problem.

It is true that occasionally in women adhesions are found between the foreskin and glans of the clitoris, trapping smegma between them. The result may be irritation and pain or discomfort during clitoral stimulation or during sexual arousal and engorgement of the glans. Dickinson (1949) has described a simple office procedure for freeing the adhesions so that the foreskin can freely retract. The work of Dr. Le Mon Clark and others is also valuable. At the Center the physician explains this to the woman; and if she agrees, he flicks a dull probe down both sides of the clitoris, in the Dickinson manner, to free the foreskin.

After the physician has examined the cervix with a lighted speculum, he holds up a hand mirror so that the woman—almost always for the first time—is able to see her own vagina, cervix, and cervical opening. The educational value of this procedure is attested to by the many questions women ask about what they are seeing.

6. *Roundtable discussion*. The two therapists and the couple participate in this discussion, usually on the third day of the program. We first ask each participant whether he or she now feels we can help, and whether they wish to continue through the two weeks. If either wishes to withdraw from the program, this is the moment to do so. (Withdrawal is very rare.) We also explore their motivations for continuing; for we have found that therapeutic results are more closely associated with motivation than with any other single factor. This is also the moment when we independently decide whether the therapy is likely to be helpful enough to warrant continuation. If we feel progress is likely to be limited, we say so frankly; but we also indicate a willingness to continue in order to see just how much can be accomplished.

7. *Developing sensuality*. Once it has been determined during the roundtable discussion that the two-week program will continue, the couple is asked not to engage in sexual intercourse for the remainder of the first week and until the ban on this activity is lifted. The most effective way to develop the sensual dimension of men and women is to forbid coital activity while many touch, pleasuring, and nondemand exercises are conducted. We explain to the couple that we wish them to get into overall warm touch (our definition of sensuality) so that when intercourse is engaged in, it is the result of a natural progressive process involving much physical and emotional intimacy and warmth before penile-vaginal contact takes place.

It is common for couples in a motel in a new city to become sexually involved rather quickly. In rare instances even dysfunctional couples, out of touch with each other for long periods of time, find themselves enjoying more intimate moments than has been true for a considerable time period. Most couples in therapy soon realize that without the basic foundation of overall warmth and intimacy through pleasurable touch contact, the heavy super-structure of coitus will not long remain on a firm foundation. Their willingness to forego intercourse during the first week of our program opens the doors to many other alternatives while experiencing warmth with each other through exercises conducted both in our offices and in their motel room wherein they learn that many emotionally close activities do not necessarily need to include coitus *per se*. Enhancing the range of these intimate activities is one of the more useful parts of our therapeutic process.

8. *Sexological examination*. Each woman fills out a marital, sexual, and reproductive history form covering frequency of masturbation, experience with orgasm, desired coital positions, and so on. There follows an examination of her breasts and genitalia by the two therapists. She is particularly asked whether she feels any vaginal effects when her breasts or nipples are stimulated, whether she nursed her children, and whether she experienced sexual arousal or orgasm during nursing.

Unless a woman objects, her male partner is invited to join in the later portion of the sexological examination. He is first shown the clitoris and then views the interior of the vagina and the cervix through the lighted speculum, and is then asked to explore the vagina with his index finger—starting just below the clitoris (the twelve o'clock position) and then proceeding around in a clockwise direction with his finger moving in and out so that all accessible points on the vaginal wall are palpated in succession. Note is made of the regions where pleasurable feelings are elicited. In rare cases where the woman reports marked pain when some area is stimulated, she is referred to a gynecologist for examination and possible vaginal surgery. We have found, however, that discomfort during stimulation as a result of vaginal tears, lesions, or scars can often be resolved through the vaginal exercises described by Kegel (1965).

The participation of the male partner in clitoral and vaginal exploration of the female partner is of particular importance for males who ejaculate prematurely; we recommend to them that they learn to provide enjoyment to the female through manual stimulation until adequate penile stimulation can be provided.

The male partner also fills out a marital and sexological history form and is examined by the two therapists to determine size of testes, sensitivity of testes to stimulation during foreplay, and similar factors. Where the male has reported pain during intercourse, the condition of the underside of the frenum is examined with particular care. The man's feelings about his genitals are also inquired into. The female partner is present for the entire examination if both partners agree (as they always have); the various portions of the penis, scrotum, and testicles are identified for her. If one of the presenting problems is premature ejaculation, she is shown the "squeeze technique" pioneered by Semans (1956) and developed by Masters and Johnson (1970). For impotence we instruct the female to gently grasp the penis with her entire hand and squeeze rhythmically at heartbeat rate.

9. *Kegel film*. The couple next views Kegel's medical film on vaginal sensation and perception ("Pathologic Physiology of the Pubococcygeus Muscle in Women," available through Morgan Camera Shop in Hollywood, California). This film, together with the direct observations by both partners during the previous sexological examination, insures that both partners have developed a familiarity with the anatomy and functioning of the vagina. The film also provides the background against which we explain the use of vaginal exercises, based on Kegel (1965), which she is asked to practice daily.

10. *Body imagery*. Both men and women with complaints of sexual inadequacy tend to undervalue their bodies and reject them. Even many handsome men and attractive women see themselves as ugly, defective, unlovable. We believe that a bodily reevaluation is an essential step in therapy.

To accomplish this, each partner is instructed to stand nude in front of a specially built three-wing mirror, resembling a tailor's mirror, with both therapists present but not the other partner. The individual is asked to touch first of all the top of his head and to report what he feels and what his emotional response is to this part of his body. He is then asked to repeat the touching and reporting for every part of the body, working downward to the toes. A dialogue ensues, in which the therapists comment on the significance of the body-image data being revealed; they also comment on the relationship between these data and the data provided earlier by the Draw-a-Person Test. The net effect of this procedure, in almost every case, is a realistic improvement in self-perception. Instead of concentrating on those few features which the individual deems ugly and objectionable—breasts too large or too small, nose too large or too small, too much or too little hair—a more realistic appreciation of the body as a whole, including its many merits, emerges.

The lights are next dimmed and the individual is asked to close his eyes and make an imaginary "fantasy tour" through the interior of his body, visiting in turn the brain, heart, lungs, vagina or penis, and anus, and describing what is encountered in each region. What parts of the body appear as sexual areas on this tour? What parts are fraught with negative emotional significance? Like the external body tour, the internal tour appears to be therapeutic as well as providing data for the therapists; a greater awareness and acceptance of the body is achieved and the chasm supposedly separating mind from body is narrowed. We have found the procedure particularly effective for those with "internal blocks" who consciously or unconsciously feel that there must be some bodily basis for their sexual dysfunction.

11. *Touching and relating (sensitivity).* The couple is brought nude together in front of the three-panel mirror, with both therapists present, and are asked to demonstrate how they like to kiss, touch, and hold each other. Many couples display a surprising amount of affection during this demonstration—despite past power struggles and psychic injuries which have resulted in serious sexual dysfunction.

The couple is next asked to hold hands, and with eyes closed, to demonstrate how they express positive and negative feelings toward each other, how they "make-up" nonverbally after fights and disagreements, and how they would say farewell to each other for the last time. This last demonstration is particularly significant, for many couples view this therapy as the last chance to save their marriage. This role-playing clearly reveals affection or lack of it, and the skill or clumsiness with which that affection is communicated or concealed by each partner. The ease or tension in the physical relationship between the partners, and the restriction on physical relations also comes into clear focus.

Steps 8 through 11, taken together, familiarize the couple with their own bodies and with each other's bodies in the presence of the two therapists. The embarrassment threshold is markedly lowered; nudity and mutual touching are no longer seen as sinister threats. We regard this as an excellent foundation for Steps 12 through 20, designed to make the couple similarly accepting of physical relations with one another.

12. *Assignment: Combing the partner's hair.* As in the Masters-Johnson program, we give each couple a "homework assignment" to carry through in their motel room after they have concluded their day's work with us at the Center. The first assignment is wholly nonthreatening: to comb the partner's hair in a manner likely to be as pleasurable as possible for the recipient. Next day both partners report their feelings, both positive and negative, when they were giving and when they were receiving this exercise.

13. *Hand caress.* The couple sit facing each other, legs entwined with eyes closed, exploring each other's hands. One is then directed to explore the other's hands while the partner is passive. This process is then reversed. Comfort in passive or active roles can be readily observed. A break is taken before the foot caress.

Foot caress. A tub of warm water is provided along with soap, towel and baby oil, and the couple is asked to decide who will give the foot caress first and who will receive it. No further instructions are given. The therapists observe the degree of warmth and ability to communicate nonverbally and to transmit feeling through the hands. This is often a most significant step in the therapy; warm water, warm touch, and warm caress of the feet can provide an emotional base which has not existed before.

14. *Film: Foot, face, body caress, and breathing together.* The couple is next taken to an audiovisual room and shown a one-hour film demonstrating how a volunteer research couple carry out the same foot caress procedure. They are then shown films of the face, body and sexual caress procedures, which will be their activities for the next few days. They are also shown by film how a couple lie together, nude and touching, and breath synchronously—one following the breathing of the other and then reversing roles. Some of these exercises can be done at the Center; others may be done in their motel room.

15. *Mutual bathing.* The couple is assigned to give each other a shower or a bath in their motel. They are instructed to do it slowly, warmly, and sensually in a manner they believe will bring the greatest amount of pleasure to their partner and themselves. At their next appointment, they discuss with the therapists their feelings during this assignment.

16. *Face caress assignment.* The partner who received the first foot caress is now instructed to give the first face caress. Here, as elsewhere in the program, the details are designed to *demonstrate* mutual give-and-take, alternate taking of the initiative, the passing back and forth of dominance and control—all features which can be much more effectively demonstrated than taught verbally. Numerous facial creams and lotions are provided. Each partner selects the one to be used on their own face.

The partner receiving the face caress lies on a specially built bed high enough to be comfortable for the giver, or sits on the floor with their head in the giver's lap. During this exercise the receiver is asked to place his hands on the hands of the giver and to show precisely how he wants to be caressed. The principle of hand-on-hand showing, pioneered by Helena Wright (1959) decades ago, is taught early in the program and reemphasized on numerous occasions. Each partner thus learns both to give and to receive hints and cues without feeling demeaned or threatened.

17. *Assignment: Wash hair.* The couple is assigned to shampoo each other's hair. Their feelings during this exercise are subsequently discussed with the therapists.

18. *Body caress.* A color film is shown of a warm, intimate body caress. Couples are asked to determine who will give the body caress first, using appropriate body lotions, with the recipient lying face down. The active partner slowly and sensually caresses the back, buttocks, and legs. Then the recipient turns over and the chest, abdomen, and legs are caressed. A special nonallergenic emollient oil (Physician's Formula Cosmetics, Inc., 230 South 9th Ave., City of Industry, California, 91746) is provided to facilitate genital caress and prevent chemical reactions on sensitive areas of the body.

19. *Breathing together.* A rest period is specified between the back caress and the front caress, in Step 18. During this respite the partner giving the caress is instructed to lie down and follow the breathing of the partner receiving the caress. Feelings of psychological and emotional warmth and closeness are the usual results. In addition, the rest period precludes the possibility of physical and emotional fatigue.

20. *Sexual caress.* Both partners are taught how to caress with a slower, more sensual movement of the hands over breasts and genitals—with special emphasis on the inside of the thighs. Finally, the female partner is taught to massage the male partner's chest, abdomen, and genitals with her breasts, using a suitable lotion. This technique is first demonstrated via film and then tried out under the direction of the therapists; but emphasis is placed on its use for arousing the sensuous and sexual feelings of both partners in the privacy of their own room.

21. *Film: Nondemand techniques—pleasuring-squeeze technique.* This is the second of the hour-long video tapes shown to each of our therapeutic couples. It primarily depicts three nondemand pleasuring techniques. This involves the male sitting with his back up against the wall or head of the bed, and with his partner's back against his chest, pleasuring her body in a position where coitus cannot take place. Another segment shows the very significant squeeze technique. This is the most important single procedure in the treatment of premature ejaculation. The couples are shown this technique when it is successful and ejaculation does not take place, and in one instance when the female partner doing the squeezing moves her thumb at the base of the frenulum and the male ejaculates. The third sequence shows the male pleasuring the female vagina in the exact physical role reversal of the preceding position. In these latter two exercises, the partner doing the pleasuring sits upright or uses the headboard or the wall for support, and the one being pleasured lies supine on the bed with legs up over the partner's legs, and with the genitalia easily available in the partner's lap.

Several other techniques are shown on this videotape including a tantra yoga position, and the insertion of a flacid penis into the vagina. Beyond the individual instruction received on the foregoing techniques, is an important desensitization process which takes place where the couple sitting alone in a darkened audiovisual room observe the genital pleasuring of both male and female partners, which will be their next assignment in their motel room.

22. *Assignment: Male-active/nondemand techniques.* The couple is shown a tape in which the male partner sits comfortably with his legs spread and his back against the head of the bed, while the female partner sits between his legs with her back against his chest. In this restful and nondemanding position, the male partner lovingly strokes and stimulates her breasts, nipples,

thighs, and genitals. (This and other films used in the program were prepared at the Center and feature volunteer nontherapy couples selected as exemplars of effective sexual functioning.) The assignment for the couple in therapy is to assume the same position and practice the same activity in the privacy of their own room.

23. *Assignment: Female-active/nondemand technique—squeeze technique.* In this exercise the female sits comfortably with her back against the head of the bed. The male lies stretched out on the bed facing her, with his buttocks between her thighs and his legs over hers—so that his genitals are, in effect, placed in her lap for easy access. In this position, she massages his penis and scrotum with the usual nonallergenic emollient oil.

Where premature ejaculation is one of the couple's complaints, and in other cases where it may prove helpful, the penis-squeezing technique of Semans and Masters and Johnson, which was demonstrated to the couples earlier, is practiced in this position. We have confirmed Masters and Johnson's finding that as a couple practices this technique, the male gradually secures autonomous control over his own initiation of orgasm, so that he can soon engage in coitus for any desired period—fifteen or twenty minutes or even longer—before ejaculating.

24. *Assignment: Male-active/nondemand technique.* This exercise represents a role-reversal of the preceding one. The man sits erect using the head of the bed or wall for support if he so desires. The female is supine with her buttocks between his thighs, her legs over his with her pelvis almost in direct apposition to his. In this position the male is easily able to digitally caress the vagina with the use of emollient oil and the knowledge learned from the sexological examination. The male is instructed to gently caress and stimulate his partner's vagina. Where premature ejaculation and insufficient foreplay have been presenting symptoms, the female is able to develop much greater vaginal perception through this exercise, and the male learns that he can bring pleasure to the vagina in a way other than through the use of his penis. In addition to the knowledge from the sexological examination, the couple have seen the Kegel film, and learned of the existence of nerve centers at the four and eight o'clock positions, about two finger joints in depth in the vagina. They are encouraged to develop maximum feeling and response in these areas through this special pleasuring technique.

25. *Assignment: The "quiet vagina."* This is another nondemand technique, initially presented via film in Step 21. The female partner is told that at some point when she feels sexually "turned on" during or following body caress or sexual caress in private, she should insert the male partner's penis into her vagina. Both parties then lie still for ten to twenty minutes, without penile thrusting or movement of any kind. Couples often report their amaze-

ment at the positive feelings which flow between them during this "quiet vagina" exercise. We have found this exercise particularly helpful for men who have difficulty in maintaining erections and for those who lack confidence in their ability to function adequately in coitus.

26. *Films of coital positions.* Couples are shown two series of 8-mm still films—slidefilms—illustrating a variety of positions for sexual intercourse. They are instructed to experiment with as many of these positions as possible during the next few days of homework.

27. *Audiotape: "How to become orgasmic."* At the same session in which the films of coital positions are shown, the couple listen to an audiotape (without visual accompaniment) in which a formerly nonorgasmic woman describes with sincerity and delight how she herself became orgasmic. She explains that she studied carefully a videotape of a multiorgasmic woman in coitus, and that on subsequent coital occasions she emulated the breathing techniques, the pelvic thrusting, and the other movements portrayed on the videotape. In the course of this emulation, she states, she enjoyed her first coital orgasm. Listening to this tape, of course, sets the stage for showing the couple in therapy the same videotape, with the suggestion implanted in advance that if the woman in therapy emulates the multiorgasmic woman on the videotape, she too may benefit.

28. *Film of coitus: "Effective sexual functioning."* Many of the steps described above might be labeled educational rather than strictly therapeutic; in our view, indeed, all therapy is educational. In our culture, however, opportunities for education in coitus are minimal or nonexistent. During the first year of our program, accordingly, we offered each couple in therapy an opportunity, if they so desired, to watch a couple—a highly effective husband and a multiorgasmic wife—engage in coitus. Every couple in the program accepted this offer. The two couples had dinner together; and for the rest of the evening the sexually effective couple demonstrated a wide range of sexual activities while the couple in therapy observed and learned. This simple teaching-by-demonstration technique, a commonplace in other fields, proved to be equally effective, quite unthreatening, and without any observable adverse side effects when offered as an educational opportunity at an appropriate point in our therapy program.

As our program expanded, however, the live demonstration step proved increasingly difficult to schedule and unduly demanding on the demonstrating couple. Accordingly, their demonstration was recorded on videotape and later made into a film. This was the videotape referred to by the woman who became orgasmic after viewing it, and who recorded her experience on the audiotape (Step 27). While we believe live demonstration has notable advantages, we have found the film demonstration an effective and convenient substitute. We feel it is our best single film in helping women experience a richer, fuller sex life. It is one of a choice of films shown clients, and the one film almost all couples see.

29. *Hypnosis when indicated.* Those couples or individual partners who, even after coming this far, still feel "up tight" and unable to relax or enjoy a sexual encounter, are offered the use of hypnosis. Hypnosis is also offered in other cases where it seems to us it may prove beneficial. The essence of the procedure is to make, while the individual is under hypnosis, appropriate posthypnotic suggestions.

We may suggest to the impotent, partially impotent, or prematurely ejaculating male, for example, that he will thereafter have firmer or longer lasting erections; and we may suggest to the nonresponding or weakly responding female that she will thereafter have fuller and more prompt arousal and more adequate lubrication. We also often suggest to the female that when arousal is complete she will *give herself permission* to enjoy orgasm; this is particularly important for women who through upbringing, religious conviction, or other factors are convinced that sex is dirty, nasty, and bad, and that only "loose" women enjoy sex.

The results of hypnosis are occasionally surprising, even to seasoned therapists. One wife who remained nonorgasmic through ten years of marriage, for example, reported to both therapists that she detested sex. She had filed a divorce action against her husband, and came to therapy with him while the divorce was pending. She both reported and exhibited an abhorrence of the penis and refused to touch any part of his genitalia. She reported infrequent sexual arousal, little lubrication when aroused, and mild discomfort rather than enjoyment during coitus. Her cooperation in the various steps of our program was minimal. She had previously experienced hypnotherapy, however, and readily agreed to cooperate in a trial of hypnosis. The husband gave his wife a body caress while the female therapist introduced a series of suggestions; that the wife would experience more and more sensuous feeling throughout her body, and especially in her vagina, and that more and more lubrication would result, together with ease of relaxation, and that she would give herself permission to enjoy orgasm. She was then brought out of hypnosis and taken to the examining room for a vaginal examination—in the course of which her whole body convulsed in a violent orgasm. She reported, remarkably enough, that she had experienced this before but had not identified it as an orgasm. At the conclusion of the two-week therapy program she cancelled her divorce action and has remained orgasmic with her husband in her continuing marriage through the past eight years.

It is notable that of all the steps in our program, hypnosis is the one that stimulates the greatest demand for repeat sessions.

30. *"Romantic" film of coitus.* The couple in therapy is shown an hour-long film of coitus in which the male never achieves orgasm, and loses

his erection on several occasions—but in which the obvious warmth and intimacy infusing the couple continue to flow delightfully throughout the hour. Viewers learn that losing an erection or finding yourself unable to achieve climax is not necessarily a disaster; they are amazed and reassured to note that affection and intimacy can be communicated very effectively without an erect penis.

31. *Play function of sex—"fun" film of coitus.* The couple in therapy views a film of a couple having fun (and coitus) on a waterbed. This fun-in-bed demonstration is particularly useful for the many couples who come to therapy with the conviction that sex is a deadly serious business, to be approached as a chore or a challenge.

Though the above coital films are the ones most often shown to couples at the Center, they are only three of a dozen such films that are used. The use of a film tends to be related to what we perceive to be the most helpful to clients. If there is no pressing need to show a specific film they may make a choice.

Other films that are often seen by clients are "Sex at Seventy," a color film of a much older couple who have been married a number of years and where the husband had never been able to make intromission. The film depicts a range of sexual activities developed by the couple where the male was totally impotent.

"Caring," is a short color film of a middle-aged couple in which the male is the more active of the couple. It isn't a "performance" film but rather is typical of their sexual functioning. The woman is free to stimulate herself while her husband is also pleasuring her.

"Together," is a color film of a middle-aged couple in which the female is fairly active sexually. It is especially good for its long afterglow and what happens sexually after coitus is technically over.

32. *Assignment: Spontaneity—How do you do your thing?* In several earlier assignments, we specify in considerable detail just what each partner is to do. In this assignment we specify instead that the couple is to "do their own thing" in their own way, to evolve their own approaches, techniques, and activities. Each is also asked to give his partner an innovative assignment which may contribute to finding "their own thing." This is a sort of graduation exercise, and results are reported to the therapists at the final session.

The last assignment involves writing up a contract incorporating what they have learned, what they are going to carry over into their life after they leave, and how they plan on implementing this. They both must agree and sign it. If either wishes to make a personal statement related to them specifically, they are encouraged to do so. However, what they plan to do together and how they will implement this is a mutual endeavor between the two of them.

If we see that they are too ambitious and what they are planning doesn't seem feasible we will discuss this, and if there is evidence that not enough is to be done to keep the problem resolved this will be discussed. This then gives the couple and us some guidelines that can be followed and some source of feedback in the follow-up contact with them.

33. *Saying goodbye.* At the final session, further homework involving body caress, sexual caress, and other activities are discussed with the hope that the patterns of learning established during the program will be continued after the therapy is terminated and the couple has returned home. A date is made for the first follow-up telephone call, or return visit which is an essential feature of the program. The couple is also assured that they may return for additional therapy, as needed, during the next two years without additional charge. They are, however, encouraged to consult with their own physician or other referring authority in all nonsexual areas. With these practical matters attended to, a feeling of mutual affection and esteem generally surfaces which the members of the therapeutic foursome express nonverbally in a ritual four-way embrace with interlocking arms.

34. *Follow-up.* This takes several forms—telephone interviews, returns for additional therapy, correspondence, and occasional social visits. As therapists, we view all this as an opportunity rather than a burden.

We are loath to report statistical "success rates" because we are eager to avoid a situation in which centers such as ours will enter into a kind of spurious competition based on a "numbers game." A center experiencing less-than-optimal success rates may be tempted to alter its definition of success, or to admit to therapy only couples with an excellent prognosis. If a center reports higher success rates than others, the range in which the numbers game is played may be further escalated.

The best-known success rates, of course, are those reported by Masters and Johnson (1970). We can report, and we can honestly assure candidates for therapy, that at the time of follow-up, couples who have completed our two-week program report significant benefits from the program in approximately the same proportions as are reported by Masters and Johnson. Favorable results are most frequent for premature ejaculation, as is the experience of others; success with impotence is also high. Orgasm is easily achieved unless the woman wants orgasm in a specific situation and place; this is harder to manage. What of couples who cannot afford to spend $2,700, and devote two full weeks of their lives to uninterrupted therapy?

The ten-day program is for couples who can't or won't give two weeks of their time to therapy or who don't need the two weeks but need more than a short term program. It varies from the two-week program in a number of ways. Less time is spent with the couples since less time is available. Fewer films are seen and there is no follow-up. The advantages are that a person need only take off work for one week since the program starts on a Friday and goes through the week to the following Sunday. The cost is less at $2,100. Follow-up if needed can be arranged at fifty dollars an hour with one therapist, which is the regular fee. Since few people need the follow-up, that isn't critical. If more help is needed, however, the fifty dollar an hour fee can rapidly mount and it is reassuring in the two-week program to know that more help is available without added cost.

During the past several years we have sought to explore ways of bringing the same basic therapeutic techniques to couples assembled in groups for short periods. Our "group workshops" have lasted from one to six days and from three to ten couples have usually assembled in each group.

To save time, we dispense with the psychological testing, physical examination, and sex history taking, and we present truncated versions of our usual body-image procedures and sexological examinations. We include foot, face, body, and sexual caress exercises and as many of the films described above as time permits. Thus the group workshop is a mini-version of our two-week intensive program.

The results can be described as promising, especially for couples whose problems are not too deep-seated. The great majority of couples participating report benefit. Research data is now available to show this is a valuable therapeutic modality for less severe problems. As might be expected, the longer group workshops produce better results. For some couples, the group experience itself seems to facilitate progress; participants encourage and support one another. Progress in some groups seems to be contagious. A few couples make greater progress during a short-term workshop than some couples make during intensive two-week therapy without a group. None of the dire forebodings of what might happen if sex education and sex therapy were offered in a group materialized.

Our experience to date has persuaded us to experiment further with group workshops and with other possible formats for presenting the same procedures more economically.

Laboratory research. Emphasis on research is essential to provide a continuing scientific foundation for sex therapy. Continuing research is the basis upon which evolving sexual therapy can realistically be regarded as "scientific." Along with its clinical program, the Center for Marital and Sexual Studies has conducted laboratory research in four major areas:

1. Studies elsewhere of "biofeedback" have produced remarkable results in several fields. It has been reported, for example, that some patients with high blood pressure have learned to lower their blood pressure when presented with a display panel or signal system which continuously informs them of their blood pressure changes. In collaboration with Zev Wanderer, Ph.D., of the Center for Behavioral Therapy, we have sought to determine whether a similar biofeedback system might benefit a particular subgroup of

individuals with sexual dysfunction. These individuals report lack of a feeling of sexual arousal despite the fact that instrumentation indicates physiological arousal is occurring. A device called the photoplathysmograph was used in this study; it provides an individual with a continuous objective indication of his own sexual arousal or absence of arousal. The procedure has proved of some value in teaching some individuals to recognize arousal when it occurs.

In later work with a physiologist, Dr. Berry Campbell, a professor of physiology at University of California at Irvine, using an audible signal system attached to a photoplathysmograph, one woman has learned to fantasize an orgasm. This work is continuing.

2. With Duane Peterson, M.D., electromyographic studies were made of muscle responses among male and female research volunteers viewing Danish pornography. Muscle tension was recorded in various regions of the hand and genitals while subjects viewed films of sexual intercourse. Male and female responses were alike in some respects and unlike in others.

3. Many sciences have progressed from a description of broadly similar features characteristic of all individuals in a group or species to a study of individual differences within a group or species. As a result primarily of the pioneering work of Kinsey and of Masters and Johnson, the broad general outlines of human sexual response in both males and females are now well established. In cooperation with Berry Campbell, Ph.D., we have launched our first studies of individual variations within these outlines. We began with a group of female research volunteers who masturbated to orgasm in the laboratory while such physiological parameters as respiration, pulse, and vaginal and anal muscle tension were simultaneously recorded.

Are all orgasms alike? Our preliminary findings, based on repeated orgasmic responses by one hundred and eleven women, indicate that the orgasm profile varies somewhat from orgasm to orgasm for a particular woman—but that much wider variations differentiate one woman's orgasms from another's. Indeed, the physiological profile of each woman's orgasms may prove to be as characteristic and as unique to her as her fingerprints. A possible interpretation is that once a woman learns to have orgasm in a particular pattern, she tends to continue in the pattern—though other interpretations cannot yet be ruled out.

To date we have recordings of fifteen multiorgasmic men. These include continuous as well as separate and discrete orgasms. Further work is necessary before a report is prepared on this subject.

4. The only objective way reported to date to gauge the "success" or "failure" of coitus is in terms of orgasm. We have sought to explore whether other objective measures can be applied using the "interaction process analysis approach" of Bales (1950). Our initial data were videotapes of coitus

of twenty-five volunteer research couples. After preliminary efforts at evaluation, we constructed a set of six scales covering both the skill-related and the
emotion-related aspects of sexual interaction. Three teams of observers, with
males and females on each team, then evaluated the twenty-five tapes in
terms of these scales. The consensus reached by one team paralleled the
consensus reached by the other team; but criteria and evaluations are being
further refined and prepared for publication.

A variety of other laboratory research studies are in various stages of
planning or pilot invesitgation. It took enormous courage, skill, tact, and other
qualities for Kinsey and Masters and Johnson to launch their trailblazing
undertakings. It is this kind of scientific research activity, however, that we see
providing the foundation for future scientific evolution of the special educational activity called sex therapy. Other scientific studies of human sexuality
also are making significant contributions and contemporary journals are
reporting increasingly valuable new research findings.

References

Bales, Robert F. *Interaction Process Analysis*. Cambridge, MA: Addison-
    Wesley, 1950.
Dickinson, Robert L. *Atlas of Human Sex Anatomy*. Baltimore: Williams &
    Wilkins, 1949.
Hartman, William E. and Fithian, Marilyn A. *Treatment of Sexual Dysfunc-
    tion*. Long Beach, CA: Center for Marital and Sexual Studies, 1974, and
    New York: Jason Aaronson, 1974.
Hartman, William E.; Fithian, Marilyn A.; and Johnson, Donald. *Nudist
    Society*. New York: Crown, 1970.
Kegel, Arnold H. "Genital Relations, Urinary Stress Incontinence and Sexual
    Dysfunction." In *Office Gynecology*, ed. J. P. Greenhill. Chicago: Year
    Book Medical Publisher, 1965.
Kinsey, Alfred C.; Pomeroy, Wardell B.; and Martin, Clyde E. *Sexual Behavior
    in the Human Male*. Philadelphia: W. B. Saunders, 1948.
Masters, William H. and Johnson, Virginia E. *Human Sexual Inadequacy*.
    Boston: Little, Brown, 1970.
Semans, J. H. "Premature Ejaculation: A New Approach." *South. Med. J.* 49
    (1956): 353–57.
Wright, Helena. *More About the Sex Factor in Marriage*. London: Benn Bros.,
    1959.

3

Sexual Identity and Sex Roles

Milton Diamond

One of the areas of recent research is in the
development of sexual identity and sex roles.
It is an area where there is still much
disagreement, and as in most areas of sex
research, conclusions remain somewhat
tentative. One of those doing research in the
field is Milton Diamond, Ph.D., professor of
reproductive biology at the University of
Hawaii School of Medicine. Diamond,
though an interested participant in the
research, attempts to assess the contributions
of various researchers with whom he is
sometimes in agreement and sometimes in
disagreement. Diamond has participated in
the Chatauqua series sponsored by the
National Science Foundation, has prepared a
series of sex education films for public
television, and has written extensively in the
field, most notably in his *Perspectives in
Reproduction and Sexual Behavior, and
Abortion Politics.*

The recent prominence in the newspapers of people like Dr. René Richards
and author Jan Morris, or movies like *Dog Day Afternoon* have brought to
common knowledge a situation which, to most average readers and movie
goers, is bizarre. The situation is one in which an individual is born and raised
as a male, yet considers himself to be a female. Such individuals are *transsexuals* and might also be individuals born and reared as unequivocal females
who nevertheless consider themselves male.

How, it is asked, could one grow up in our American society and yet, as if
in disregard of "all that is holy" or acculturated, effect such a complete switch
in sexual identity and gender role? And further, even if one could make the
switch, why would one? Certainly, the question of how one might come to
change and why one might want to are two separate but related questions.

39

Occuring as they do at the same time confuses the matter further to provide an intriguing enigma.

Understanding of these changes has only really developed in the last two dozen years or so. While these cases are intriguing for their novelty, an underlying question is of much broader interest: how does anyone come to "know" he or she is male or female? What follows is a somewhat historic account of how we now come to answer this question. As a participant observer to this history over the past twenty years, the development presented will obviously have a personal perspective.

In the late fifties and early sixties (when Christine Jorgensen was the popular focal point of such questions) the answer would be quicker in coming than it is today. At that time, one would simply be informed that one comes to "know" what he or she is by what is taught or learned.

At that time this would not have been hard to accept. It is common knowledge now, and was then, that from birth society treats males and females differently. Starting at birth, boys are given masculine names and blue blankets, while girls are given female names and pink blankets. If these types of distinctions are not always true literally, they certainly are true figuratively. But forces other than common experience were at work.

For example, social forces of the post-Korean War era were attempting to correct problems of social bigotry with demonstrations and academic confrontations. The marches and sit-ins were effective; they raised a public consciousness to the injustices of discrimination and laws were forced to change. Academics for their part showed how many of the differences between the races could be attributed to differences in societal pressures and teachings. Going further some then asked why, if basic features of race were not innate, should basic features of sex necessarily be innate? Perhaps, it was hypothesized, stereotypes in sexuality were due to an acculturation that would bear elimination.

Another social movement of the times was the emerging feminism. The social awareness of women being treated differently from men—and the minority, second class nature of this treatment came essentially after the publication of *The Feminine Mystique* in 1963. This movement had the effect of giving political and emotional force to the emerging academic theory that sex differences were made, not inborn, and to rectify past wrongs, society ought to remove these differences.

Another somewhat different yet still related zeitgeist was occuring in psychology. Psychologists at this time were strongly into learning theory—human behaviors are learned, not inborn—and those on our side of the Atlantic were merrily scoffing at our colleagues in Europe who, using terms like innate, considered behavior to be controlled to a large degree by instinct.

In many ways everyone was right and wrong at the same time. With the benefit of hindsight we can see that the situation was akin to the blind men investigating the elephant. Without an appreciation for a very broad picture, understanding of the development of sexual identity or sex role was impossible.

One of the first tasks among those interested in the issues involved (and to us for this discussion) was to agree on definitions for some terms. Many commonly-used terms were erroneously used interchangeably and went undefined. We now, however, have come to a consensus. An individual's *sex* refers to being male or female, as related to having testes or ovaries respectively. This is biological and fixed. An individual's *sexual identity* refers to that person's private and personal assessment of his or her sex. It is the person saying inwardly, "I am a male" or "I am a female," "which may or may not be in concert with my gonads." The ways in which a person's inner identity may be reflected to the public via lifestyle and activities is the person's *gender* or *gender identity*. The *gender (sex) roles* for males and females are sex-appropriate behavior patterns accepted by society as sex-related. Patterns that, in our society, are most often displayed by men are considered *masculine* and those most often displayed by women are considered *feminine*. *Sex-appropriate* or *sex-typed behaviors* are those that are culturally accepted as associated with either being male or female. So far so good. The arguments begin to multiply and get more heated when one now restates the original question thusly: how does society's institutionalizing of a gender role relate to a person's sexual identity and vice versa? In terms of transsexuals like Rene Richards and Jan Morris, or others like you and me, how does society's ordering or structuring gender roles, knowingly or not, affect our sexual identity and vice versa?

In the late fifties and sixties several areas of research were expanding to help view the elephant. Investigators watched children at play, with or without their parents, in mixed sex groups, in family situations and in different cultures from within our own borders to far-flung anthropological haunts. Researchers interviewed normal adults to find out how they understood their own development and checked to see how they behaved in their lifestyles. Clinicians began to review patients with various sexual orientations and biological and social incongruities (hermaphrodites, pseudohermaphrodites, homosexuals, transvestites, etc.) to try and understand their development. And significantly, scientists began to look to other species, primates as well as nonprimates, to see what light these could shed on the subject.

In those "early" days, the findings of psychologists often seemed contradictory in explaining the development of sex-appropriate roles. For example, children of either sex were found to imitate a powerful model when the model was successful, but models could be of either sex and the behaviors acquired may even be a result of punitive consequences. Early studies on aggression indicated that physical aggression was expected more in boys and rewarded for them more than girls, while dependency was more acceptable in girls. Though data was admittedly scarce and recognized as such, it was easy to consider a *theory* that posited that individuals developed their sexual behaviors due to societal pressures ("social-learning" theory); i.e., gender appropriate behaviors are brought about by suitable external social rewards influencing the child. According to this theory, a suitable identity develops with appropriately rewarded behavior.

Supporting a learning model were studies that indicated that there were many models of male and female behaviors from which the child could learn how to behave in sex-appropriate ways. In the development of sex behavior patterns, this modeling, as the presence of such individuals to model, ("role modeling" theory) were believed crucial. Indeed, studies were available to support what people know—namely that children learn by imitation. Some researchers, however, considered this modeling as the most important element in the development of identity; almost as if the child assimilates a sex role identification as the indelible outcome of a satisfactory relation between the subject and model. To most psychologists, thus, identity was a *product* of social learning or modeling.

The findings of anthropologists were also somewhat conflicting yet informative. Their major contribution was to show that while cultures may vary immensely in that many tasks are divided by sex or ranked in order of prestige, some consistencies held cross-culturally. One finding is that in all cultures, children are generally raised by women and this doesn't seem to pose problems for development of appropriate sex roles. More significantly for the present discussion, many societies have established mechanisms within them for individuals to abstain from accepting assigned gender roles they think inappropriate for themselves. And cultures exist in which, even though gender roles are *not* strictly assigned, the development of sex-appropriate behaviors follows a normal nonambivalent course. For example, among American Plains Indians, male individuals might develop and act as females in the absence of any role models or cultural script for them to follow and in the absence of cultural reinforcement. These males, called *berdache*, were accepted and categorized on the basis of their behavior. How different they are from our own society where we give first priority to the genitals and gonads.

Most of the clinicians concerned with questions of identity were psychotherapists. For them in the fifties and early sixties, transsexual individuals and, indeed, *homosexuals* (individuals whose sex and sexual identity are in concert and who have sexual preferences for members of their own sex) as well were considered sick. The former were classified delusional and the latter regarded as suffering from "arrested development." These interpretations were based on clinical impressions rather than experimentation or studies where normal individuals were also examined. The individuals they did get to see, in the main, were troubled persons seeking help. Small wonder these therapists saw such people as disturbed. The heterosexuals they saw were also disturbed. The transsexuals and homosexuals (and heterosexuals) who were functioning well in society and not disturbed didn't seek help. The theoretical rationale used by most clinicians was Freudian theory which was

considered "normal" sexuality—identity and preferences—the natural predestined outcome which would lead to heterosexual coitus with the biological underpinning of reproduction.

In one clinical area, however, a line of research was developing which
was significant to understanding sexual identity. This involved the study of
hermaphrodites and pseudohermaphrodites. These individuals were seen at
clinics for various reproductive, fertility, endocrine and genetic concerns.
According to the prime researchers in that area, Money, Hampson and
Hampson, despite disparity between an individual's genetic sex, gonadal sex,
hormonal sex, internal and external genitalia and the way the child was
reared, in the vast majority of cases, the gender role assumed by the child was
consistent with the sex of rearing. In their own words:

> In the light of hermaphroditic evidence, it is no longer possible to
> attribute psychologic maleness or femaleness to chromosomal,
> gonadal or hormonal origins, nor to morphological sex differences
> of either the internal or external genitalia. . . . From the sum total of
> hermaphroditic evidence, the conclusion that emerges is that sexual
> behavior and orientation as male or female does not have an innate,
> instinctive basis. In place of a theory of instinctive masculinity or
> femininity which is innate, the evidence of hermaphroditism lends
> support to a conception that psychologically, sexuality is undiffer-
> entiated at birth and that it becomes differentiated as masculine or
> feminine in the course of the various experiences of growing up.

In essence, this, for the period 1955–1965, represented the prevailing
opinion of most clinicians and American psychologists; i.e., newborns were
psychosexually neutral-at-birth and developed their sexual identity and behaviors via learning or modeling forces.

Meanwhile, two sets of laboratory experiments were being conducted
which had wide ranging repercussions. One, set in the laboratories of William
C. Young and his collaborators, showed conclusively that the adult sexual
behavior of animals could be programmed (organized) simply by the animals
being treated with hormones prenatally, even though the treated mothers
showed no effects from the treatment. Females subjected to male hormones
before birth by injections given to mother did not show their typical female
behaviors. Instead, they displayed male-like sexual activities which otherwise
would not be seen. The extent of this adult behavior could be regulated by the
amount of hormone, the timing, and the duration over which the material was
administered prenatally.

The second series of experiments involved work from several laboratories which demonstrated that not only was the nervous system of animals
programmed as male or female from birth, particularly in regard to sexual
behavior and reproduction, but that effecting this system was relatively
simple. The hypothalamus was observed to be "switching effective sex," as

the result of a single hormone injection. For example, a female rat given a single injection of male hormone the first week of her life would never ovulate nor exhibit typical sexual receptivity.

The implications of these laboratory experiments, that animals indeed come into the world sexually programmed to a large extent, obviously was at odds with the clinical, psychological and general impressions mentioned above. And as discussed, the psychological studies were in conflict within themselves. An attempt at synthesis or reconciliation of the disparate reports was needed and, within a year, two appeared: an article in the *Quarterly Review of Biology* by the present author in 1965, and a book edited by Eleanor Maccoby in 1966. These works, each in their own way, pulled together material from many different studies and various disciplines in an attempt to understand the nature of sexual behavior and how various behaviors developed.

My article dealt primarily with the biological and clinical aspects of the problem, while Maccoby's book considered, in the main, the psychological aspects. Both were again looking at different parts of the elephant. Unfortunately, but predictably, the article and book were generally read by different audiences and received with mixed reviews. Nevertheless their publication provided a backdrop with which subsequent thought, theory and research had to deal.

My article, I think, along with my subsequent work, did several things. First: the prevailing opinion of how psychosexuality developed was severely challenged by placing the biological studies on animals into human perspective and showing humans and animals on an evolutionary continuum. All other species are sexually programmed although the extent varied with the species. Humans may show the least of any species, but there is no evidence for believing there is a complete divestiture of evolution in this regard. Second: the rapidly accumulating research on animals showed how relatively simple it was to permanently alter adult sexual behavior patterns by treatment paranatally; something that had implications for humans. Third: the interpretation of the work with hermaphrodites and pseudohermaphrodites was disputed since the same findings could (and in my opinion do) result from these individuals being particularly flexible and labile to postnatal experiences due to their biological abnormalities. And fourth: most crucially, many clinical cases were presented where individuals emerged with sexual identities and behaviors at complete odds with their upbringing. Instead of being sexually neutral at birth, it was argued that:

> primarily owing to prenatal genic and hormonal influences, human beings are definitely predisposed at birth to a male or female gender orientation. Sexual behavior of an individual and thus gender role, are not neutral and without initial direction at birth . . . we are dealing with an interaction of genetics and experience; the relative

contribution of each, however, may vary with the particular individual concerned. . . . It is the genetic heritage of an individual which predisposes him to react in a particular manner so that the learning of a gender role can occur.

This appeared to be the first strong contemporary statement that humans, not only other animals, were so significantly subject to their biological heritage in regard to sexuality. This inherent sexuality was seen as a built-in "bias" with which the individual interacted with the environment. This was not a theory that denied the effects of learning or experience, but rather one that suggested how this interaction most probably was organized. The article went further, however, and gave the theory a clinical aspect by recommending that individuals, like transsexuals or hermaphrodites, be allowed to choose for themselves how they might live (their gender roles) rather than have their roles imposed by others.

Many in the field reacted quite affirmatively to the theory but not everyone was convinced. To many, the reaction was "maybe for animals, but for humans the rearing events are apparently so overwhelming that sexual identities are socially learned. And allowing individuals like transsexuals to change their sexual lifestyle would be catering to their delusion rather than curing them."

My intention was not to set up a nature versus nurture, or heredity versus environment controversy, but to argue for a synthesis wherein an individual's biological heritage provided a predisposition which was potentially setting limits to a pattern greatly modified by life's experiences. The individual interacted and learned from life's situations in a manner biased by his or her biology. The theory was thus referred to as a "sexuality-at-birth" theory, in distinction to a "neutrality-at-birth" theory. Another name for the "sexuality-at-birth" theory, focusing on the postnatal period, was "biased-interaction" theory. The impact of the argument and the data presented was significant. No longer could one give a simplistic denial to the crucial role biology plays in sexual orientation and behavior.

The Maccoby book had a greater influence in the social sciences. In it, several authorities reviewed the status of various theories of psychological sexual development, including "social learning" and "role-modeling." These theories were well-supported.

To the review of the established psychological theories, however, a relatively new one was offered by Lawrence Kohlberg. In essence, Kohlberg theorized that:

sexual development starts directly with neither biology nor culture, but with cognition . . . by the child's cognitive organization of his social world along sex-role dimensions. . . . This patterning of sex-role attitudes is essentially "cognitive" in that it is rooted in the child's concepts of physical things—the bodies of himself and others—concepts which he relates in turn to a social order that makes functional use of sex categories in quite culturally universal ways.

With this cognitive-theory base, learning is believed to be influenced by reward in the following way: the child first somehow conceives of himself as a boy or girl and internally says to himself something like, "I am a boy, therefore I want to do boy's things and doing so is rewarding." The inner identity the boy has determines what will be rewarding.

Research findings providing support for this theory were available. For example, kindergarten children were found to hold strongly to their "masculine" or "feminine" values regardless of punishment or reward and these masculine or feminine values could actually themselves determine the value of situational rewards. With these types of finding, cognitive theory has identity as a *cause*, rather than *product* of social learning and modeling.

Since all behavior must be somehow rooted in the nervous system, one might rhetorically ask where this initial self-concept of the child comes from and answer: "the biological heritage." Is it a chicken and egg puzzle? I do not think so. We have a good idea where we humans come from. We come from other species in which the mammalian biology preceded the human socialization processes, but invariably they must interact in concert to be adaptive. With all theories in the Maccoby book considered, the author of the summary chapter, Sanford Dornbusch, a sociologist, stated, "We have seen again and again in this volume that it is difficult to separate the cultural product from its biological base."

Another significant book was published in 1966; *The Transsexual Phenomenon* by Harry Benjamin. This book focused on the clinical condition which, by its very nature, gives immense support to the sexuality-at-birth thesis. The book reviewed the largest collection of cases of known transsexuals to that time. These were individuals brought up in concordance with their unambiguous gonads and genitals, yet as adults considered themselves members of the opposite sex. Despite rearing as males, for example, they claimed to be (not just *wanted* to be) females. The transsexual says, "I am a female but, for some unknown reason, have the body of a male. I am wrongly imprisoned." In the overwhelming majority of cases reviewed, there was no evidence or doubtful evidence of any childhood conditioning toward this expression. Certainly the usual view of social learning and role-modeling was called into question.

A significant volume of work sympathetic to the understanding of transsexualism appeared in 1969. Edited by Green and Money, this book explored transsexualism from social, psychological, clinical and legal aspects. This volume with its highly respected contributors added a great deal of support to the cause of transsexuals and understanding of their situations among the medical profession. Most psychologists and sociologists, however, due to its specific focus of this volume and its predecessor, were unaware of the publication and the implications it contained for understanding the wider area of sexual identity and gender roles.

The years from 1966 until 1974 saw an abundance of research and writing relating sexual identity and gender roles. Some of the work was exceedingly significant with contributions from various disciplines. Inevitably, a share of the work was repetitious with advocates of social learning and modeling mustering strong arguments and theory for their side, while no fewer were being presented in favor of biology's force. It is regrettable that none were able to achieve a synthesis of the nature and nurture interaction sufficient to capture a consensus of psychologists, clinicians, biologists and sociologists (not to say anything about special interest groups like feminist or gay organizations). Two attempts occurred in 1968. One in a book I edited entitled *Perspectives in Reproduction and Sexual Behavior* and a major effort by Stoller in his book *Sex and Gender*. Both presented clinical cases which supported the biased-interaction theory. Stoller said it this way:

> A sex-linked genetic biological tendency toward masculinity in males and femininity in females works silently but effectively from fetal existence on, being overlaid after birth by the effects of environment, the biological and environmental influences working more or less in harmony to produce a preponderance of masculinity in men and of femininity in women. In some, the biological is stronger and in others weaker.

Two books appeared in 1972 and 1973 which strengthened the arguments of the social learning advocates and those who attended to the significance of environmental forces as being deterministic in shaping human sexual behavior: *Man and Woman, Boy and Girl* by Money and Ehrhardt and *Sexual Conduct* by Gagnon and Simon.

Money and Ehrhardt appeared to repeat and expand on the material presented in 1965 regarding sexuality and biased-interaction-at-birth. While allowing for the prenatal force of biology they still interpreted the majority of findings to give postnatal rearing the final say in organizing an individual's sexual identity and gender role. One new report included in their material has become classic and influential in maintaining anew the questions "How does anyone come to know he or she is male or female?" and "What organizes behavior?" The report described a set of male twins who were circumcised by cautery. Due to an accident, one had his penis burned off. With the belief that sex is primarily a social phenomenon and identity is learned, in the absence of a penis, the decision was ultimately made to raise the penectomized boy as a girl. The other brother would be raised as a boy. The experimental stage was obviously set to test if the rearing as a female would overcome the biology of the male. Several years later, when about six years old, the twin reared as a girl, aside from some tomboyish behavior, was reported by Money and Ehrhardt to identify and generally behave and accept the role of a girl. According to them she dresses, plays and plans as a girl. The twin brother identifies and behaves as a normal boy. This was certainly seen as good fuel for the power of rearing and social forces over biology. But is it?

Instead of letting rearing compete with biology, the penectomized twin was subsequently castrated to remove the androgen source, had surgical reconstruction begun to enhance appearance as a female and placed on a schedule for female hormones. Indeed, while the wisdom of the original decision might be questioned, these practices would be in keeping with such a decision and humanitarian motives should take precedence over experimental niceties. It must be realized, however, that as much as possible was done to defeat the male biological realities and enhance female biological maturation.

Sexual Conduct provided a theory that would support the force of social experience in organizing sexual behavior. This theory of *"sexual scripts"* reinforced the twin study report and continues to have a significant impact particularly with learning theorists, psychologists and sociologists.

A *sexual script* is described as an internal rehearsal to describe sexual behavior. It is supposedly a sexual script that defines not only the situation but the actors and the plots in a sexual experience.

> Scripts are involved in learning the meaning of internal states, organizing the sequences of specifically sexual acts, decoding novel situations, setting the limits on sexual responses, and linking meanings from nonsexual aspects of life to specifically sexual experience.

According to the theory's proponents, these scripts are learned and provide: "the ordering of bodily activities that will release these internal biological states. Here, scripts are the mechanisms through which biological events can be potentiated." The script, a product of experiences and learning of what is and is not appropriate in our society, not only provides a social reference for each actor in a sexual situation, but provides an intrapsychic motivating force to produce arousal or at least a commitment to a sexual activity.

Gagnon and Simon provided much anecdotal material as well as some correlated data from other studies to bolster their theory of sexual scripts. Their explanation had a great deal of appeal since it combined social learning and biological forces in a socially acceptable comprehensive package.

If 1972 and 1973 were good for environmental theorists, the next year went to the biologists.

An experiment of nature was reported on in 1974 by Imperato-McGinley and coworkers. In its own way, it must be considered classic. For those who were keeping score, it reinforced the predictive value of the "biased-interaction" theory, and cast doubts on the "twin-experiment" and theory of "sexual scripts" as formulated.

In a small community in the Dominican Republic, due to a genetic-endocrine problem, a large number of males were born who, at birth, appeared to be females. These males had a blind vaginal pouch instead of a scrotum and, instead of a penis, had a clitoris-like phallus. (They thus looked "more female" than the penectomized twin.) The uneducated parents were unaware of anything unusual and these males were raised as typical females in the community. There was no reason to do otherwise. At puberty, a spontaneous change in their biology induced a penis to develop and their psychological orientation to change. These males, born years ago and raised as females, nevertheless, at puberty individually gave up their living as females and assumed life as males. The medical researchers concluded:

> Psychosexual orientation (postpubertal) is male, and this is of considerable interest, since the sex of rearing in eighteen of the affected males was female. Despite the sex of rearing, the affected were able to change gender identity at the time of puberty. They consider themselves as males and have a libido directed toward the opposite sex. Thus, male sex drive appears to be endocrine related, and the sex of rearing as female appears to have a lesser role in the presence of two masculinizing events, testosterone exposure in utero and again at puberty with development of male phenotype.

These individuals obviously did not agree that the sex of rearing and assigned gender roles were more important than their own inner sexual identity and preferred roles. Any "scripting" obviously was not potent enough to organize the biological events relative to sexual identity and sexual preferences—these individuals, despite being raised unambiguously from birth to puberty as females, saw themselves as males and found females to be their erotic choice.

Of equal importance for another 1974 review of our elephant of sexual identity and gender roles was an impressive publication by Maccoby and Jacklin—*The Psychology of Sex Differences*. As its 1966 predecessor, it again provided a major reference for work on psychological and social aspects of sexual behaviors. Although the book did not directly address the question of sexual identity nor present a new theoretical approach to its study, it did question the basis for psychological sex differences, and in the process provided a valuable review of scores of studies pertinent to the popular theories of role-modeling and social learning.

This review contradicted many commonly held impressions and stereotypes in regard to sex-typing of behavior and the organization of gender roles. For example, mothers were not found to treat their sons or daughters differently in encouraging cooperation or dependency, or discouraging aggression.

Moreover, fathers punished their sons more than their daughters for being aggressive. Neither parent encouraged aggression as a way of resolving disputes. There was also no evidence that, for small children, mothers chose different toys to offer sons as compared with daughters. The children themselves behaved or chose differently according to sex, while the parents did not.

In regard to frank sexual matters like masturbation, display of nudity, genital play with peers and asking questions about sex, parents were equally likely or unlikely to punish or accept the behavior in young sons or daughters. There is no doubt, according to the classical Kinsey studies, however, that these behaviors are not displayed equally as often by males and females.

Some of their conclusions, best stated in their own words, are:

> Our analysis of the arguments concerning the role of modeling in sex-typing and our review of the research on selective imitation have led us to a conclusion that is very difficult to accept, namely *modeling plays a minor role in the development of sex-typed behavior.* This conclusion seems to fly in the face of common sense and to conflict with many striking observations of sex-typed role playing on the part of children. (emphasis added)

The volume was not a complete loss for role-modeling or social learning theory. While these theories were not seen as crucial in the *acquisition* of a behavior, they were seen as important in the proper *performance* of the behavior. Boys and girls may both know how to farm, cook, sew or fight, be aggressive, dependent or nurturing. Independent of the sex and behavior of the available models, however, typically males and females seem to acquire and perform these traits with different ease and predisposition. A further conclusion was:

> It is reasonable, then, to talk about the process of acquisition of sex-typed behavior—the learning of sex-typed behavior—as a process built upon biological foundations that are sex-differentiated to some degree.

It certainly seems in the main that from 1974, evidence as interpreted not only by biologists but among some psychologists as well, was pointing to a strong constitutional influence in structuring sexual identity and gender roles. The influence of nature on identity proved most strong and independent of subsequent socialization and learning. The influence of nature on gender role seemed less absolute and more a matter or providing a bias to what is learned and most suitable for individual expression.

The effects of the 1974 publications are yet to be fully appreciated in regard to how the average professional or lay individual would now answer the question "How does one come to know he is male or female?" While the bulk of evidence available, when seen in toto, seems to argue for an inner biological "voice," an "innate feeling" that develops quite young, many find this concept unacceptable, or at least not yet proven. For me, the research and reviews of 1974 provided even greater assurance that humans develop sexually in line with a "biased-interaction" theory. Reflecting on the twins referred to earlier, I became more fully convinced that, as I predicted in 1965 for such cases in general, with puberty the penectomized twin has a good likelihood of rebelling at the assignment of rearing which is in conflict with biological heritage. Acceptance of female identity, if it occurs, may be due more to the biological intervention than the social situation.

During 1974, the broader issue (zeitgeist) of feminine activism and social justice prompted, and still prompts, evaluation of these findings in regard to various public conscience issues. On the one hand, it has been advocated that if biology calls the tune, societies should socialize children to enhance sex differences and maximize biological tendencies, e.g., aggression should be fostered in men and nurturance in women. This supposedly would lead to greater self-satisfaction and less social disappointment. On the other hand it has been argued that to increase self-satisfaction of individuals and better society, efforts should be made to moderate male aggression downward and male nurturance upward.

I suggest a third option is available: allow anyone, male or female, the freedom to choose what they want to learn and what they want to do and how they prefer to be viewed without societal condemnation for any choice as long as it doesn't conflict with the public good. The individual himself/herself then becomes the arbiter of his/her own lifestyle.

Since 1974 there has been additional synthesis and integration. Studies from various disciplines have added significantly to the research pools, but the basic theoretical arguments remained relatively unchanged. In 1976, a new compilation and analysis has appeared. Only time will tell if its attempt at synthesis and integration of the various data and theories has been successful. The compilation and analysis are presented in *Human Sexuality in Four Perspectives* edited by Frank Beach. Investigators of various stripes presented their views on broad issues in human sexuality. With recognized authorities as spokesmen the likelihood that the thought of one "school" may more quickly become known and integrated with those from another is increased and hoped for. A more comprehensive synthesis may therefore evolve. Certainly such an attempt was made by the editor in choosing the participants. However, it remains for each reader to do the same for himself/herself for a major effect.

In regard to the book's treatment of sexual identity and gender role development there appears to be agreement that "sexuality-at-birth" is accepted by all and, instead of a nature-nurture dichotomy, there is a nature-nurture interaction. That a programmed "biased-interaction" for postnatal behavior exists is less generally accepted. Disagreement persists in the significance of postnatal experiences relative to postnatal biological maturation. That there is interaction is admitted, but how and how much remains at issue.

The volume contains an update of various theoretical positions. For my part, I proposed that a single continuum does not provide an adequate model of masculine or feminine behavior development. While male and female are different and separate, masculinity and femininity are not necessarily poles apart; rather their consideration warrants separate criteria. Further, to better specify categories of behavior for study in relation to possible influential factors, *four behavioral levels* must be assessed for an individual; *sexual identity* as defined above is only one level. In addition three others must be evaluated: *patterns* (those behaviors easily modified by learning and culture, such as dress codes and hair styles), *mechanisms* (those behaviors relatively free from learning and culture, such as penile erection, vaginal lubrication or orgasm), and *object choice/preference* (those behaviors relative to choosing an erotic or love partner). These four levels of behavior are believed to be each associated with its own neural tissues controlling them. These tissues are hypothesized to develop independently under different influences and with varying rates. Their independent development allows for typical development when in phase but atypical development, e.g., transsexuality or homosexuality, when out of phase.

Money has developed his thesis to now fully incorporate the idea of "sexuality-at-birth" which he calls "phyletic programming." In Money's concept, however, there is considerable amount of leeway for this "phyletically-written program." The program as he sees it may be altered by idiosyncrasies of personal history.

> Postnatally, the programming of psychosexual differentiation becomes, by phyletic decree, a function of biographical history, especially social biography. There is a close parallel here with the programming of language development. The social-biography program is not written independently of the phyletic program, but in conjection with it, though on occasions there may be disjunction between the two. Once written, the social-biography program leaves its imprimatur as surely as does the phyletic. The long-term effects of the two are equally fixed and enduring, . . .

Kagen reviews some pyschological aspects of sex differences. His approach is, to a large extent, cross cultural and results in another good view of our elephant. His analysis points to a high degree of agreement in the interpretation of or understanding of what is male and female across the world.

> The cross-cultural uniformity on these symbolic dimensions of masculinity-femininity has important implications. All individuals possess a set of basic assumptions about the essence of maleness and

femaleness. Even if we could change the familial treatments to which children are exposed and could arrange the social environment so that all adults treated boys and girls equivalently, we might not totally eliminate sex differences, because of the symbolic interpretations of masculinity and femininity derived from irrevocable differences in size, strength, differential anatomy, and life functions . . . psychological differences between the sexes are, in large measure, the result of differential socialization; nevertheless, the general agreement on the content of sex-role standards across many cultures suggests that different societies are responding in the same way to differences in physical qualities and normal life functions. As a result, they are constructing similar sets of sex role standards.

The underlying theme of personal symbolic interpretations of maleness and femaleness is reminiscent of Kohlberg's cognition theory. It presupposes some internal standard against which individuals compare possible behavioral or physical attributes. This internal symbolism is seen as the possible result of biological forces interacting with experience. However, the interaction is such that men and women are universally seen "sensitive to different aspects of experience and gratified by different profiles of events." This last statement seems reminiscent of a "biased-interaction" philosophy.

Beach, in his introductory chapter to the volume considers the presentations of Diamond, Money, and Kagen and concludes:

the developmental perspective centers upon the origins and ontogeny of differences between the sexes . . . and the reasons are not far to seek. A moment's thought will prove that any concept of sexuality would be impossible without the accompanying concepts of male and female . . . *there cannot be sexuality without sex.* . . . We cannot understand sexuality until we understand sex. We must comprehend differences between male and female before we can grasp differences between masculine and feminine.

Beach then proceeds to synthesize from the volume's chapters and his own analysis how the basic male-female differences are evolutionarily consistent and congruent with "congenital sex differences in the predisposition to learn and perform [discriminable sex] roles [which] accounts in part for the existence of those male-female differences which are observable today in most, if not all, human societies."

How long will it take for these ideas to catch hold, be disseminated and widely accepted remains to be seen. As orginally discussed, ideas change slowly and those with vested interests, although well meaning, often prefer to maintain their idea of the status quo or urge acceptance of certain systems instead of others. We can, however, now offer a theory that synthesizes all the above to answer our original question about sexual identity and sex roles with

Figure 1. A Proposed Model of Sexual Development Which Incorporates Contemporary Theories

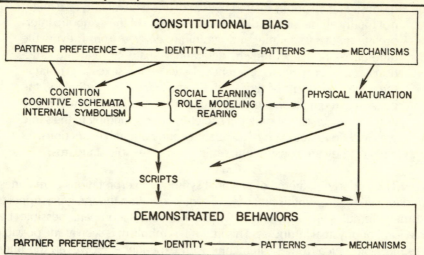

An individual constitutional bias organizes four levels of sexuality: partner preference, identity, patterns and mechanisms. Via the intervention and interaction with internal (e.g., cognition) and external (e.g., social learning) and physical processes, one arrives at observed demonstrated behaviors.

a little more certitude, albeit with a little more complexity. The test of this theory, as any other, is how well it provides for past findings and allows prediction of future ones. (See Figure 1.)

An individual is born with a certain biased predisposition to interact with the world in certain ways. Part of this bias leads to a cognitive frame (cognitive schemata and internal symbolism) which provides a preprogrammed standard against which possible behavior choices will be considered. The basic feature of this standard is sexual identity—an internal and personal conviction as to being male or female. Different male and female forces bias which behaviors are modeled and what learned from the environment. The experiences to which one is exposed may be likened to a smorgasbord offering from which certain things will be chosen and others left according to one's individual taste. During the experiences of growing up the forces of rearing are crucial in providing reinforcement or challenge to one's concept of self but they are normally not deterministic. Rearing and experiences will provide socially and culturally possible models and scripts from which the individual might choose and order future behavior. An individual reared in a sex incongruent with his/her sexual identity (e.g., a transsexual or malassigned child) will manifest this incongruity by not accepting sex roles or impositions that are out of character. But part of the "smorgasbord" offering of experience must include the possibility of free choice.

For normal individuals in open societies the "smorgasbord" choice is wide since so many different patterns, sex roles and gender roles are possible and indeed are seen cross-culturally. It is for this reason that masculine and feminine patterns may appear so admixed in normal males and females. Many families or situations do not allow free choice and stifle attempts at individual expression. The fact that many so-called sexual aberrancies appear in families where there is an absent parent would, according to this theory, not be due to the absence of a proper role model or guiding influence, but rather *due to the absence of severely inhibiting influences* that that parent would present. An individual's basic natural tendencies (to have *gender identity* conform to *sexual identity*) would be allowed to develop. The presence of overly rigid forces (parents, or others) would also prevent free choice and thwart the emergence of natural tendencies.

To provide the healthiest normal environment for sexual growth it is humanistically proposed that all individuals be provided the richest possible banquet of experiences from which to learn and model freely without fear of social censure. Then in regard to sexual identity, preferences and roles, they ought to be free to act as they wish. Males and females will then be truly free to express who and what they are.

References

Beach, Frank A., ed. *Human Sexuality in Four Perspectives*. Baltimore: Johns Hopkins, 1976).

Benjamin, Harry. *The Transsexual Phenomenon*. New York: Julian Press, 1966.

Diamond, Milton. "A Critical Evaluation of the Ontogeny of Human Sexual Behavior." *Quarterly Review of Biology* 40 (1965): 147–75.

_____. "Genetic-Endocrine Interactions and Human Psychosexuality." In *Perspectives in Reproduction and Sexual Behavior,* ed. Milton Diamond. Bloomington: Indiana University Press, 1968.

_____. "Human Sexual Development: Biological Foundations for Social Development." In *Human Sexuality in Four Perspectives,* ed. Frank A. Beach. Baltimore: Johns Hopkins, 1976.

_____, ed. *Perspectives in Reproduction and Sexual Behavior*. Bloomington: Indiana University Press, 1968.

Dornbusch, S. "Afterword." In *The Development of Sex Differences,* ed. E. Maccoby. Stanford, CA: Stanford University Press, 1966.

Friedan, Betty. *Feminine Mystique*. New York: Norton, 1963.

Gagnon, J., and Simon, W. *Sexual Conduct: The Social Sources of Human Sexuality*. Chicago: Aldine, 1973.

Green, Richard, and Money, John. *Transsexualism and Sex Reassignment*. Baltimore: Johns Hopkins, 1969.

Imperato-McGinley, J.; Guerrero, L.; Gautier, T.; and Peterson, R. E. "Steroid 5 α Reductase Deficiency in Man: An Inherited Form of Male Pseudo-hermaphroditism." *Science* 186 (1974): 1213–15.

Kagen, J. "Psychology of Sex Differences." In *Human Sexuality in Four Perspectives,* ed. Frank A. Beach. Baltimore: Johns Hopkins, 1976.

Kohlberg, L. "A Cognitive Developmental Analysis of Children's Sex Role Concepts and Attitudes." In *The Development of Sex Differences,* ed. E. Maccoby. Stanford, CA: Stanford University Press, 1966.

Maccoby, E., *The Development of Sex Differences.* Stanford, CA: Stanford University Press, 1966.

Maccoby, E., and Jacklin, C. M. *The Psychology of Sex Differences.* Stanford, CA: Stanford University Press, 1974.

Money, John. "Human Hermaphroditism." In *Human Sexuality in Four Perspectives,* ed. Frank A. Beach. Baltimore: Johns Hopkins, 1976.

Money, John, and Ehrhardt, Anke. *Man and Woman, Boy and Girl.* Baltimore: Johns Hopkins, 1972.

Money, John; Hampson, J. G.; and Hampson, J. L. "An Examination of Some Basic Sexual Concepts: The Evidence of Human Hermaphroditism." *Bulletin of the Johns Hopkins Hospital* 97 (1955): 301–9.

Phoenix, C. H.; Goy, R. W.; Gerall, A. A.; and Young, W. C. "Organizing Action of Prenatally Administered Testosterone Propionate on the Tissues Mediating Mating Behavior in the Female Guinea Pig." *Endocrinology* 65 (1959): 360–92.

Stoller, R. J. *Sex and Gender.* New York: Science House, 1968.

4

Transsexual Surgery

Julius H. Winer

One of the results of the research described by
Diamond in the preceding article is an
increasing willingness by surgeons to perform
operations on patients who feel their
biological identity is not their true sexual
identity. Transsexual surgery was pioneered
in the 1920s and 1930s but the public did not
become aware of it until the Christine
Jorgensen case. One of the surgeons presently
engaged in performing transsexual surgery is
Julius H. Winer, M.D., F.A.C.S., a Beverly
Hills urologist, who is also affiliated with the
University of California at Los Angeles.

In recent years, as increasing numbers of individuals have sought surgical sex
change operations, the need for careful selection and screening of these
patients has assumed greater and greater importance. This is because there
has been and still is a high incidence of emotional and physical complications
associated with the operation. The most effective approach, and the one we
recommend is team management of this group of patients. Preoperative
evaluation, both surgically and psychologically, is essential; the types and
progress of the surgery must be carefully and regularly evaluated, and long-
term follow-up studies are essential. In our opinion, the management "team"
should consist of at least a urologist and a psychiatrist or psychologist, but
might also involve the help and contributions of individuals in numerous
other specialties.

No patient should be given urological sex conversion unless he or she is
able and willing to undergo prolonged psychological evaluation followed by
adequate preoperative endocrine and social management. Surgery should be
preceded by the hormone management, and in the male to female patient
with a preliminary implant mammoplasty (breast implant) at least six months
prior to the proposed genital surgery.

The above is a minimum. For patients who come to us we insist that they have a confirmed lifestyle of crossdressing for at least five years prior to the proposed procedure and that they have at least two years of careful evaluation and contact with competent psychiatrists or psychologists. We also require at least one year of hormonal management. Since our criteria are so strict, our dropout rate has been high, and many have rushed off either to foreign countries or to other surgeons for a more easily obtained surgical procedure. This, in our experience, has resulted in the return of a significant number of those patients back to us with a large number of complications or incomplete procedures. Some of this might be inevitable, since when surgery has been initiated elsewhere, such as orchiectomies (castration), the ethical urologist often will go ahead with the reconstructive surgery. Unfortunately, however, a distinct number of these patients have returned with complications, not only surgical, but psychological, and some are suicidal. Still we have not hesitated to do our utmost to help in their rehabilitation.

When patients for urological sex change present themselves for their initial consultation, their opening statements are almost routine, probably having been passed along by gossip from other applicants. Males who want to change their sexual identity state that "I have always felt that I was a woman in a man's body," or "I always played with dolls as a child, and did not engage in sports," or "I was always considered a 'sissy'." Females to males have similar stereotyped answers. As a matter of routine we refer all patients to a psychologist or psychiatrist. If they express reluctance to go we explain to them that we are not referring them for therapy, since if they needed psychological therapy we would not have considered them for any type of surgery; rather, our referral is essential to the management of their case, including the screening to find appropriate patients, and in providing postoperative support. If any mental aberrations are noted, surgery in our opinion should be deferred until after the need for any psychiatric therapy is over.

The greatest number of patients who come in requesting sex-change surgery are found to be poor candidates for this surgery. Some of them turn out to be intersex patients who need more complicated procedures and investigation. Others are not true transsexuals, but have considerable emotional conflicts with regards to their self-concepts of masculinity or femininity. In the patients who have had adequate crossdressing and psychiatric evaluation and clearance, our next step is to advise the performance of breast implants which will then still be a reversible procedure. This procedure is much less serious than the more rigorous surgery to follow.

Following the use of large doses of female hormones, the patient's skin softens, there is development of breasts and atrophy of the gonads. The insistence on breast augmentation operations and plastic surgery for other purposes undergone by these patients also aids in their feminization. A number of surgeons have performed initial castrations, occasionally as office procedures, and we have had the occasion to be consulted for scrotal hematomas and infections.

The surgical vaginoplasty, transplantation of the urethra and penectomy are the most strenuous of the procedures. The need for careful postoperative follow-up, particularly in those patients where a vaginal stent is required which must be kept in situ, is necessary. The patients must be impressed with the need to continue their follow-up procedures. With the appropriately selected patients and properly performed surgery, most of these patients have been enthusiastic and could almost be considered exhibitionists when in the medical office.

Surgical complications resulting from surgical procedures have been noted in some patients operated on abroad. Complications include those following excision of residual corpora cavernosa and excess corpus spongiosum of the penis where the presence of these structures adjacent to the vagina caused it to occlude on erection.

Inadequate construction of a deep perineal vagina has also been common in our experience with complications. These have occurred in patients operated on in sections of this country (where patients are kept in the hospital and in the area for only a brief period of time following their surgery, then returned to their home locality for surgical follow-up, if any). A number of urethral strictures have required dilatation.

The transsexual must be differentiated from atypical homosexuals, transvestites, and personality disorders and neuroses.

Though transsexuals are so dissatisfied with their sexuality as to seek surgical therapy, it is important that the therapy be aimed at total complete rehabilitation. The surgeon should attempt to meet expectations of the patient. As stated above, many of these patients seem to be coached and give a completely "pat" story by rote, answering all questions that could be asked, before they are asked. Therefore in many of these cases, the history is no longer pertinent, even when supported by a battery of the common psychological testing procedures. The occasional hypogonadal types may be indicative of some degree of intersex, emphasizing the need for chromosomal karyotype studies. As mentioned above, the large number who are rejected, or should be rejected, include the homosexual, exhibitionist, psychotic, psychopath, the highly devout, celibate, and those who threaten suicide. The reactions of the patient's family should be carefully integrated into the evaluation. These studies should be explained to the patients as necessary preoperatively to avoid any postoperative regrets.

The patient should be evaluated and advised in regard to hospitalizations, insurance, creation of an identity prior to surgery, and the possible surgical complications, risks, and options. Some of the investigations may require the assistance of endocrinologists. Plastic surgeons, obstetricians, and gynecologists may also participate in this interdisciplinary procedure. Guid-

Table 1.   Urological Timetable for Transsexual Management

Urologist

Gynecologist
Plastic Surgeon
Endocrinologist

Psychiatrist-screener
Psychologist
Counselors, Rehabilitation, etc.
Sociologist

Male to female	Female to male
Live as a female for up to 5 years	Live as male for up to 5 years
↓	↓
Female hormone Rx 1+ years (testicular atrophy, adequate breast enlargement in minority)	Male hormone Rx 2+ years (testosterone enlarges clitoris, beard, etc.)
↓	↓
Breast augmentation surgery at least 6 months prior to vaginoplasty	Lower abdominal penile tube graft
↓	↓
Vaginoplasty (Preliminary orchiectomy if adequate atrophy) Penectomy, partial perineal dissection and perineotomy. Skin grafts and peno-scrotal inversion and clitoroidal-labial construction.	Stage I 6 months Release Upper End tube-graft and glans penis phalloplasty
	↓
	Stage II Combined with Mastectomies Salpingo-oophorectomies Hysterectomy
↓	↓
Follow-up IVP's Vaginograms Hormone therapy Prostatic-vaginal exams Rehabilitation Psycho-social and behavioral	Stage III (?) Insert inflatable F. Brantly Scott type of prosthesis
	↓
	Follow-up Urethral calibration Hormone therapy Psychological Behavioral Rehabilitation

ance by lawyers, sex counselors, vocational counselors and theologians is also necessary. Although primarily the procedure is male to female, occasionally the urologist is called upon to do the female to male procedure. For many years only the urethral tube was formed, since the insertion of a rigid plastic stent lead to erosion of this type of implant. However, the use of an inflatable penile prosthesis is well suited for use in this type of patient.

Greater emphasis must be made on the need for educating our colleagues and the hospitals concerning these patients. The prime consideration is their rehabilitation into their new sex identities. The psychological and sociological diagnoses and rehabilitation of this group of patients are emphasized.

In evaluating these patients, it is important that the surgeon take a neutral attitude both toward the final diagnosis and the steps involved in transsexual surgery. A number of these patients will appear with atrophic testes or traumatized testes and request surgery, insisting that their insurance hospitalization will take care of this particular portion of the procedure.

The urologist, as a part of a gender identity team multidisciplinary group, has the primary responsibility for the performance of the surgery and care for the patient's postoperative surgical status and follow-up. The urologist who comes in after surgery has already been initiated and some preliminary care has been performed. He has the unenviable job of correcting the complications and assuming some responsibility for the patient's rehabilitation. The necessity of a second formidable procedure has been frequent. The complications of the various operations used in transsexual surgery include the introital stenoses, the requirement for use of long-term stents; the use of isolated bowel segments; the frequent sloughing due to rigid stents; rectal injuries; infections; hydronephrosis due to urethral trauma behind the bladder; urethral fistulas including urethrovaginal fistulas; urethral strictures; recto-vaginal fistulas; and the hair growth in the vagina; this last has not been too great a complication in those cases where the scrotal skin becomes inverted into the vagina.

The complications occurring in the female to male procedures with or without the addition of an os penis to the penile tube, include strictures, sloughs, scars of the donor sites; hair in the urethra; fistulas, infections, calculi and urinary dribbling. Extrusions of the permanent implants of cartilage or rigid silastic can also complicate this procedure. Efforts at avoiding complications have been reported by various investigators. The use of the Lowsley prostatic tractor during the construction of the vaginal orifice has improved the procedure. The use of an O'Connor drape for perineal dissection with the rectal finger in place is also a safeguard. The importance of fishmouthing the urethrovaginal anastomosis also eliminates some of the complications. The follow-up prophylactic therapy includes: (1) Periodic intravenous pyelograms, to assure immediate or delayed non-involvement of the lower ureter; (2) Vaginograms periodically to forestall vaginal stenosis; (3) Constant hormone therapy with the knowledge of the need for frequent physical examinations, because hormone therapy will not prevent cancer of the prostate in the transsexual, one case of which has been reported by Markland. The prostate and breasts should be checked periodically in the patient who is receiving hormones.

Summary

The surgical schedule of a patient for sex change procedures must allow for the sociological, endocrinological and preoperative management, in addition to the psychological and psychiatric screening. This must be timed as noted in this paper, but may be varied depending on the psychological needs of the individual patient. Guidance by the various counselors, including the vocational and theological advisors, is important.

References

Brosman, S. *Personal Communication*. January 1977.
Laub, D. R., and Gandy, P., eds. *Second Interdisciplinary Symposium on Gender Dysphoria Syndrome*. Stanford: Stanford University Medical Center, 1973.
Money, John. "Intersexual and Transsexual Behavior and Syndromes." *American Handbook of Psychiatry*, Rev. ed. Edited by S. Arieti. New York: Basic Books, 1974.
Stoller, R. J. *Sex and Gender*. New York: Science House, 1968.
Stone, C. B. "Psychiatric Screening for Transsexual Surgery." *Psychosomatics* January 1977.

5

A Social Psychologist Looks at Scientific Research on Homosexuality

Richard W. Smith

Sex researchers, like researchers in other fields, have learned to be cautious in reading into their findings more than might actually be there. Though research into the physiology of sex has enabled many sexual therapists to deal more effectively with sex dysfunction, and research into sex and gender development has made us more understanding of transsexuals and others who do not conform, there is still much that we do not know. Richard W. Smith, Ph.D., a professor of psychology at California State University, Northridge, and one of the founding members of the Center for Sex Research there, offers some words of caution based upon his own research.

In the late 1940s, a social psychologist named Stanley Schachter wrote his doctoral dissertation on how people in a group typically react when there are some members who do not conform. The results of his carefully designed research, which other psychologists, anthropologists, and sociologists have later substantiated and generalized, can be summarized as the "Schachter effect." It has three basic parts:

1. In any set of human beings, the majority of individuals conform to the accepted beliefs and behaviors of their group, and this majority pays a great deal more attention to *deviance* from social standards than it does to *conformity*, which it usually takes for granted.

For example, people who consider cows sacred, such as orthodox Hindus, notice when other Hindus deviate and eat beef, but don't particularly observe the large numbers of their comrades obeying the taboo against such behavior. And, in any group, members wearing a frowned-upon kind of clothing (such as a woman dressed in a bikini or a nun's habit in a synagogue, or a man walking down Wilshire Boulevard in a kimono) often draw more attention from people than do the many who conform to the ordinary attire.

This attending primarily to those who deviate seems to be especially pronounced when the social standards are emotion-laden.

2. The conformers often perceive the deviants in negative ways—as "sick," "dangerous," or "unhappy," and so on. Such negative labeling occurs whether the nonconformist is a practicing Christian Scientist in Leningrad, Russia, or an avowed atheist in Tuscaloosa, Alabama. (Indeed, in many languages the words meaning "deviant" frequently have a pejorative connotation: to be "different" is to be "bad.")

The conformers then pressure the "unsatisfactory ones" to behave in a manner accepted by the group.

3. If the conformers cannot convert the variants into following the majority's emotionally-tinged norms, the conformers usually try to eject the nonconformers from the group.

The Schachter effect appears to be something like an automatic social mechanism which insures that most people perceive the world, and behave, similarly to the gut-level ways of the individuals around them. Those who drift away from accepted attitudes and behaviors are observed suspiciously by others. Persons who continue to deviate are ostracized.

Some version of the Schachter effect seems to occur in all fairly cohesive human agglomerations, from the smallest face-to-face discussions to the largest ongoing civilizations—no matter how naive, sophisticated, religious, atheistic, or whatever, the human collectivities are. The executive who wears nothing but jockey shorts in his office, the Marine who insists on always keeping his pants on in the barracks, the orthodox Jew who eats lobster, or the Englishman who keeps two wives, are equally targets of the effect. Only the *style* of the "schachtering" varies from one group of people to the next, from one era to another.

The phenomenon does not depend on whether the disliked activity is objectively harmful, neutral, or beneficial. The action simply must be taboo in that particular group.

The Schachter Effect and Scientific Research on Homosexuality

Anyone who has studied the writings of scientists on homoeroticism, and also the research of Schachter and his coworkers on human reactions to deviance, can't help but be struck by obvious connections. With the exception of Kinsey, some societal reaction theorists, and a few gay liberationist researchers (who will be discussed later), most scientists studying homosexuals (and, for that matter, most ordinary citizens looking at that minority) behave exactly as the Schachterians have found *any* majority of people reacts to *any* kind of gut-level nonconformity. (Parenthetically, we should note that the scientists we are talking about come almost exclusively from societies that have strong emotional taboos against homoerotic activity. Although there are cultures that permit, encourage, or require various gay acts, such groups are usually small and nonliterate, and do not produce investigators on this topic.)

If we relate the Schachter effect to work on homosexuality, we find that:

First, scientists and clinicians from western societies have done a lot of research on homosexuality—especially on theories regarding its possible causes, and on how to discover homosexual tendencies in people. The scientists have not, however, done a correspondingly large amount of research on *hetero*sexuality and its possible causes, and how to detect it. ("The majority pays a great deal more attention to *deviance* from social standards than it does to *conformity*, which it usually takes for granted.")

Second, much of the language that the investigators use to label gay persons and gay acts shows that the researchers perceive the nonconformists in nonneutral terms. ("The conformers often perceive the deviants in negative ways—as 'sick,' 'dangerous,' or 'unhappy,' and so on.") Words such as "perversion," "degenerate," "psychopathology," "aberration," "abnormal," "sodomite," "disturbed," and "distorted" occur frequently in the supposedly neutral scientific literature. (Such pejorative terminology continues to be used after the American Psychiatric Association's change in nomenclature regarding gay people. The scientific writers thus parallel the average citizen's continued use of words like "queer," "dyke," "fag," "fairy," "fruit," "sinner," "sissy," "pansy," and so on.)

The scientists have also devoted (and are still devoting) a substantial part of the research literature to trying to find ways to convert the gay people in their societies to heterosexuality. ("The conformers pressure the 'unsatisfactory ones' to behave in a manner accepted by the group.") The unfriendly attitudes of the researchers carry over to the techniques they sometimes use to convert. These techniques have included castration, lobotomies and localized brain ablations and electroshock, and often still include drugs that induce nausea, vomiting, and cessation of breathing, as well as various intensely stressful kinds of psychotherapy. (These painful and dangerous techniques resemble the methods used by the Inquisition, although the rationales are opposite. The Church tortured "faggots" because the gays supposedly had *freely* chosen to behave that way, and hence were "sinners." The clinicians still sometimes treat homosexuals because the latter supposedly *cannot* make free choices in their sexual behavior, and hence are "mentally ill"—despite the American Psychiatric Association's recent revision of its categories.)

An important special case of the conversion literature is that devoted to finding ways in which heterosexual parents can discover homoerotic tendencies in their children, and then pressure those potentially gay children to grow up heterosexual instead. Presumably, the philosophy behind such work is the old saw "As the twig is bent, so grows the oak."

Finally, at least some of the research writing has concerned itself with how to eject unconverted homosexuals from various groups, such as by imprisoning gays, forcing them into psychiatric hospitals, passing laws forbidding them to immigrate into the country, having informal understandings that expel gays from medical practice or teaching or psychoanalytic training, and so on, as well as by refusing to give jobs or welfare to homoerotic persons, or to allow them to rent or buy houses, etc. Science thus joins religion, law, the military, governmental investigating agencies, and other social institutions in ostracizing those nonconformists it cannot convert.

Gay people who have noticed that they were being "schachtered" have often been thought of as paranoid. (Indeed, psychiatrists and psychologists have produced a number of theories precisely on this topic: so many individuals with homosexual tendencies seem to think they are being spied upon, whispered about, converted, deprived of jobs, or harassed in different ways, that "delusions of persecution" must obviously be part of the homosexual "syndrome" or vice versa.)

In contrast to the gay people's awareness of being observed, pressured to conform, and ostracized, the nongay scientists—again like the ordinary citizens of the same societies—seem to show little awareness that anything like this is going on. In fact, the whole Schachter effect appears to be actually *invisible* to the very people whose perceptions and behavior it *best* describes. (A majority's proclivities are often unconscious to them—precisely because everybody has the same ideas and behaviors. Most of us continually and subliminally compare our perceptions of reality, and our actions, with those around us. If everybody else perceives things, and then acts, in the same way we do, we go ahead and live and act comfortably in our perceived reality. If disliked "deviants" disagree with our perceptions or behavior, and a huge majority agrees with us, then part of our perception is that the nonconformers must be rationalizing, or lying, or somehow psychologically denying the obvious truth which we and the vast majority perceive and act upon. If a formerly heterosexual woman turns gay and announces that she is much happier as a lesbian, then the poor wretch has clearly gone haywire. If a previously homosexual man changes to heterosexual and claims that, as a member of the majority, he is now much happier, then the fortunate fellow has finally given up all those earlier defense mechanisms which caused him to misperceive so badly. The socially-defined version of reality is thus the only one that most of us perceive and act upon. And part of this perception and behavior is the Schachter phenomenon.)

Because we are so totally enculturated in a heterosexual mode of behaving and perceiving reality (many American children learn to call anybody they dislike a "queer" or "fag" by about the age of three or four, and millions of adults in western societies uncritically accept sweeping, hostile generalizations about gay people), it is difficult for most researchers to see themselves engaging in the Schachter effect. For such researchers, and other members of the majority, it sometimes helps to compare the scientific literature on homosexuality to the literature on roughly comparable phenomena, such as homoraciality. Doing this sometimes makes the invisible visible.

If homo*sexuality* is defined as "restricting one's sexual and other intimate activities primarily or exclusively to members of one's own *sex*," then homo*raciality* can be similarly defined as "restricting one's sexual and other intimate activities primarily or exclusively to members of one's own *race*." Whereas homo*sexuality* is taboo in the societies most researchers come from, homo*raciality* is not. (Even the most vociferous critics of "racism" are usually homoracially married themselves. "Racism" is somewhat taboo in terms of *non*intimate, *non*sexual areas like jobs, schooling, public housing, and so on, but same race *intimate* relations are at least emotionally *accepted,* if not unconsciously *preferred,* in science-oriented societies.)

Going through the components of the Schachter effect again, we find:

1. Very little research has been done on homoraciality, even though scientists could ask approximately the same questions about it that they ordinarily ask about gayness. ("Is homoraciality hereditary or environmental? Is it caused by prenatal hormonal influences on the brain, or early learning experiences? Is it a kind of imprinting? At what age do homoracial tendencies begin? How can parents spot incipient homoraciality in their children? Can it be completely reversed, or only partly?") Again, the majority of scientists have been unable to see the conformity surrounding them (and which they often share), even while spending hundreds of hours curiously wondering about the deviance.

2. Very little unfriendly writing occurs in the scientific literature about homoraciality. Whereas the common attitude about gays is "What is *wrong* with them for being homosexual," it is almost impossible to find parallel negative questions being asked about preferring same *race* sexual relations. But, to coin a few such questions: "Is homoraciality caused by an aversion for the bodies of people of a different race? Or is it caused by a fear of people whose bodies are different? Is it caused by a bad sexual experience with someone of another race? Or is it caused by seduction by a member of the *same* race when the child's sexual preferences are still developing? If animals engage in it, then is it natural? Do animals living in their native environment ever restrict their mating to members of their own color? (For example, do white dogs mate only with other white dogs? As an aside, we might note that we occasionally have observed dogs mounting another member of the same sex—homoeroticism—but we haven't personally seen, say, a tan canine restrict its sex exclusively to other tan dogs—homoraciality.)

According to the Schachter effect, hostile questions about homoraciality should be infrequent, whereas those about homosexuality should be almost the only kind asked. Thus, *positive* inquiries about gays should be unlikely. ("Do lesbians find that most women are more loving than most men, and consequently choose same-sex intimacy over opposite sex relations? Just how do gay men manage to avoid all the pressures to conform? Do members of the same sex give each other more intense pleasure than do members of the opposite sex? Is homosexuality a beneficial and natural way to reduce the overpopulation problem?") And *negative* questions about *hetero*sexuality should also be unlikely. (e.g., "What is wrong with heterosexuals? Is fear of being sodomized by another man the cause of male heterosexuality? Are heterosexual men unconsciously afraid of being castrated if they are in a sexual situation with another male? Do heterosexual men have an aversion to the bodies of other males? If so, what traumatic or otherwise unpleasant experiences did they have which caused these aversions? Was it wrestling with a stronger boy as a child? Was it being tackled in football? Was it smelling bad body odors in sweaty gyms and dirty locker rooms and public toilets? Is heterosexuality caused by a need to conform, or by a lack of creativity? Do nongays get that way because they did not have close-binding, intimate mothers? Do people become heterosexual by psychologically over-identifying with the parent of the same sex? Or with siblings of the same sex? Or playmates? Are children or teenagers made heterosexual by being seduced by a member of the opposite sex? Do straight women have an unconscious contempt for other women? Do such females have an aversion to the bodies of other women? Is having an excess of hormones of one's own sex in the bloodstream, or a deficiency of hormones of the opposite sex, a factor in the etiology of heterosexuality? Must heterosexuals use unnatural objects and chemicals to avoid causing overpopulation?") Such negative questions are seldom asked, because heterosexuality and male fear of castration and being sodomized, and aversions to the bodies of one's own sex, and an excess of same-sex hormones in one's body, and psychologically identifying with same-sex parents, and so on, are all socially accepted, and common. Such conformity thus, given the Schachter effect, goes relatively unnoticed, and certainly unpunished, by the majority.

It is impossible to find any parallel scientific literature on conversion away from homo*raciality* (as opposed to *racism,* which, as a nonintimate phenomenon, *is* written about) as on conversion from gayness. If a scientist wrote an article suggesting brain surgery, castration, drugs that stop breathing, etc., to try to cure those who prefer sex with their own race of their hypothesized fears and aversions to members of another race, would such an article be acceptable to the editors of scientific journals? (*Many* such articles on gay persons have been published.)

3. Finally, the literature on how to eject homo*racials* from various groups (medical practice, teaching, etc.)—because they may affect others by their homoraciality—simply does not exist. If a black female high school teacher is married to a black man, not even George Wallace or Anita Bryant

would probably worry that this might cause some students to want to marry a person of their own race. According to the Schachter phenomenon, groups do not try to eject conformers—no matter what caused the conformity, or what possible fears or aversions keep them conforming. Once again, the research literature follows the Schachter effect. (And so do the researchers. How many evolutionary theorists are willing to speculate, in print, about possible adaptive functions served by homosexuality—adaptive functions that may have guaranteed that gayness survived in our species? Speculations about nearly everything else abound in highly theoretical areas like evolutionary theory, but to hypothesize *too* much about homosexuality is to run the risk of being "schachtered" as a possible gay oneself. Thus, the orthodox scientific view continues to be that homosexuality could not have had any survival value for our ancestors, and hence everybody must be biologically totally heterosexual today. This idea then becomes the basis for "schachtering" the gays as "unnatural" which, in turn, makes it professionally dangerous for a biologist to challenge—or even to conceive of alternatives to—the current paradigm, which is then used to "schachter," and so on. The socially-defined reality is once again the only one perceived by the majority.)

Deviations From the Schachter Effect Itself

The Schachter effect states that the *majority* of individuals in a group study nonconformists, perceive them in negative ways, try to convert them, and attempt to eject them from the group. *Not all* group members do these things, however.

There are *some* individuals who conform to the group's norms in their own attitudes and behavior, but are totally unconcerned about variants. And, of course, the nonconformers may themselves adopt the majority's attitude towards their own deviance. ("Why am I this way? How can I change? Society's beliefs are those of God, Science, and Truth, so mine must be sinful, unscientific, and false. Perhaps I should leave town or commit suicide if I cannot convert to society's definition of acceptable feelings and behaviors.") *But,* the nonconformers may also define their *own* norms, and in so doing refuse to be "schachtered."

Among sex researchers, a few—such as Kinsey and his coworkers and later members of his Institute, some sociologists involved in social labeling theory and societal reaction theory, and others—have avoided incorporating the Schachter effect into their research (although the effect takes into account the fact that not *everybody* "schachters" deviants). And, of course, the nonconforming gay liberationists have steadfastly refused to be "schachtered."

Whether or not Kinsey's methods were perfect or his results unassailable, whether or not social labeling theory is true or even a particularly clear or scientifically precise view, or has been adequately tested by research is not at issue here. What *is* the point is the fact that some researchers *do* set aside unconscious majority biases and yet theorize and gather data. The gay liberationists are now more and more insisting that *all* researchers do this.

Such research would seem to be eminently more objective and dispassionate than much recent work has been. Perhaps behavioral "science" would evolve from pseudoscience to real science.

References

Becker, Howard S. *Outsiders: Studies in the Sociology of Deviance*. New York: Free Press, 1966.

Dank, Barry. "The Homosexual." In *Outsiders, U.S.A.*, ed. Patricia Keith-Spiegel and Don Spiegel. San Francisco: Rinehart Press, 1973.

Hoffman, Martin. *The Gay World: Male Homosexuality and the Social Creation of Evil*. New York: Basic Books, 1968.

Saghir, M. T., and Robins, E. *Male and Female Homosexuality: A Comprehensive Investigation*. Baltimore: Williams & Wilkins, 1973.

Schachter, Stanley. "Deviation, Rejection, and Communication." *Journal of Abnormal and Social Psychology* 46 (1951): 190–207.

Scheff, Thomas J., ed. *Labeling Madness*. Englewood Cliffs, NJ: Prentice-Hall, 1975.

Weinberg, George. *Society and the Healthy Homosexual*. New York: St. Martin's Press, 1972.

6

Interpreting Data on Sexual Conduct and Social Change

Veronica D. Elias

The cautionary note sounded by Richard W. Smith in the previous article appears in the article by Veronica D. Elias, Ph.D. A professor of sociology at California State University, Northridge, Elias was also one of the founding members of the Center for Sex Research at Northridge and is currently its director. Professor Elias studied at the Institute for Sex Research at Indiana University founded by Alfred Kinsey.

There is a disturbing inclination among contemporary scholars studying human sexual behavior to invest their research findings with interpretations that are, for the most part, unwarranted. While this statement may displease some of my colleagues involved in the study of human sexuality, it is important to come to grips with the possible causes and effects of such misinterpretations, so as to present accurate observations to others outside our field.

If we are to correctly assess changes in sexual attitudes and behaviors over recent decades, we must first recognize that such changes can only be understood within the context of the part played by sexuality in relation to other elements making up the fabric of our social structure, including the family, economy and polity, and certain values regarding the phenomenon of social change. The frequent failure to place sexual conduct in perspective has encouraged the present confusion regarding changes in the sexual area relative to those in other sectors of life.

The work of William Simon and John Gagnon, in *Sexual Conduct: The Sources of Human Society,* is a notable exception to what I see as a disturbing tendency toward lack of academic responsibility in interpretations of our observations of human sexual conduct. In *Sexual Conduct: The Sources of Human Society,* they point out that:

. . . as a society, we are saddled with and delighted by an imagery of change—indeed, of revolution—when we talk about sexuality. This climate of opinion clouds our ability to judge accurately whether or not there is change, and, if there is, what direction it is taking. The demand for novelty, even in scientific research, distorts the process of data collection. It highlights the dramatic to the detriment of the pedestrian and forces the creation of theories that are overweighted in the direction of change. At the same time, the imagery of change becomes a variable not only in scientific activities, but in social life itself.[1]

In my own career as a sex researcher I have noted the receptivity to the "novel" versus the "pedestrian" to be reflected in the relative willingness not only of the media (where I expect it) but of scholarly publications (where it dismays me) to accept far more readily research that is novel than that which is less stimulating, perhaps, but nonetheless important. For example, I have relatively little difficulty finding a forum to discuss research in such dramatic areas as "changes in female attitudes toward male nudity" but a less welcome reception toward work dealing with the more mundane inquiry into sources of sexual learning among children.

Simon and Gagnon also observe that an " . . . even greater difficulty which affects any discussion of sexual behavior is our profound lack of information."[2] I do not discourage research in novel areas; since our field reflects a relative paucity of data, any information that may be gathered has the potential to further understanding of this segment of human activity. By the same token, in a broader sense, it is not my place, nor that of any scholar to dictate which areas of behavioral and attitudinal phenomena are legitimate scholarly concerns. Having said this, nonetheless I must observe that too often what little research exists rests on a negligible theoretical foundation and reflects evidence of bias based on our love affair with the new and different. It contains too little reference to social and psychological dynamics and the place of sexual behavior in the context of total life experience. More particularly, I find disturbing the inclination on the part of some investigators to adopt a noncritical attitude toward either theoretical underpinnings or quality of research methodology in the face of that which is "unique" or "different" in approach. Not a few academicians recently espoused to students the "innovative" *findings* of *The Hite Report* [3] only to find on closer inspection that on methodological bases having to do with sampling and return rate *alone*, their willingness to accept results uncritically was an embarrassment to the field. Without detracting from the importance of the topics Ms. Hite addresses, I must echo Dr. Wardell Pomeroy, coauthor of the original Kinsey studies, who was quoted as saying in response to Hite's work, "I do not favor biases or politics when they enter the portals of science."[4] While we cannot eliminate bias, and while I do not believe there can be, nor should be, such an endeavor as "value-free" social research, surely we must not let the demand for novelty guide either the collection of data nor the interpretation of its results.

Let us then briefly examine the question of change in sexual conduct and attitudes, looking beneath "the surface of facts" in an attempt to understand more clearly the social dynamics shaping sexual conduct. As Pavlov wrote to the academic youth of Soviet Russia just before his death, "Do not become the archivists of facts. Try to penetrate to the secret of their occurrence. . . ."[5]

The need to assess sex data (as all social data) in the context both of historical trends and current social influences is reflected in the prevalent interpretations of the original Kinsey volumes.[6] Ignoring both whatever prior data exist, as well as Kinsey's own cautious observation of a decline in sexual activity—especially of prostitution—from the nineteenth to the midtwentieth century, students of sexual behavior translated what was an effort to record present patterns of sexual conduct into incautious (at best) interpretations asserting the sudden burgeoning of premarital, extramarital, and homosexual activities indicating the existence of a virtual "sexual revolution." Such an interpretation was unwarranted. The Kinsey team assessed these data as descriptive of current patterns, and, if anything, indicative of a more balanced, less exploitative pattern of sexual relationships than had existed historically. From that time to the present, researchers familiar with this knowledge have spent an inordinate effort in trying to correct myths attesting to a wholesale sexual revolution. The persistence with which these data have been misinterpreted in the quest for the dramatic and new—over nearly three decades—since these volumes were published, is sufficient evidence for the need for a more careful, more informed, and less emotion-laden approach to sexual data. Indeed, the very propensity in our society to separate sexuality from the whole of human experience, investing it with a power and mystique quite likely unwarranted,[7] encourages magnification and misinterpretation of findings on the part of those studying sexual conduct, who bring their own social histories, including perhaps an overemphasis on "things sexual" to their work.

So long as social science adheres to the view of sexual behavior as a drive that is both strong and persistent, though admittedly variable at different times in personal life careers, we shall implicitly if not explicitly conceive of a sex drive that will propel itself out of control where external social controls are relaxed. Hence we find "authorities" predicting with strong conviction and little evidence, that a significant proportion of preadolescent children will engage in sexual intercourse in the near future—as early as ages seven or eight, where existing data do not in any way warrant such prognostications. More predictably, perhaps, we find the news media featuring articles with headings such as "Many Prepsters Admit Having Premarital Sex," where isolated quotations from thirteen and fourteen year-olds are used to build a case for the argument of widespread prepubertal or pubertal sexual activity. This is done despite the statistics cited at the end of the particular article to which I refer, which indicate that slightly less than one-half percent of the total population in a recent national survey report having had intercourse at age twelve or younger.[8] By the senior year of high school, 60 percent still report not having had sexual intercourse, indicating that evidence pointing to a sexual revolution among young people is somewhat less than warranted, based on examining data from the time of Kinsey to now. If the model of sex as a persistent drive reaching high intensity in late adolescence (especially for males) is valid, then the present relaxation of attitudes regarding such conduct should be reflected in a concomitant rise in such behavior—which apparently is not the case.[9]

While academicians and clinical practitioners have openly scorned (and rightly so) predictions by some that dancing styles, choice of dress, the advent of the automobile and so forth, must inevitably lead to sexual promiscuity on the part of young people, can we really be sure that those engaged in "scientific" inquiry are any less guilty of such unfounded predictions? How else can we explain "expert" predictions that increased relaxation of attitudes will result both in earlier and greater incidence of coitus among the very young when there is an absence of data to support such predictions? It would seem that Simon and Gagnon are hitting painfully close to home when they observe, "There is a certain commitment to finding the world more sexual than it is, more exciting, more pornographic. This pastime serves the self-interest of both sexual radicals and sexual conservatives."[10]

While sexual radicals predict a positive result from reduced social controls where conservatives predict the destruction of society as we know it, nonetheless both ends of the continuum invest sexuality with a great deal more power and autonomy than any examination of existing data would warrant.

Regretfully, I must agree to a large extent with Simon and Gagnon that our present faulty models of human sexuality do not allow for serious discussion about the future of sexuality—if by "serious" we mean discussion that not only will allow for reduction in ideological bias and adequate interpretation of sexual conduct within the context of the total society. Until we overcome these flaws, we can hardly expect to look into the future with any degree of certainty.

Having said this, there are certain statements that can be made regarding future changes in sexual patterns. If there is one societal variable setting the stage for the future in the sexual area, it is the economic factor. The rise in the standard of living since the Second World War has made alternative life styles increasingly more viable for a significant segment of the population. Not only do young people find it possible to attain economic independence from their families at earlier ages, with an increased freedom to choose alternatives, but to the degree women gain independence from economic domination by men, we can expect an increment in sexual activity prior to marriage. Given the dismaying statistics on the widening gap between the earning power of women versus men in the last decade, I expect such changes will not markedly affect those currently in the adolescent stage of life. The present decline in birth-rate coupled with improvements in the standard of living in the United States may be expected to encourage divorce where couples might otherwise live out their lives together in unhappy marriages. Without the demanding economic, emotional, and temporal commitments required of parents, those who remain childless would be expected to explore alternatives in many areas of living—cultural and recreational activities, prolonged education, and, quite possibly, sexual experimentation both within marriage and after divorce. As the Women's Movement encourages women to expect sexual fulfillment as well as the attainment of goals historically reserved for men, and as related changes in male gender styles continue in the direction of more emotional commitment and less instrumentality in respect to heterosexual and heterosocial relations, we *may* find an expected increase in sexual activity to be accompanied by a reduction in the salience given to sexual conduct in the context of one's total life situation.

In other words, I would predict that future generations will likely engage in more, and varied sexual activity, but at the same time probably will invest sexuality with less power and less mystery and it will assume more balance with the rest of life's activities. Insofar as sexual conduct is more accurately assessed in future as part—and only part—of the integrated whole of life and our value-system, I feel we can be assured that investigations into sexual conduct will benefit. Sexuality can then be seen more accurately, and our theories and explanations of sexual pheonomena will be more valid and reliable than is now the case. We will be able to predict more accurately patterns of sexual behavior across groups and through time. In the meantime, I would suggest we proceed with more caution in interpreting research results and in predicting the future. On a note of careful optimism, we would do well to heed Sir Francis Bacon: "If we begin with certainties, we shall end in doubts, but if we begin with doubts, and are patient in them, we shall end in certainties."[11]

Notes

1. John Gagnon and William Simon, *Sexual Conduct: The Social Sources of Human Sexuality* (Chicago: Aldine, 1973), p. 283.
2. Gagnon and Simon, *Sexual Conduct,* p. 284.
3. Shere Hite, *The Hite Report* (New York: Macmillan, 1976).
4. *Hustler,* Spring 1977.
5. Pavlov, *Sciences* (April 17, 1935): 369.
6. Alfred C. Kinsey et al., *Sexual Behavior in the Human Male* (Philadelphia: W. B. Saunders, 1948); and *Sexual Behavior in the Human Female* (Philadelphia: W. B. Saunders, 1953).

7. William Simon and John Gagnon, "On Psychosexual Development," in *Handbook of Socialization Theory and Research*, ed. David Goslin (Chicago: Rand McNally, 1969), p. 736.
8. *Valley News and Green Sheet* (Van Nuys, CA), April 3, 1977, p. 8.
9. Veronica D. Elias, "An Exploratory Study of Differential Sources of Sexual Socialization for a Sample of Urban Adolescents," in *American Family Relations: The Analysis of Salient Issues*, ed. Lawrence E. Sneden II and Veronica D. Elias (Lexington, MA: Xerox, 1974).
10. Gagnon and Simon, *Sexual Conduct*, p. 286
11. Sir Francis Bacon, *De Augments*, Book 1.

References

Bell, Robert R. *Premarital Sex in a Changing Society*. Englewood Cliffs, NJ: Prentice-Hall, 1966.

Bell, Robert R., and Gordon, Michael, eds. *The Social Dimension of Human Sexuality*. Boston: Little, Brown, 1972.

Elias, Veronica D. "An Exploratory Study of Differential Sources of Sexual Socialization for a Sample of Urban Adolescents." In *American Family Relations: The Analysis of Salient Issues*, ed. Lawrence E. Sneden II and Veronica D. Elias. Lexington, MA: Xerox, 1974.

Gagnon, John G., and Simon, William. *Sexual Conduct: The Social Sources of Human Sexuality*. Chicago: Aldine, 1973.

_____, eds. *The Sexual Scene*. Chicago: Aldine, 1970.

Hite, Shere. *The Hite Report*. New York: Macmillan, 1976.

Hunt, Morton. *Sexual Behavior in the 1970's*. New York: Playboy, 1974.

Kinsey, Alfred C. et al. *Sexual Behavior in the Human Male*. Philadelphia: Saunders, 1948.

_____. *Sexual Behavior in the Human Female*. Philadelphia: Saunders, 1953.

Reiss, Ira L. *The Social Context of Premarital Sexual Permissiveness*. New York: Holt, Rinehart, 1967.

Sorenson, Robert C. *Adolescent Sexuality in Contemporary America*. New York: World, 1973.

Wagner, Nathaniel N. *Perspectives on Human Sexuality: Psychological, Social and Cultural Research Findings*. New York: Behavioral Publications, 1974.

7

Three Issues Relating to Sexuality and Adolescence

James Elias

James E. Elias, like his wife Veronica, studied
at the Kinsey Institute and is now affiliated
with the Center for Sex Research at California
State University, Northridge. In this article he
reports on some of his own studies relating to
adolescence and sexuality.

Current literature abounds with discussions and definite opinions regarding
three distinct topics:

1. The question of a sexual revolution among adolescents with regard to
their sexual activities

2. The place of erotic stimuli (pornography) in the adolescent community

3. The possible relation of sex education to adolescent attitudes and
behavior patterns.

We would like to relate some of the findings of four different studies,
three of which I personally directed, which deal with the above topics and
which were conducted at the Institute for Sex Research, Inc., Indiana University, over the past four years.

The Sexual Revolution

Increased premarital coitus indicative of a sexual revolution among our
adolescent population is *not* supported by data. An analysis of the etiology of
this belief will provide some answers and perhaps help to clarify the situation
by bringing it into proper perspective. There are three levels that must be
reviewed when we discuss a sexual revolution: (1) *The media level,* where
products, programs, and performances pervade the contemporary scene,
providing an image of a sensate and sexually-oriented society; (2) *the attiudi-*

nal level, which represents those feelings and opinions that are expressed by adolescents; and (3) *the behavioral level,* which deals with those activities actually engaged in by adolescents.

First, the revolution really exists in *the media,* which bombards the public with sexual stimuli. If the population in question responded to these stimuli, and if the promises of sexual success offered by the media were fulfilled, then a real sexual revolution would have taken place. The changes that have occurred in the media are great indeed. Only thirty-five years ago there was a public outcry when Jane Russell appeared in the film *The Outlaw* (Howard Hughes), which involved the partial exposure of a breast, accompanied by the *inference* of sexual intercourse. Some may even remember that eventful December of 1954 when the first issue of *Playboy* magazine was published. The media, and its entertainment and advertisements, have moved a long way from this period, as evidenced by films such as *I am Curious (Yellow),* or by the numerous pseudonudist sexual magazines or even the explicit scenes of sexual activity shown in "adult magazines." The stag show, until recently shown mainly in V.F.W. Halls and other men's clubs, is now part of the "lunch-time special" along with toplessbottomless dancers. The most recent move has been toward live public sex shows depicting sexual intercourse on stage with one or more couples. From this, it legitimately may be said that regarding the media, a definite revolution *has* occurred. This revolution in the media has occurred rather rapidly, facilitating exposure of the population to explicit sexual behaviors and a sexual openness which in the past was only implied. Parental reaction to many of the current media presentations is one of shock—yet the parents are the prime consumers of this material, not their children. This "schizophrenic" aspect of our society clearly seems to be evident in our *normative* system, which is not in agreement with our actual practices.

Secondly, adolescents have become more permissive in their attitudes toward sexual behavior, and are openly discussing sexuality and sexual relationships as a natural part of our everyday life. Open discussions of sex often startle parents, because sex, as a discussion topic, was taboo in *their* childhoods; therefore expressed curiosity, questions about nonmarital intercourse, or even the mention of a word like "homosexuality" at the dinner table, gives parents the idea that their children have completely escaped their grasp and gone astray. Parents fail to realize that the openness of dialogue and discussion evident in today's youth, a reflection of societal changes and concerns, is not automatically accompanied by a change in *behavioral* activities.

The attitudinal change is an interesting one, because it is in this sphere of attitudes that the possible ambiguity between parental and adolescent attitudes is most evident. The last generation engaged in nonmarital and extramarital intercourse more than they apparently admitted. That is, their professed attitudes were more conservative than their behaviors. The present generation provides a *reverse* effect—that is, they are more liberal in their attitudes than in their *behaviors*. Therefore, for both parents and adolescents, their attitudes are generally inconsistent with their behaviors. Adolescents are willing to accept the fact that people sleep together outside of marriage without negative feelings toward such people. Unfortunately, parents tend to misunderstand the reversal of *attitudinal* positions, and translate their confusion into an equation that states: "Attitudinal change equals behavioral change." They also tend to project their adult frustrations, anxieties, and guilt feelings on the adolescent who has few of these "residue feelings" from the past generation.

The oral contraceptive is seen by some as a technological achievement that many assume to be responsible for encouraging an adolescent sexual revolution marked by promiscuous coital encounters—a series of indiscriminate sexual encounters without any significance attached to the *quality* of the relationship. Data do *not* support this position, but instead indicate that for the majority of the contemporary adolescent females who engage in coital activity, this occurs mainly where accompanied by strong feelings of affection for the sexual partner. Adolescent female coital patterns are strongly correlated with behavior patterns formed within the context of the family, and as such, a pattern of promiscuous coital encounters usually is not evident. The use of the oral contraceptive has changed the "marital scene" but has not made significant inroads among adolescents. Besides, the use of oral contraceptives or the nonuse of them is *not* the chief factor in deciding whether to participate in coitus, for most adolescents.

In terms of actual sexual *behavior,* adolescents have not changed radically from their parents. The frequency of nonmarital coitus has been increasing for females (Kinsey indicates approximately 20-25 percent for college females, and a more recent study at the Institute for Sex Research of college students, shows this nonvirginity rate to have risen to 33 percent). This increase has occurred over a twenty-five year period and certainly cannot be termed "revolutionary." As for males, there has been little change in the frequency of nonmarital coitus among males—it remains around the 60 percent level for college males. There is a definite increase in petting activities, including petting to orgasm, which may be a substitution for coital behavior, but a high nonmarital coital frequency, one that would accompany a promiscuous society, is not in evidence. We might add a note at this point: Those who are engaging in nonmarital intercourse are doing so more frequently, and enjoying it more than did their elders and with less guilt feelings.

Therefore the *idea* of a sexual revolution regarding nonmarital coitus is encouraged and perpetuated by the mass media, *not* by research data. Behavior increases are found mainly in the area of petting, with only a 10-13 percent increase of *nonvirginal* college females. The so-called revolution may be viewed as one of *attitudinal* change rather than behavioral changes on the *coital* level.

Erotic Stimuli

It seems most strange to us that our society chooses to restrict, repress, and condemn any material that can create a feeling of sexual arousal. Yet it is the same vocally critical members of the middle class that are among the chief consumers of erotic materials. This conflicting aspect of our society, holding disparate public and private norms, is reflected in the inconsistant enforcement of "community standards." There is no unified agreement on the evaluation of erotica.

Our studies of erotica and its place in adolescent sexual development show some interesting results: one such study dealt with depth interviews of adolescents of varying social classes. Respondents were questioned as to what material they would consider "unacceptable." The range of responses was considerable; the most frequent response especially on the part of males, was that there was little erotic material (such as nudist books, sex action graphics, stag or "blue films") depicting explicit sexual activity which they would consider unacceptable. Differences in social class and sex were evident, with the higher social classes providing a less definitive view of what was unacceptable, defining materials relative to their aesthetic value. This was most evident among adolescents with highly educated parents. One upper-middle class male reported a drivers' education film depicting accident victims as the most unacceptable material that he had encountered. In this group, while nothing was considered unacceptable, materials were assessed in terms of their "tastefulness" and "aesthetic value" rather than by any set sexual standard. In the lower socioeconomic groups, there is a more rigid standard of absolutes, especially on the part of the female. Females in the lower socioeconomic groups seem to find even the marginal materials unacceptable in contrast to their male counterparts who find very little of even the "hard core" erotica as unacceptable. Other differences concerning the definitional view of erotic materials can be seen when the adolescent places his or her views on a comparison basis with "significant others."

Definitionally, erotic material is often assessed in terms of "significant others," which in this case are peers, parents, teachers, and the community. Differences occur in terms of generational variance, sex, and socioeconomic level. It is generally accepted that males break away from home ties earlier than females, but with this occurring at an earlier age both among lower class males *and* females. We find that females adhere to the family value-system longer than do males and maintain a closer association with the home environment. Females, then, are more likely to espouse the family value-system than are males, and this is indicated in the data, especially with respect to the females in the lower socioeconomic levels. The females in the higher socioeconomic level also adhere to the family value-system, but the family is generally more liberal than their lower SES counterparts. The males, upon breaking away from family ties and the family value-system, move to the peer group for support, and the peer group becomes the "norm interpreting agency" for many male adolescents. In most cases males see themselves as similar to their peers in terms of their definitions of erotic material. Adolescents seldom see themselves as similar to their parents and this "seldom" group usually is represented by upper and upper-middle class males. At this level, often the peer and parental views are quite similar. It is significant to note that *none* of the males saw their definitions of erotica as similar to that of their teachers or the community.

Females on the other hand, strongly identify with the family value-system, and over two-thirds of the respondents indicated definitions similar to those of their families. The other one-third of the females see themselves as similar to their peers.

Any discussion of exposure must deal with the type of erotica to which the adolescent is exposed: (1) general material of a sexual nature, e.g., *Playboy* magazine, (2) marginal erotica, (3) erotica, and (4) hard-core erotica.

1. *General sexual material* such as *Playboy* magazine contains no explicit sexual activity or exposed sex organs (fellatio, cunnilingus, or coitus).

2. *Marginal erotica:* The marginal erotica category contains nudist magazines, pictures and books that show sex organs or pubic hair, but not sexual activity. This category also contains live shows of the strip tease variety which do not contain masturbation or sexual activity, shows classified commonly as "beaver," due to the exposure of pubic hair or sex organs.

3. *Erotica:* This category contains those types of materials that depict sexual activity as found in "action" pictures or drawings. Pictures of coitus, oral-genital activity, etc. are found in single photographs, picture books, on decks of cards and other objects, and cartoon books depicting sexual activity through the media of cartoon drawings and live shows in which there is masturbation or "fondling" of the sex organs, "rough beaver," but not actual sexual activity.

4. *"Hard-core" erotica:* The "hard-core" category has been reserved only for stag films and live shows where sexual intercourse is explicitly depicted. None of the adolescent sample had ever seen a live show depicting actual sexual activity.

Nearly all adolescents had been exposed to magazines such as *Playboy* on a regular or semiregular basis. *Playboy* is the most popular of its type on the current market, and the consumption among the adolescent community is high. In terms of erotic content, *Playboy* allows "fantasy to replace fact" in the depiction of female nudes. Males make up the more avid audience for the magazine and increased socioeconomic status is reflected in increased interest in the content and articles rather than focus on the pictorial layouts.

Marginal erotica are found primarily in the male sector of the adolescent subculture, with nearly all males being exposed to this material. The orientation of the "nudist type" magazines and the "girlie magazines" of the marginal erotic classification to the male culture, and the public openness of places of distribution may account for the low exposure rate for females.

Erotica, on the other hand, is not as easily available and must be sought out, or found, in private rather than public displays. The middle, lower-middle, and lower class males, as opposed to the upper and upper-middle class males and the majority of the females, have the widest variety of exposure to erotic materials. Decks of cards depicting sexual behavior, cartoon books of comic strip characters, and photographs are not uncommon in this sector of the young males' world where peer acceptance and status, as well as sexual arousal, are all-important.

Exposure occurred most frequently in the accompaniment of peers where the respondent or peer had the material in his possession. Most frequently, the first exposure consisted of pictures of nude females, and later, heterosexual materials. The adolescents professed strong interest in the materials, and the entire area of sexuality seems of strong concern to the adolescent subculture. Ages at initial exposure begin in the early years, with adolescents reporting first exposure at ages seven or eight. Reaction to the erotic material was positive for the majority of the males and neutral or negative for the majority of the females.

For the males, the general reaction was one of sexual arousal, shock, and interest. Peer group acceptance of the individual based upon his reaction to the material is quite dependent—therefore, "appropriate" reactions on the part of the viewer will bring positive sanctions from the peer group. Status is achieved by possession of, and knowledge of, sexual information and erotic materials. As the peer group is the main source of sexual information, those who can produce the "relevant materials" for sex education are held in a higher status position.

Females exhibit a curiosity toward erotic materials with that material usually being labeled as "bad" or "nasty." Their reactions range from embarrassment to, "It makes me feel dirty inside." As indicated previously in this discussion, females are more likely to adhere to family standards than are males. The exposure of the females was mainly to the more marginal erotic materials in contrast to the exposure of males. A contributing factor is that the majority of the material produced is directed to the male market.

Among uses for erotica were (1) for arousal, and in some cases, subsequent masturbation, (2) sex education, especially where sex education has not been provided for the adolescent, and (3) peer group status through ownership of the medium of information. The use of the material for arousal and masturbation is rather explicit and does not require extensive analysis. Masturbation is often denied—sexual arousal is admitted in the male group because arousal is seen as a masculine trait, but masturbation is not. The use of fantasy and masturbation as an outlet is less frequent in the lower socioeconomic levels than in the middle and upper classes. In many cases, the outlet for the lower socioeconomic level adolescent is sexual intercourse. In terms of sex education, the lower class males are introduced to sex education through the medium of erotic materials—in addition to the peer group being the initiator of the adolescent to explicit sexual information.

Efforts to provide sex education at school fall short because the lower socioeconomic groups have had exposure and experience long before the courses are offered. Perhaps one of the more significant and least explored uses of erotica is to gain peer approval and status in the peer group. Ownership or possession of erotic materials promotes status within the peer group, and materials "take on new meaning" with the additional value of the erotic material being realized in terms of peer group values and acceptance. Many of those interviewed indicated the enhanced value this material assumed when they discovered the status achieved by ownership or possession of erotica. This "status-enhancement" also increased their interest in such materials above the level of curiosity and prurient interest, because of the inherent value it promises the adolescent in terms of peer acceptance and status.

Sex Education

Sex education, or education about human sexuality, begins as a matter of course very early in life, and continues throughout the life span of the individual. Much of this education is indirect. For example, the child who walks into the occupied bathroom will soon find that this is "verboten," though he does not know why; nor, frequently, is he given any explanation. The interesting part of this "informal socialization" is that little or no explanation is offered for the negative sanctioning often given by parents. The curiosity which is aroused in the child invites him to discover that there are differences between the sexes, and he begins to ask questions in relation to these differences; bathroom habits, birth, pregnancy, and reproduction. These are the early beginnings of sex education and all too often these questions are turned aside and the child seeks out other children to answer his questions. Formal sex education should start as early as the child starts formal education because many of these questions have already been asked, and, in the majority of cases, left unanswered or answered in terms of poor analogies and harmful psychological reprimands.

As the child reaches puberty, he begins to view his parents less as interpreters of the social norms, and looks to his peers for social interpretations and peer-group norms persist. Direct questions (often pretending prior knowledge) about human sexuality are common topics of discussion, especially among males. Young adolescent females seem heavily oriented toward the romantic aspects of love, rather than the instrumental approach toward sexuality taken by the males. Many times the sexual information shared by adolescents consists of "pooled ignorance" on the part of the participants.

The adolescent with the "answers," whether accurate or not, gains status in the eyes of his peers, and the quality of his information is frequently unchallenged.

Our study of high school students and their sources of sex education reinforces past research, as the peer group is cited as the major source of sex information. Looking only at those sources that provided a "great deal of information" we found that, for males, their major source was other males of their same age and for females, their girl friends. The second major source of sexual information given is peers of the opposite sex. One category, the teacher, who in the past provided little, if any instruction in this area has emerged as a major source of sex information. For those adolescents who have taken a course in sex education, and for those who have not done so, our research indicated that *today* the teacher functions as a strong source of information in the area of human sexuality.

The parental role in sex education seems to be lacking except in the case of the mother-daughter relationship, where 65 percent of the females indicated that their mother had discussed sex with them. The discussions between mother and daughter often are centered around menstruation and the "negative" aspects of premarital sexual intercourse. The father served as a source of information for daughters in only 2 percent of the cases, and neither parent talked with their daughter in 33 percent of the cases. For males, parents do not provide this type of instruction, as 64 percent of the males indicated that neither parent had discussed sex with them. Twenty-six percent did indicate that the father-son relationship existed in a discussion about sex and 10 percent answered positively to a mother-son discussion. Interestingly enough, neither parent is indicated as the *first* source of information on any of the nine topics mentioned to the males. For the females, the mother is the first source of information regarding pregnancy, menstruation, menopause, and contraception. The other areas (of sexual intercourse, erection, masturbation, prostitution, and homosexuality) are left mainly for peers to provide the first source of information. For males, parents are not the first source of information in *any* area.

In summary, the sources of learning about human sexuality came from various areas, with the most frequent single source being the peer group. Much of the information is learned at ages earlier than previously expected, and the idea of "innocence of youth" doesn't apply to the question of human sexuality.

Attitudes Toward Sex Education

From a short series of questions concerning the teaching of sex education in the schools asked in the post–test situation, it was evident that the students have a very positive position toward this curriculum of the school system.

Over 90 percent of the students who had taken the course indicated that sex education should be taught in the schools.

Religious teachings are often cited as being in direct conflict with the educational teaching of sex education; however, 95 percent of the students in the predominantly Catholic community, *after* having taken part in the program, did not find sex education in disagreement with their religious beliefs.

Information from home is also often viewed as being in conflict with this type of educational instruction, but over 90 percent of the students after having taken the course, disagreed with this idea of conflict of information.

Since the school system did not take an overt "moral" stance with regard to sex education, perhaps this explains why there was little conflict between the school, home, and church. There seems to be more made of the conflict than actually exists *in reality,* and the schools' presentation of information does not seem to encroach on the discussion of human sexuality in the home or by the church. As indicated in an earlier discussion, the home and the church are not major sources of sex education for the child.

One of the most significant changes that the students seem to indicate is their projected handling of sex education with their own future children. This change may be due to their dissatisfaction with the handling of sex education by their parents as contrasted to how they as parents plan to deal with the subject. Part of the classroom discussion was oriented toward the question of when children should be presented with information, with all of the participants exploring their own experiences in the home situation.

What to look for in a mate and how far to go on a date also seem to be areas of more extensive change. The pragmatic situation of dating is of great concern for the high school adolescent as he is intimately involved in this situation and often the extent of petting is determined without a frame of reference, or based upon peer group norms. Mate selection is especially important for those who will soon enter into marriage, not seeking further education on the college level.

Conclusion

Sex education as currently presented in the educational system offers "too little too late" and in many instances the most it can do is present accurate information to correct the misinformation that students have learned. Sexual learning occurs much earlier than the institution of programs of formal learning in the schools, indicating that education in the area of human sexuality should begin with conventional formal education. Informal sources of sex education still rank as the major sources of sexual learning. The sex education programs surveyed in this study did not conflict with the home or church, contrary to popular belief. As a result of the sex education program, most of the students felt that they would handle sex education differently with "their" children. Formal sex education did not conflict either with religious teachings or information provided in the home. This may be the result of the program not taking an "overt moral stance" with regard to sex education, but serving more as a source of objective sexual information.

References

Berger, A. S.; Simon, W.; and Gagnon, J. H. "Youth and Pornography in Social Context." *Arch. Sex. Behav.* 2, 4 (1973): 279–308, table 21.

Blaine, Graham B. "Sex Among Teenagers." *Medical Aspects of Human Sexuality* (September 1968).

Burleson, D. L., "Evaluation in Sex Education: A Wasteland." *SIECUS Report* 1 (1973): 1.

Calderwood, D. "Adolescents' View on Sex Education." *J. Marriage Fam.* (May 1965).

Chess, S.; Thomas, A.; and Cameron, M. "Sexual Attitudes and Behavior Patterns in a Middle-Class Adolescent Population. *Am. J. Orthopsychiatry* 46, 4 (Oct 1976): 689–701.

Elias, James E. "Sex Education in the Public Schools." *Awareness* 69 University Seminars, Indiana University, 1969.

————. "Sexual Attitudes and Practices on Campus." In *Human Sexual Development—Perspectives in Sex Education,* ed. Donald L. Taylor. F. A. Davis, 1971.

————. "Teen Age Sexual Behavior Patterns." In *Examination of the Risk-Taking Behavior of Youth.* New York: American Social Health Association, 1970.

Elias, James E., and Elias, Veronica. "The Sexual World of the Adolescent." *The Counseling Psychologist* 5, 1 (1975).

Elias, James E., and Gebhard, Paul. "Sexuality and Sexual Learning in Childhood." *Phi Delta Kappan* (Education Research Journal) March 1969.

Mathis, J. L. "Adolescent Sexuality and Societal Change." *Am. J. Psychother.* 30, 3 (July 1976): 433–40.

McCary, J. *Sexual Myths and Fallacies.* Princeton: Van Nostrand and Reinhold, 1971.

Rosenthal, M. B. "Sexual Counseling and Interviewing of Adolescents. *Primary Care* 4, 2 (June 1977): 291–300.

Rutledge, A. L. "Sexual Intercourse Among Adolescents, a Behavioral Review." In *Sexual Maturity,* ed. E. S. Hafex and J. J. Peluso, pp. 167–73. Ann Arbor, MI: Ann Arbor Science, 1976.

Sorenson, R. C. *Adolescent Sexuality.* New York: World, 1973.

Vener, A. M., and Stewart, C. S. "Adolescent Sexual Behavior in Middle America Revisited: 1970–1973." *J. Marriage Fam.* 36 (1974): 728.

8

Prostitution, Psychiatry and History

Vern L. Bullough

Sex research today is carried on by
individuals in a number of different
disciplines. So far in this book we have had
contributions by physicians, social workers,
psychologists (and biologists), sociologists,
marriage and family counselors, but there are
also historians, theologians, philosophers,
and others who can offer valuable insights
from the point of view of their own discipline.
I have included one of my own papers
viewing one aspect of sexual behavior,
prostitution, and the psychiatric research
done in the field, from the viewpoint of the
historian.

Prostitution has a long and ancient history but it has also gone through periods
of being rediscovered by the media. During the past couple of years almost
every newspaper in the country has carried articles about the increase in
prostitution. It has come to be regarded as a "new" problem in the cities, and
various "new" solutions have been adopted, from setting aside designated
areas (a failure in Boston) to arresting the customers of the prostitute. A Utah
congressman, in fact, lost his reelection campaign in 1976 because he had
been arrested by an undercover vice officer in Salt Lake City. In the process of
dealing with prostitution, western society has evolved from treating it as a sin
to regarding it as a crime and a sickness. It is neither. Historically it has been
an occupation, often the only one open to women, and it is only in these terms
that we can understand it and deal with it.

   This historical concept of prostitution as an occupation goes counter to
much of the psychiatric research of the past few decades. These studies,
however, leave much to be desired, but it is necessary to recount them to
show their deficiencies. Almost all such studies start from the premise that the
prostitute herself is a sick person. The origins for this approach lie in the
history of medicine, but the concept became most influential in the nineteenth century when sexual variation came to be classed as an illness rather

than a sin. This model has been discussed in considerable detail in some of my earlier work. Among the writers who impressed upon the public the dangers of sexuality were Sylvester Graham, Claude Francois Lallemand, William Acton, John Harvey Kellogg, George M. Beard, Paul Moreau, Richard von Krafft-Ebing, and even Sigmund Freud.[1] A popular nineteenth century summation of this concept was by Cesare Lombroso who held that man represented an advanced stage of animal life and had progressed from a hermaphroditic or self-fertilizing stage to a higher heterosexual phase. In the process of evolution some degenerate forms of man had been left at the level of bisexuality, since the higher man progressed the less his sex drives became. Lombroso believed that the life cycle of each individual went through the same society as a whole, ontogeny recapitulating phylogeny, and that those who were unable to achieve the higher standards of today were pathological cases, perverts, morally insane, and so forth.[2]

Though the twentieth century investigators have been somewhat more sophisticated than Lombroso, one of the favored approaches to prostitution during the past few decades has been to look upon it as an illness. Karl Abraham, for example, theorized that it was only when a woman could not enjoy the sex act with one partner that she felt compelled to change partners in the Don Juan fashion. Taking pay for the sex act demonstrated her own hostility to men; she took revenge on men by emphasizing that the sex act which men held important, meant nothing to the prostitute.[3] Edward Glover whose work has been called the outstanding psychiatric contribution to the study of prostitution,[4] interpreted prostitution as evidence of an unresolved Oedipus conflict; the woman still hated her mother and was disappointed with her father. Glover agreed with other psychoanalytic writers that the prostitute was sexually frigid, hostile towards men, and had homosexual tendencies. He also argued that many customers of prostitutes were able to enjoy the sex act only with people they held in low esteem.[5]

The theme of latent or open homosexuality runs through both these analyses, but was most strongly advocated by Frank Caprio. In 1953, Caprio toured the world visiting brothels in most of the major cities, interviewing prostitutes. He found two or more lesbians in every brothel he visited, and these women reported that they engaged in homosexual activities for their own gratification, or at other times put on exhibitions for customers. Using this data, Caprio argued that prostitution was a deviant behavior which appealed primarily to women with strong homosexual tendencies; their activities with their customers were a pseudoheterosexual defense against their true desires for lesbian love; eventually, however, many of them lost their inhibitions and turned to open homosexuality. He stated that prostitutes were emotionally sick people whose activities were manifestations of their illness.[6]

Taking a different tack was Tibor Agoston who maintained that the prostitute erected a pseudopersonality to escape her feelings of guilt. By denying her true identity and offering a pseudopersonality for hire, the prostitute was able to proceed to complete infantile regression with her rented pseudopersonality.[7] This emphasis on the identity problem of the prostitute was accepted by Helen Deutsch, but she saw the problem in a different way. For her the prostitute suffered from disconnected identities. Identification was with the masochistic mother, and the deriding of social institutions, law, morality, as well as the men who imposed such authority, since all represented a focus of paternally directed hostility. Another type of prostitute, however, was the woman who renounced tenderness and feminine gratification in favor of the aggressive masculinity she imitated, similar to Caprio's idea of the lesbian prostitute.[8] H. Lichtenstein identified prostitution as representing symbiosis with the original love object, the mother, and the prostitute achieves a symbolic phallus by permitting "castrated" men sexual use of her body as a prostitute,[9] another version of the secret lesbian.

J. Lampi de Groot also saw prostitution as a manifestation of homosexuality. He hypothesized that in the Oedipal struggle the prostitute turned to the man out of revenge upon her mother, not with an attitude of feminine surrender but of masculine assertiveness and activity, making the client the "feminine" partner in the sexual act.[10] Marc H. Hollander visualized prostitution and hypochondriasis as closely related in that both were one step removed from a totally objectless state. Bodily and sexual contacts became the regressive substitutes for interpersonal relationships, and the male, after achieving orgasm, was felt to be powerless and castrated, thus gratifying sadomasochistic and hostile dependent wishes.[11] The objectless state was further amplified by Thomas Szasz who implied that prostitution was a mechanism by which a woman through indiscriminately participating in sexual intercourse, could give up parts of her body (the genitals) and experience these as nonexistent.[12] F. Wengraf emphasized the latent homosexuality of the prostitute,[13] as did P.L. Gotoin.[14]

Maryse Choisy, a French psychoanalyst, wrote that the union of the prostitute with her client was one of debasement in which both partners expressed their aggression and hostility in a sadomasochistic relationship. The women were seeking revenge against their fathers and the men against their mothers; the money that changed hands was a symbol of the mutual contempt they felt for each other.[15] Her source of data included interviews with patients as well as a month's firsthand experience working as a waitress in a brothel while she collected material for a newspaper series.[16] There are other psychiatric explanations, to a large extent dependent upon the view or school of the investigator.[17]

Looking at these studies objectively, one can note many deficiencies. One of the more obvious difficulties is that they generalize from a patient population to a population at large. Most of the samples were small. Though Vesalius revolutionized anatomy through the detailed study of one female corpse, female psychology is much more complicated than female physiology. Another difficulty is that the clinicians placed diagnostic labels on everyone they saw, and regarded them as sick or troubled persons. Perhaps this is natural since most of the subjects were patients or clients undergoing therapy. Is a patient, unhappy enough to seek therapy, however, typical of all prostitutes? When the question is put this way, it becomes obvious why the studies permit such great distortions.

Historically, however, the greatest difficulty with these studies is that they have lumped all prostitutes into the same category without looking at the social conditions that led the women to prostitution, their educational level, their competence, and a whole host of other variables. They also tend to regard prostitution itself as abnormal in society when in point of fact it has always been a part of history. Moreover, the psychiatrists have made a serious mistake of examining only one part of the prostitution relationship, namely the female part. If prostitutes are ill, what about the males who go to prostitutes? Do they create a symbiotic relationship, matching neuroses with neuroses? If it is normal for men to seek sex, is it not also normal for women to want to participate in sex? Though several generations of women are acculturated to believe that sex was only for the purpose of procreation, this is simply biologically not the case.

Still another problem with the psychiatric studies is the primitive state of the research methodologies. The best psychoanalytic study in this respect is that by Harold Greenwald. His initial sample of prostitutes went beyond his own practice. He sought out prostitutes, and his study is based upon twenty, a pitifully small sample, yet psychiatrically speaking, it is far beyond what anyone else has done. Greenwald is also more cautious both in specifying his source of data and in his conclusions, but there is no control group to match his conclusions against. How, for example, do prostitutes differ from other women in the same economic or social setting? Greenwald argued that for his sample, the primary predisposing factor to prostitution was a history of severe maternal deprivation. This loss of mother love caused the child to turn increasingly to her father for affections, but usually the father failed to give the necessary emotional support; this led the girls to turn to self-abasement in an attempt to hurt their mothers. Prostitution then represented a way of search for the security, warmth and love that the adult woman had not received as a child.[18] Is Greenwald any more adequate in his explanation than any of the other psychiatrists who had gone before? Is he again putting an onus on mothers which might have origins elsewhere? What evidence is there for lack of mother love causing prostitution? Does every girl who lacks it turn to prostitution? Obviously the answer has to be no. What do men who lack mother love turn to? Why do some women turn to prostitution and not others from the same emotional setting?

Although some of the arguments of the psychoanalytic school about the psychopathology of the personalities of the prostitutes might well contain elements of truth, inevitably they leave unanswered more questions than they answer. It is still impossible to know whether prostitutes dislike men more than nonprostitutes do or whether prostitutes are more likely to be lesbians than a group of teachers or nurses or any other occupational group dominated by women. Even if prostitutes are shown to be lesbian in orientation beyond other groups of women, it is not certain whether this is a cause or consequence of their occupation. Women who continually have to fake orgasm with men might well turn to other women for satisfaction. In sum, then, it would seem to be a distortion of the evidence to conclude that prostitution is a mental illness. It would also be in contradiction to the historical data which suggests, if it does not prove, that the position of the individual in the social structure is a signficant variable in the person's choice of occupation. Social class is also significant in the case of prostitution in distinguishing between the common prostitute and the higher status of courtesan. The psychiatric oriented investigator might well be able to explain why a particular woman turned to prostitution, but his research is far too incomplete to tell us why women become prostitutes. That prostitutes might be troubled women is perhaps evidenced by their high rate of drug addiction and alcoholism. The skeptical researcher, however, has to wonder whether drug addiction results from prostitution or prostitution from drug addiction. Prostitution, demonstrably is often the easiest way for a drug addict to support her habit.

There are statistical studies of prostitutes that have used somewhat more scientific approaches than the psychiatric ones although most of the solid research, comparable to that in other areas of social science, is of relatively recent origin. One of the more significant studies in this respect was a 1955 English study entitled *Women of the Streets* which included a sample of 150 prostitutes with in-depth interviews of a smaller portion of the sample. The author, who chose to remain anonymous, indicated that there were many different personality types as well as outlooks among the streetwalkers, although she did describe a type of alienation which she called a state of not belonging. She also reported that the women in her sample worked hard, transferred any guilt feeling (which the author apparently felt they should have) to their customers; the prostitutes felt that they were honest, hardworking women while they regarded their customers as cheating on their wives or acting in other dishonest ways. There were social class differences among the group. The more well-to-do streetwalkers who worked in affluent neighborhoods seemed charming, educated, and sympathetic, while those who worked in poorer neighborhoods were more embittered and more obviously out to get the best of their customers.[19]

The Kinsey group also gathered information about prostitution although much of the data has never been published. Wardell Pomeroy in 1965, however, reported some of the findings based on a sample of 175 prostitutes although the sample is somewhat skewed since 154 of the subjects were in prison when they were interviewed. Significantly, and in contrast to the assumptions in the psychiatric literature, these women were not frigid. In fact, they were more sexually responsive than the women interviewed for the major Kinsey study on female sexual behavior.[20] Ninety percent of the prostitute group reported that they had orgasms in their nonprofessional contacts, and even in sexual contacts with clients approximately 80 percent reported having orgasms at least occasionally. Nearly two-thirds of the group reported that they felt no regrets about their choice of occupation, although the prison inmates did regret being sent to jail. The women reported that they chose prostitution as a work role because it offered a good income, an opportunity to meet interesting people, was comparatively easy, was fun, and gave sexual pleasure. Pomeroy emphasized that these were only the conscious reasons for the choice, and that undoubtedly there were also unconscious factors entering into their selection of occupation. Nevertheless, what we have in two studies that went beyond the psychiatric couch is a view of prostitution that is much different than that given by the psychiatrists. One of the difficulties in researching prostitution is that it remains a temporary occupation for many women who leave it if something better turns up. This temporary nature was emphasized by a British study of some 400 wayward girls, many of whom turned to prostitution usually on a temporary basis as they attempted to find an adjustment to life. These girls who did become prostitutes had normal intelligence and superficially little more emotional difficulties than those who did not.[21] Other studies have shown that though the general social values have some impact on the isolated individual prostitute, she rationalizes a justification such as financial success or ability to unselfishly assume the financial burdens of people dependent upon her.[22]

Another way of examining prostitution is through the biographies and autobiographies of the more literate prostitutes of which there are several dozen. Many of the prostitutes reported suffering feelings of degradation which made them the willing victim for the dope salesman, the beatings of a pimp, for the sadistic practices of a client, and even for suicide. What comes through strongest, however, is that prostitution turns out to be hard work, and while some women demand extremely high fees, very few manage to hold on to the money they earned. The call girl has to see the same show night after night and yet act enchanted and delighted with her sponsor while the lowly streetwalker has to snag a customer in order to pay her light bill. The girl who works in a brothel has her life carefully circumscribed; in fact, she is more carefully supervised than a girl in a dormitory in a strict religious college. Most of the biographies fail to fit into the psychoanalytic model, even though many wrote as part of their own self-analysis. Most of the women undoubtedly were concerned with some sort of self-justification and might not tell the truth even if they knew it, yet a surprising number reportedly found pleasure in their work.[23]

Historically, what can we state about prostitution? Prostitution in a sense is the traditional women's role in life except that it is restricted to the sex act. The prostitute is giving the male pleasure, and that has been her prime purpose for her occupational role. Occupation as defined by Stewart and

Cantor in their book on the subject is a "social role performed by the adult members of society that directly or indirectly yields social and financial consequences."[24] Prostitution is clearly an occupation, it has filled a social need, and it offers financial rewards to its participants. Though it is a deviant or stigmatized occupation, the stigma varies significantly from the highly paid courtesan or call girl to the low level prostitute. Generally speaking, the higher the fee, the less the stigma. Both prostitution and marriage have the same basic objectives of filling the sexual and social needs of men, but marriage also has other goals. The occupational explanation is not inconsistent with modern sociological theory which accepts the fact that both deviant and acceptable behaviors and conditions can be built upon the same social structures and values.[25]

Most prostitutes probably drift into the occupation, and historically this has most often been the case. Usually they experiment hesitantly with accepting payment and then ultimately decide to become professional. Though they go through a process of working into the new identity, the crucial factors in their coming to think of themselves as prostitutes are the reactions of society towards them, and the labels that others attach to their work.[26] Though the prostitute identity is not sought and can be painful at first, eventually it can also be supportive as the subculture gives a world view to the prostitute which defines her work as significant and allows her to develop friends in the life. Since it is an occupation in which the mobility tends to be downward as the woman ages, most people tend to seek other roles. If the legal or other barriers are not too rigid, ultimately most leave the life for other occupations or marriage. Legalized or highly organized prostitution acts as a barrier to the mobility out of the profession, and for this reason, if not any other, I feel prostitution should not be regulated or legalized.

What in effect history tends to show about prostitution is that prostitution essentially is an occupation, a traditional one for women, but most women have left it when something better came along. If history has any meaning in dealing with prostitution it would indicate that we have to abandon both the medical and criminal treatment of prostitution. The psychiatric explanation is not valid, and the criminal treatment punishes women for doing what they have been trained and acculturated to do, namely satisfy the man. They just do it for cash on the line instead of services. In summary, the prostitute is the traditional woman in a specialized occupation. Perhaps as women begin to assert themselves, the prostitute herself will change. But to label a woman sick for what all women have been acculturated to do is ahistorical.

Notes

1. See Vern L. Bullough, "Sex and the Medical Model," *Journal of Sex Research* 11 (1975), and "Homosexuality and the Medical Model," *Journal of Homosexuality*, 1 (1974). Both of these articles were reprinted in Bullough,

Sex, Society, and History (New York: Science History Publications, 1976), pp. 161–85.

2. See Cesare Lombroso, *Criminal Man* (reprinted Montclair, NJ: Patterson-Smith, 1972).

3. Karl Abraham, "Manifestations of the Female Castration Complex," in *Selected Papers,* trans. Douglas Bryan and Alix Strachey (London: Hogarth, 1942), chap. 22, p. 361. This paper was originally written in 1920.

4. Arnold S. Maerov, "Prostitution: A Survey and Review of 20 Cases," *Psychiatric Quarterly* 49 (1965): 675–701, especially p. 680. His survey was helpful.

5. Edward Glover, *The Psychopathology of Prostitution* (London: Institute for the Scientific Treatment of Delinquency, 1945); the paper was also reprinted in Glover, *The Roots of Crime* (New York: International Universities Press, 1960), pp. 244–67.

6. Frank Caprio, and Donald Brenner, *Sexual Behavior: Psycho Legal Aspects* (New York: Citadel Press, 1961), pp. 249–52.

7. Tigor Agoston, "Some Psychological Aspects of Prostitution—The Pseudo-Personality," *International Journal of Psychoanalysis* 26 (1945): 62–67.

8. Helen Deutsch, "The Genesis of Agoraphobia," *International Journal of Psychoanalysis* 10 (1929): 51–69; and Vol. I of *The Psychology of Women* (New York: Grune & Stratton, 1944).

9. H. Lichtenstein, "Identity and Sexuality," *Journal of the American Psychoanalytic Association* 9 (April 1961).

10. J. Lampi de Groot, "The Evolution of the Oedipus Complex in Women," *International Journal of Psychoanalysis* 9 (1928): 322.

11. Marc H. Hollender, "Prostitution, the Body and Human Relatedness," *International Journal of Psychoanalysis* 42 (July–October 1961): 404–13.

12. Thomas S. Szasz, *Pain and Pleasure—A Study of Body Feelings* (New York: Basic Books, 1957).

13. F. Wengraf, "Fragment of an Analysis of a Prostitute," *Journal of Criminal Psychopathology* 5 (October 1943): 247–53.

14. P. L. Gotoin, "The Potential Prostitute," *Journal of Criminal Psychopathology* 3 (January 1942): 359–67.

15. Maryse Choisy, *Psychoanalysis of the Prostitute* (New York: Philosophical Library, 1961).

16. Maryse Choisy, *A Month Among the Girls,* trans. Lawrence G. Blochman (New York: Pyramid Books, 1960). The book was first published in 1928.

17. See, for example, Sandor Ferenczi, *Contribution to Psychoanalysis* (Boston: Richard C. Badger, 1916), p. 269; Sandor Rado, *Psychoanalysis of Behavior* (New York: Grune & Stratton, 1956), p. 116; Eustace Chesser, *Live and Let Live* (New York: Philosophical Library, 1958); and Siegfried Borelli and Willy Starck, *Die Prostitution als Psychologisches Problem* (Berlin: Springer-Verlag, 1957). For a more complete listing see

Vern Bullough, Barret Elcano, Margaret Deacon, and Bonnie Bullough, *A Bibliography of Prostitution* (New York: Garland, 1977), pp. 333–44.

18. Harold Greenwald, *The Call Girl: A Social and Psychoanalytic Study* (New York: Ballantine, 1958), passim; a revised edition of this was published under the title of *The Elegant Prostitute* (New York: Walker, 1970).

19. C. H. Rolph, ed., *Women of the Streets* (London: Seeker and Warburg, 1955), pp. 46–50.

20. Wardell B. Pomeroy, "Some Aspects of Prostitution," *Journal of Sex Research* 1 (November 1965): 177–87.

21. T. C. N. Gibbons, "Juvenile Prostitution," *British Journal of Delinquency* 8 (July 1957): 3-12.

22. Norman R. Jackman, Richard O'Toole, and Gilbert Geis, "The Self-Image of the Prostitute," *Sociological Quarterly* 4 (1963): 150–61.

23. Among the nonfictional biographies and autobiographies are the following: *Madeline: An Autobiography* (New York: Harper, 1919); Sheila Cousins, *To Beg I Am Ashamed* (New York: Vanguard, 1938) which was reprinted under the title *Prostitute* (New York: Lancer Books, 1962); Serge G. Wolsey, *Call House Madam* (San Francisco: Martin Tudordale, 1942); Polly Adler, *A House is Not a Home* (New York: Rinehart, 1953); O. W. [Marjorie Smith], *God Have Mercy on Me* (New York: Sheridan House, 1931), as well as *No Bed of Roses* (New York: Macaulay, 1930), and *With My Eyes Wide Open* (New York: Sheridan House, 1949) by the same author; Nancy Dean with Jack Powers, *Twenty Years Behind Red Curtains* (Chicago: Newsstand Library, 1959); Carol Erwin with Floyd Miller, *The Orderly Disorderly House* (New York: Doubleday, 1960); Ben L. Reitman, *Sister of the Road: The Autobiography of Box Car Bertha* (New York: Sheridan House, 1937); Susan Kale, *The Fire Escape* (New York: Doubleday, 1960); Sara Harris, *Nobody Cries for Me* (New York: Signet, 1959); Virginia McManus, *Not for Love* (New York: Putnam, 1960); *Street Walker* (London: Bodley Head, 1959); Martha Watts, *The Men in My Life* (New York: Lyle Stuart, 1960); Madame Sherry [Ruth Barnes] with S. Robert Tralins, *Pleasure Was My Business* (New York: Lyle Stuart, 1961); Helen Cromwell with Robert Dougherty, *Dirty Helen* (Los Angeles: Sherbourne, 1966); Sally Stanford, *The Lady of the House* (New York: Putnam, 1966); Iolana Mitsuko, *Honolulu Madam* (Los Angeles: Holloway, 1969); Helen "Rocking Chair" McGowan, *Big City Madam* (New York: Lancer Books, 1965); Pauline Tabor, *Pauline's* (New York: Fawcett Crest, 1973); Xaviera Hollander with Robin Moore and Yvonne Dunleavy, *The Happy Hooker* (New York: Dell, 1972), Ms. Hollander made herself into an industry and there are several additional volumes in her series; Terri Randall, *Hooker* (New York: Award Books, 1969); Kristin Anderson with Linda Du Breuil, *The Wholesome Hooker* (New York: Norton, 1973). There are many more, see Bullough, Elcano

et al., *A Bibliography of Prostitution*. Some of the accounts are probably more fictional than real.

24. Phyllis L. Stuart and Muriel G. Cantor, eds., *Varieties of Work Experience* (New York: Halsted Press, Wiley, 1974), pp. 7–8.

25. Edwin M. Shur, "Reactions to Deviance: A Critical Assessment," *American Journal of Sociology* 75 (November 1969): 309–22.

26. Shur, "Reactions to Deviance," and Howard S. Becker, ed., *The Other Side* (New York: Free Press, 1964), pp. 1–6; Becker, *Outsiders* (New York: Free Press, 1963). See also Erving Goffman, *Stigma* (Englewood Cliffs, NJ: Prentice-Hall, 1963); and Method, *Social Problems* 9 (Winter): 247–56; and Edwin M. Shur, *Crimes Without Victims* (Englewood Cliffs, NJ: Prentice-Hall, 1965). There are many other works.

9

Erotic Sex and Imagery in Sexual Hangups

John Money

Sex, as indicated in the previous articles, is more than physiology. It involves all of what we call being human. John Money, Ph.D., of the Department of Psychiatry and Behavioral Sciences as well as the Department of Pediatrics at Johns Hopkins University and Hospital is one of the preeminent researchers in the field today. Some of his work was recounted in the article by Diamond earlier in this book, and his work in gender and sex role has been of the utmost importance in establishing new areas for sex research. In this article he deals with the importance of imagery. Research for this article was supported by USPHS Grant HD 00325 and by funds from the Grant Foundation, New York.

Imagery and Pair Bonding

Male and female created He them, the Book of Genesis proclaims, thereby giving recognition to nature's vast utilization of sexual dimorphism in her scheme of multiplying the species. Genesis is reticent on the other aspect of nature's scheme, namely the bonding or attraction of the separated sexes in pairs so that they will multiply. Within the animal kingdom, pair-bonding has two alternatives. That is to say, either the organs of smell or vision are the primary vehicles of sexual attraction; either odor or visual image is the primary stimulus or sexual attractant. Typically, among those mammals in which odor is the primary attractant, it is the female that emits the odor, and the male that is attracted. The rule of the eye may well be the same. Among us human beings, striking evidence to this effect exists in the phenomenon of the so-called wet dream which personalizes the announcement of sexual maturity in the life of most boys. The imagery of the wet dream is nature's own pornography show, and its content varies according to earlier erotic history, so to speak. It carries over into the masturbation fantasy. There is no corresponding dream phenomenon in the adolescent girl. This is not to say that the female is unresponsive to the visual erotic image, but rather that the male has a lower threshold of visual erotic response in the initiation of erotic arousal. For the female, generally speaking, the romantic encounter and especially the sense of touch have the lower threshold.

Imagery that announces itself in the wet dream and the masturbation fantasy may be said to serve as a rehearsal of what may subsequently take place in action. Some individuals find that their imagery is orthodox, relative to the eroticism that society sanctions, and some do not. Those whose imagery is socially unsanctioned will be erotically aroused by visual representations of, or actual participation in, activities for which they will be condemned.

Religion, History, and Eroticism

It is common in the history of mankind for religious doctrine to have encompassed erotic imagery and behavior, prescribing some and proscribing other erotic manifestations. Some religions have celebrated eroticism, others have negated it. In our own tradition, the early Christian fathers preached in the fifth century a doctrine of asceticism and mortification of the flesh. The pendulum began to swing in the twelfth century, the era of the Crusades and the Troubadors. This was an age of new religious doctrine, denounced by the church as heresy, giving new prominence to the Mother of God, and new tolerance of love and eroticism. The Troubadors lifted the ban on eroticism in their songs and poems, but only to celebrate an idealized romantic love not fulfilled in sexual intercourse. Along with the new openness in sex, academic formalism and antiscience gave way to a reawakening of interest in science. This was the age of Roger Bacon.

The pendulum swung again as the forces of reaction gathered momentum in the fifteenth century in the form of the Inquisition. The spirit of free inquiry was extinguished and the church became so obsessed with sex as a sin that literally hundreds of thousands of Europeans were tortured to confess imagery of erotic encounters with the devil, for which they were then publicly burned alive. Entire villages in southern Germany and Switzerland were literally exterminated.

Italy escaped the worst excesses of the Inquisition, which no doubt helps account for the fact that it was in Italy that the High Renaissance first came into full flower in the sixteenth century. From there the new learning spread to the north and was in part responsible for the Reformation, a revolt that the masses, sick from so many burnings, espoused without too much resistance. The Renaissance and the Reformation rehabilitated eroticism after the excesses of the Inquisition, but confined it, in northern Europe and America, within the rigid boundaries of Puritanism and, in southern Europe, within the tradition of the double standard and the virgin bride.

In the eighteenth century, the Age of Enlightenment, there was a relatively brief interlude of sexual liberalism in northern Europe. It was an interlude more for the aristocracy than the population at large. The Inquisition still cast its shadow in the form of Fundamentalism and, in turn, Fundamentalism began to cast a shadow in the form of Victorianism.

Victorianism was less a resurgence of Puritanism, as we are so used to hearing, than a masterful blend of secular and religious dualism in both science and sex. Thus it taught the literalness of Biblical creation, while secularizing the Book of Genesis with the theory of evolution. It tabooed sexual frankness, but produced Freud and other great founders of sexology. It preached the sanctity of the family while making big business of prostitution. It imposed a church-appeasing censorship on erotica, and ran burlesque shows in its big cities. It warned against the moral and psychic degeneracy of masturbation, and encouraged it by supplying no other outlet. It abhorred homosexuality, while segregating boys from girls in the adolescent years. To the young, it identified sex as sacred, spiritual and beautiful, but then vetoed it until marriage, while simultaneously identifying it as carnal, lustful and dirty, but to be kept specially for the one you love. It believed in universal education, but excluded sexual knowledge from the curriculum. It wanted its children to grow up sexually healthy, but it punished them for showing any signs of healthy primate sexuality of childhood and instilled an abiding sense of sexual guilt.

The move toward a greater liberalism in sexual matters in the present day and age is associated with a greater secularization of sexuality—a greater separation of sex and church. As a reaction to this secularism there is a dabbling with oriental religions and the occult as a consequence of discontent with Christian doctrine. But the ultimate import of these trends is that they constitute a new mysticism and antiscientism which, if history is a guide, will consolidate with antisexism.

Other societies, for example Buddhist societies, have been able to function quite well without a sexual taboo and without a tradition of sexual punishment and guilt. We do not have a good record in this respect. We have become dependent on tabooing and punishing the natural erotic functions of sexuality in childhood as the means of establishing a sense of guilt, and thereby establishing a mechanism for the control of behavior. Once established, a sense of guilt can be played upon to control behavior far removed from sex. Politicians and judges inchoately know this when they vote or decide against liberalization of the erotic censorship laws.

Hypersexual, Hyposexual, and Paraphiliac

Nature exacts her price for the thwarting of sex to generate guilt. When the normal heterosexual expressions of sexuality in the play of early childhood are not approved of and positively reinforced, then the stage is set for behind-the-scenes psychic maneuverings of exotic sex to take place. One possibility is that the imagery of sexual arousal will become obsessively hypertrophied and will express itself with excessive frequency, as in the compulsive Don Juan or the compulsive prostitute. Another possibility, and one more frequently encountered clinically, is that of hypofunction of sexual arousal imagery. Hyposexuality manifests itself as sexual apathy or inertia, anorgasmia, or, in women, vaginal phobia and, in men, impotence and premature ejaculation.

A third possibility, also frequently encountered clinically, is one in which the erotic image that induces sexual arousal is switched from orthodox to unorthodox. The switching may be a simple transposition of male and female image, as in the sexuality of men whose love affairs are with men, and women whose love affairs are with women. In more complex form, the transposition may become a true paraphilia by assimilating with a clothing fetish to become transvestism. In this condition the person needs to change his own gender image in order to achieve erotic arousal and perform sexually. The change of self-image may involve actual transexualism, the compulsion for hormonal and surgical sex reassignment.

In addition to transpositions, paraphiliac imagery switching may take the form of an intrusion of imagery that is unorthodox. The list of possibilities is long, especially if all the known fetishistic images are included. The appearance of the partner may be involved, as in the prepubertal compulsion of the pedophiliac, or the grandparental compulsion of the gerontophiliac. Or the partner may have to be of a race, creed, class or color socially stigmatized in one's own family, or to be dead (necrophilia), or to have specific characteristics, such as an amputation. There may be a compulsion to alter one's own image by means of elective amputation, before sexual arousal can be consummated. The self-image may need to involve the experience of pain, bondage and humiliation, that is to say masochism, which may be associated with smearing or ingestion of feces and urine. The masochist may need sometimes to take the obverse role of sadism, though he may be aroused only in the role of slave to a sadistic master—and vice versa for the sadist. Sadism is akin to rape and lust murder, the difference being that the rapist is compelled to have an unwilling partner subjugated by force. The exhibitionist does not want to harm his partner, but he is sexually aroused by the reaction of amazement or shock in the stranger to whom he unexpectedly shows his penis. The voyeur is likewise dependent on the surprise of doing something forbidden, but in his case it is the surprise of glimpsing a woman undressing or naked, without her knowing of his peeping, as he runs the risk of being discovered. Compulsive fascination with forbidden images is the primary compulsion in the erotic vulgarities of the illicit telephone propositioner. In narratophilia, the person is compulsively dependent for erotic arousal on erotic talk, to or from his partner, of the type he has been reared to consider pornographic. In pictophilia he is similarly dependent on pictures or movies. In both instances the person may need his partner to play the role of impersonating a prostitute, so as not to be too respected and respectable for coitus; or he may need her to have sex with a third party, in a trio, so as to make the impersonation more realistic.

It is not fortuitous that the pronoun in an enumeration of the paraphilias should be "he," because in fact most of the paraphiliacs have been recorded in men. Those recorded in women tend to be fetishes related to tactile sensations, submissive masochism, and possibly kleptophilia—though the new frankness regarding woman's sexuality may extend the list. That paraphilias are mostly a male phenomenon is consistent with the hypothesis of the initiation of erotic pair-bonding in human beings by visual arousal of the male. To complete the hypothesis, one needs the further proposition that the content of the imagery of visual arousal is not preordained at birth but is, like native language, subject to early childhood social experience. During this period there is vulnerability to error, and the result tends to be permanent. There is clinical documentation to this effect in longitudinal studies of childhood development. But such studies are still rare and need to be increased, for the necessary information generally cannot be retrieved and authenticated retrospectively in adulthood.

Tomorrow's Children

It requires, as above, only enumeration of the exotic images of sex, the paraphilias to reveal that they all represent a circuitous or tortured way of maintaining substitute imagery of sexual arousal when the simplest way of heterosexual pair-bonding has been displaced or inhibited by an excess of punishment and guilt. The paraphiliac activity itself is socially forbidden and punishable, but in the young child's developing awareness of sex, it was less so, one infers, than was heterosexual imagery and rehearsal play. The socioreligious climate that dictates a family's negation of their child's emergent sexuality paradoxially engenders patterns of behavior which are officially more abhorrent than the heterosexual orthodoxy that it attempts to keep in check.

The resolution of this paradox constitutes a very difficult challenge in social medicine and public health, for there are no guaranteed techniques for changing adults' methods of child rearing on a widespread basis. Nor are there effective guidelines on how to establish a healthy sense of guilt in childhood development without creating sexual disability. One step in the right direction would be enlightened legislation so that factual information on childhood sexuality might be gathered without fear of trial and imprisonment, and without loss of research funds. In the meantime, society needs a more frank acquaintance with the paraphilias, and a more honest discussion of education for ordinary heterosexual copulation. It is toward this end that I recommend you expose yourself to a panorama of explicit sexual movies. In this way, you may be able to become less apprehensive of the phenomena involved, and more capable of guaranteeing masculine or feminine psychosexual development, respectively, free of sexual hangups, generations ahead. In the human species, pair-bonding is effected by the visual image rather than odor as the attractant. The threshold for visual arousal leading to initiation of sexual approval appears lower in the male than the female. The imagery of arousal announces itself to a boy in the wet dreams and masturbation fantasies of puberty. In Western culture over the ages, religious doctrine has alternated antisex and sexual leniency, but application of the taboo on natural primate sexual rehearsals in early childhood has always been maintained in some degree as a means of establishing behavioral control through guilt. The resultant psychosexual cost is excessive in terms of sexual hangups, including the exotic forms of imagery that constitute the paraphilias. Preventive research is socially prohibited because it would involve frank and overt study of the sex lives of children.

10

What Kind of Sex Is Natural?

Richard W. Smith

In this article and in the following one, two
researchers address the kinds of questions
invariably asked of every sex researcher.
Smith is also the author of Chapter 5 in this
collection.

A few years ago, a jittery student walked into my office at the college where I
teach. He was clearly suffering some kind of emotional crisis. After closing the
door, he told me in a quivering voice that he had been having sexual
intercourse with his girl friend for the past several months, and he had what he
called a "beautiful relationship" with her until the night before he came to see
me. During that night, when they were alone in her apartment, he had talked
his girl into engaging in oral intercourse with him—for the first time in his, or
her, life. He timidly told me that he had enjoyed it very much. But, after
leaving her apartment, he had begun to have overwhelming guilt feelings.
Anxiously averting his eyes from mine, he said that he was seeing me that day
because he now wanted me, as a psychology professor, to cure him of his
"sexual perversion" of wanting oral intercourse.

I asked him why he considered oral copulation to be a perversion. He
replied, "Because it's unnatural." Trying to alleviate his obvious misery, I said
that, while many people in *our* culture avoid that kind of sex, because *we*
apply to it the concept of "unnatural sex," there are other cultures that don't
use that concept at all, and that accept mouth-genital contacts as totally
normal, so he shouldn't feel especially guilty.

Surprisingly, he seemed to become even *more* agitated at my remark,
and he said . . . "Wait a minute. It's got nothing to do with culture. Look at
dogs. *They* don't have any culture, and *they* don't do it, do they?" I replied
that, as a matter of fact, dogs often do lick each other's genitals as part of their
mating act. He stopped cold, and spent about two minutes struggling with
apparently powerful, but mixed emotions. Finally, with a shaking voice and
trembling hands, he said, "That *proves* that it's wrong. We're supposed to be
more *civilized* than dogs."

The fact that this student had completely reversed himself within two minutes—telling me first that humans are supposed to behave the way dogs do (because such behavior is intended by nature), and then telling me we are supposed to *avoid* behaving like dogs (because such behavior is patently uncivilized and animalistic)—made a deep impression on me. Was this poor young man an unusual case of neurotic anxiety, whose guilt reaction had temporarily led him into making logically contradictory statements, or was he an example of a prevalent confusion in the sex mores of our society?

Since that time, I've been doing research for a book on culture and personality. For a section of the book concerning contemporary American attitudes towards universal human problems, I've conducted participant-observer interviews with people in several cities and in many everyday situations: for example, with people on the steps of churches, before and after services on Sunday; with officers of the Los Angeles Police Department, as they were preparing to play handball at a YMCA in the San Fernando Valley. I've talked with members of the Hare Krishna religious group, as they chanted and proselytized on Hollywood Boulevard. In Denver and Minneapolis and Miami and San Francisco, I've chatted with patrons at taverns (both straight and gay) as they were drinking and conversing with each other. I've attended services of street Christian groups (or "hippie Jesus freaks" as they are some-times called) and questioned them about a variety of topics.

During these interviews, I've always inserted questions about "natural" and "unnatural" sex. (Incidentally, I've never told my respondents that I am a social psychologist, because in such casual, street-corner discussions, it turns out that nothing creates a worse barrier to free-flowing conversation about sexual attitudes than people's fear that there is a psychologist present who is "psychoanalyzing them.")

I've found that the logical contradiction that occurred in my student's anxiety-ridden manifesto about oral intercourse and dogs is highly prevalent in the casual conversations of the general public. In fact, my student's incon-sistency of first declaring that we should imitate dogs, and then denouncing anybody who does so as uncivilized, was rather mild compared with some of the contradictions and ambiguities I've run across—even among educated, and otherwise coherent, individuals. And, I also found myself uncovering contradictions in my own views by challenging the ideas of others.

I've heard people announce in stentorian tones, for example, that we must avoid doing anything "unnatural" related to sex—because deviating from "nature" is the root of evil. I confronted some of these folks (and myself as well) by asking them if wearing clothing over the genitals was "natural" or "unnatural." Some of them announced loudly that it was the only "civilized" thing to do—and that we must avoid being like "those primitive savage tribes who run around naked and then do perverted things." In other words, we apparently must cover ourselves "unnaturally," in order not to be tempted to do anything "unnatural."

I've heard individuals pontificate that we must never frustrate the "natural purpose" of the sex act—which, they say, is obviously to squirt male semen into a female vagina. All forms of sex that don't do this—such as masturbation and homosexuality—violate the "natural purpose" of the sex organs, and are wrong. When I asked such individuals what the "natural purpose" of the hair follicles on various parts of our bodies was, they usually said "to grow hair." When I asked them if a man's shaving his beard off, or getting a haircut, or a woman's shaving her underarms and legs did or did not frustrate the "natural purpose" of the hair follicles, several people said that we must avoid being like "those long-haired, bearded hippie perverts." In other words, we must use artificial instruments, such as razors, scissors, hair clippers, shaving cream, depilatories, and so on, to reverse the "natural purpose" or our beard and hair growing organs, in order to avoid being like those bad people who ignore the "natural purpose" of their bodies.

When the people I talked with brought up the rather frequent example that animals behave the way nature intended (because animals—especially in their wild state—have never been subverted from "natural behavior" by a currupt civilization), and so humans should follow the example of animals, I often asked such persons if voluntary *celibacy* (which seldom occurs among animals in the wild) is therefore "unnatural." If so, then girls who voluntarily remain celibate until marriage, and unmarried men and women who are lifelong virgins, and Catholic priests and nuns, should perhaps be called sexual "perverts." I was frequently told no, they shouldn't, but such voluntary celibates would have been doing something unnatural if they had "behaved like animals." And when I told such individuals who had suggested imitating animals, that various species, in their natural environments, sometimes engage in incest between mother and son, between father and daughter and so on, and in homosexuality, I was often told that we shouldn't pay any attention to what animals do.

The results of these paradox-ridden conversations have led me to propose the following general formulation, which fits my conversations into a wide range of observations made by many other behavioral scientists: Namely, because of our differing social environments, we humans have likes and dislikes (about sex and food, etc.) that are quite variable—particularly between *societies*.

For example, a person is engaged in the same behavior if he is naked in public, whether he is a citizen of the United States or a member of the Chavantez Indian tribe in Brazil, but most people in our society apply a strongly *negative* value judgment to being nude in public ("It's obscene"), and most of the Chavantez give a *neutral* or *positive* judgment ("It's normal").

Thus *variability* in human value judgments about sex or food or whatever—especially across societies—is part of the human condition (and it is tempting to say that it is the only really "natural" thing about our behavior). But, when we are challenged to give reasons for our varying likes and dislikes, we often fall into confusing and contradictory half-explanations, as did many of the people I interviewed.

The Concept of "Natural Behavior" in Western Civilization

Aversion to public nakedness is, for most of us Americans, a socially transmitted attitude. As such, it is part of the collection of socially-communicated feelings (like disgust at homosexuality), beliefs (like faith in one God), and behaviors (like driving automobiles), that anthropologists call "culture." (Our American culture is part of a broad complex of cultures—along with those of France, Germany, and so on—comprising Western civilization.)

But while most of us humans are born into a culture, and pick up its ideas and outward mannerisms, we are nevertheless mostly unaware of its existence. The women in traditional Moslem countries who wore a veil over their faces, did not think they did this because they had "interiorized a culture," but because appearing bare-faced in public was "shameful." (This explanation, like the guilt feelings it "explained," was also part of their Moslem culture.) Those of us occidentals who are sickened at the thought of eating snake meat (like the people of India who are disgusted at the thought of eating beef, or the people in Ceylon who have a repugnance to drinking milk), don't think of these aversions as an "interiorized bit of culture," but simply as a reflection of the fact that snake meat is "disgusting" (or cows are "sacred" or milk is "horrible"). Thus, the culture that surrounds us (and is invisible to most of us—like the oxygen we breathe), supplies us with an "explanation" for our feelings of guilt and disgust about certain foods (and the culture itself remains invisible). Indeed, we are often so convinced of this cultural "explanation" of our cultural food aversions that we find it hard to believe that some societies think snake meat (or beef, etc.) is quite delicious! (Some scientists once had trouble giving up the culturally-transmitted theory of phlogiston and accepted instead the newer view that oxygen—which surrounded them, which they were constantly breathing in, which was part of their very own molecular structure—really existed and had an effect on them.)

So, when our women feel guilt and disgust at the idea of being topless (while women in many nonoccidental societies are topless all their lives), when we feel religiously-based revulsion at the thought of homosexuality (while some societies permit it quite freely, and others even *require* it in their sacred ceremonies), when we arrest men who exhibit themselves in public places (while in certain societies, males are uncovered all their lives, even though females are clothed), we are *not* likely to be aware that our guilt and disgust are interiorized bits of the occidental culture which surrounds us, and which has become part of our personalities. We are likely, instead, to say that our socially sanctioned behavior is "natural" and our condemned acts are "unnatural." And we use typically Western definitions of "nature" to explain our occidental sexual feelings, and we are incredulous when we learn that *other* societies feel differently. We sometimes even label such acts as women's wearing of bras, and the circumcision of our males, as "natural," even though an objective external observer would probably think of these acts as rather "unnatural."

It is only when someone probes for inconsistencies in our socially transmitted use of the label "natural" (as I did in the interviews I conducted) that we begin to think deeply about why we *really* feel the way we do.

The Concepts of "Natural Sex" in Contemporary America

Beneath the inconsistencies in their explanations about their sexual aversions that most people gave me during our conversations, implicit definitions of the words "natural" and "unnatural" kept recurring. It appeared to me that there were about three such definitions which I will call the "logical," "biological," and "metaphysical" definitions, respectively. There was also a "theological" view which avoided the term "natural," but which usually led to the other three usages. I will mention the "theological" viewpoint first:

The "theological" view

Although many contemporary theologians have begun to absorb the discoveries of modern science into their writings, the people I talked with were not professional theologians, and a few gave a rather black-and-white traditional view of sex acts: All forms of sex, except penis-vagina intercourse, in private, between a man and wife, are forbidden by religion. Hell-fire and damnation await anybody who knowingly and deliberately does anything else (such as masturbation or oral intercourse).

Many people switched from this explanation to other ones (listed below) when I asked them if that particular theological view was the *only* cause of their feelings. For example, I asked if the Christian politicians who wrote the legal codes for most American states (such as California, where oral intercourse used to be forbidden by law) were forcing their religion onto others by use of secular injunctions. Most people told me, no, that there were *other* reasons for their aversions ("logical," "biological," etc.), so that the courts were not forcing an exclusively *theological* view onto others.

Also, when I asked such individuals if God was being arbitrary when He forbade all kinds of sex—except one kind—they usually responded negatively: there were "logical" or "biological" or "metaphysical" reasons for the prohibitions. This leads to the second view.

The "logical" definition of nature

According to the second, or "logical" view, our society's rules against sex are entirely logical, not arbitrary. Certain forms of sex are *natural* and *good*. Other forms are *unnatural* and *bad*. When I asked people who talked this way to define "natural" they often replied with something like "Any damned fool knows what kind of sex is natural." When I asked them if *un*natural sex could ever be good, they usually gave replies such as, "Of course not. What are you, some kind of a Communist?"

Taking their views literally, then, I assume that they perceive our sex mores as a logical system rather like Euclidean geometry, in which the terms "natural" and "unnatural" are undefined, basic terms which are intuitively clear (like the words "point" and "line" in Euclid's system). We can define other words in relation to them, but cannot define these words themselves. For example, we can define a perversion as an "unnatural sex act," but we can't define "unnatural"—although we can give examples of unnatural acts such as oral intercourse.

Although this has recently changed, in my own state of California, the State Penal Code used to contain the following: "Every person who is guilty of the infamous crime against nature, committed with mankind or with any animal, is punishable by imprisonment in the state prison not less than one year." It also stated, "Any sexual penetration, however slight, is sufficient to complete the crime against nature." Nowhere in California's Penal Code could I find a definition of the "infamous crime against nature," although the Code was careful to define the *amount* of penetration. (Incidentally, at the time the poor student came to see me with his dilemma about dogs, the law made oral-genital copulation a felony, not a misdemeanor, carrying a one-to-fifteen-year prison sentence. Apparently, when I tried to alleviate his guilt over having oral intercourse with his girl friend, I was aiding and abetting his possibly committing future *felonies*.)

When I looked into legal dictionaries for "infamous crime against nature," they frequently defined it as a "perverted sex act," and a "perverted sex act," in turn, was defined as the "infamous crime against nature." Such circular definitions, in logical systems, usually mean that a bedrock, basic undefinable term is being used. And, since none of the folks I interviewed seemed to need to prove that natural sex is good and unnatural sex is bad, I assume that such a proposition is taken as self-evidently clear.

Using the analogy between this view of our sex norms and Euclidean geometry, I asked several people if a sort of *non*-Euclidean set of sex norms was possible. For example, I asked them if it was possible to change the axiom "Unnatural sex is bad," to its reverse "Unnatural sex is good," and then test to see which postulate worked better in the real world. Most people asked me, at this point, if I was crazy. Apparently, they look upon alternative ethical systems about the same way that Euclidean geometers used to look at non-Euclidean systems: as utter nonsense.

When I mentioned that other societies consider as "natural" forms of sex which we label "unnatural"—such as homosexuality—I was often told that such societies needed to have the truth preached to them. When I asked why these societies didn't *already* know what was natural and what was unnatural, seeing as how the concepts of "natural" and "unnatural" were self-evident ones, I often got replies such as "stop bothering me." Sometimes I was told that those other societies really knew as well as we do what's natural and what's unnatural, but they aren't as honest and clear-thinking as Americans, that's why we've got to make them similar to us. At other times, I was accused of lying when I said that other societies have different norms than ours.

At several bars, after people had told me that "any damned fool knows what kind of sex is natural and what kind is unnatural," I asked my respondents whether mutual masturbation between a husband and wife was natural or not. I got replies such as "It's *unnatural*" and "It's *natural*, if they're *married*," and "It's *unnatural*, but it's *okay* if they're *married*." I asked my respondents why they didn't agree with one another, if the concepts of natural and unnatural were self-evident to any damned fool, and how unnatural sex between married people is good, if it is axiomatic that unnatural sex is bad. At this point, they usually began to define "natural" and "unnatural" and to try to prove their "axiom" about unnatural sex—and this leads us to the next explanation that many people gave for their aversions.

The "biological" definition of nature
In the third, or "biological" model, the terms "natural" and "unnatural" are no longer basic, undefined ones. Rather, "natural" behavior is that which is defined by the more basic term "inborn," and "unnatural" behavior is that which goes against our "instincts"—another basic term.

According to this "biological" definition, we are all genetically predetermined to engage in certain kinds of sex, and genetically predetermined to avoid other kinds. Thus, some sex is *biologically* given, and other sex is *biologically* avoided. (Apparently, animals in the wild state *naturally* engage in *unnatural* sex.)

When I asked such individuals whether all humans have the *same* biological predetermination, or whether some people are genetically predisposed to engage occasionally in, say, oral intercourse, I was usually told that every human has exactly the *same* genetic predetermination. This makes this layman's view of heredity somewhat different from scientific genetics, because geneticists know that anything hereditary—like eye color and height—can vary, although some traits that are immediately lethal (like a genetic determination not to breathe), end up as not occurring in surviving members of the population. Behavioral traits that scientists have found to be hereditary and nonlethal—such as the ability of rats to learn mazes—are extremely variable within a species.

But, our society has never passed laws requiring people to engage in *other* forms of innate, universal behavior. (There are no legal rules telling us we must breathe, or urinate, or defecate, and so on.) And society has never passed laws forbidding *other* forms of noninstinctive and even counter-instinctive behavior. (There are no laws against cooking food, parachute jumping, and so on.) So, I asked my respondents why laws have been passed to force people to engage only in "natural sex"—which all people are biologically predetermined to engage in anyway—and to avoid "unnatural sex"—which all people are already predetermined to avoid. I was usually told that most people *do* engage only in "natural" sex, except for a few "perverts." When I asked why their form of sex was a "perversion," I was told "because it's unnatural." When I asked if it was against *everybody's* nature, or just the nature of the *majority*, I got different answers from different respondents. Some said that it goes against the *majority's* nature, but "perverted" people have *different* natures (thus contradicting the earlier statement that we all have the *same* nature). When I asked if that means that our laws are forcing some people—the erotic minorities—to behave in ways that are unnatural to *them*, although natural for the rest of us, I was again not infrequently called a Communist or "some kind of nut."

But other respondents said that erotic minorities have the same "nature" as everybody else. So, I asked them how it was that so-called "perverts" (such as homosexuals) were able to avoid behaving according to the way they were biologically predetermined to behave. The answer I got led to the fourth, or "metaphysical" concept of nature.

The "metaphysical" definition of nature

In this explanation for people's sexual aversions, "nature" is no longer heredity, but is an intrinsic factor in each of us which our accidental traits have to match if we are to be good people. We are free to make a match between our external behavior and our internal nature, or not. (This "nature," incidentally, is Aristotle's concept of "essence." It was once used to "prove" that heavy objects fall faster than light ones, that women are "inferior" to men—because they don't correspond as closely to basic human nature as do men—that American Indians are "inferior" to whites, and so on.) When I asked for evidence that such a nature really exists, and that it is the same in all of us, I was usually referred back to a version of the "logical" definition—namely, that these things are self-evident to any damned fool.

Those are all the definitions of "nature" I have been able to extract from the rather casual conversations I have engaged in. More systematic research would probably modify the concepts somewhat, and perhaps discover more of them.

I've mentioned these concepts as if they were fairly rational pictures which people have about "natural" and "unnatural" sex. Actually, however, most people I talked with seemed somewhat anxious or hostile when I questioned them closely—even those who had previously talked freely about sex. Natural and unnatural sex, it seems, are supposed to be self-evident to all people, and it is threatening to find inconsistencies between *your* version of "nature" and those of *other* people. It is even *more* threatening to detect inconsistencies *inside* your own strongly-held value judgments—especially when there is no place to localize the causality for those culturally-transmitted, but interiorized, guilts and aversions, except in your basic "nature." Consequently, I was often accused of being un-American, Communistic, perverted, and so on. The accusations and obvious physical manifestations of anxiety that accompanied these casual conversations led me to believe that my student, with his problem about oral intercourse and dogs, was exhibiting just an acute version of a chronic sickness which infects many people—and even the penal codes—in our society.

Psychologists and psychiatrists, it seems to me, have an obligation to alleviate this social illness—not by helping this society to force people to conform to ethnocentric views about what sex is "natural," but by educating people, instead, about the variability and healthiness of human sexual behavior.

11

Am I Normal?

Elizabeth Canfield

One of the values of current research into human sexuality is that it can help those who deal with children, adolescents, and young adults answer the age old question "Am I normal?" more effectively. Elizabeth Canfield, though technically not a researcher in the field of human sexuality, has been able to apply the research to real life problems. She offers some effective advice to those engaged in counseling, and in the process tosses in a large amount of good common sense. At present she is a health and family planning counselor at the University of Southern California in Los Angeles. She has written numerous articles on birth control and pregnancy counseling.

For the past twenty years I have been involved with family planning, abortion law reform, pregnancy counseling and education in human sexuality. First came birth control work among low income families, then community education on abortion, followed by the founding of the Los Angeles Free Clinic and the organization and launching of the Clergy Counseling Service for Problem Pregnancies. For the past seven years I have been involved with student health services on the college level.

I have had the opportunity of talking with thousands of girls and boys, women and men, ranging in age from thirteen years to the seventies; thousands of questions have been asked—both verbally and in written form, following lectures and discussions on sexual subjects. Striking has been the similarity of concerns across racial, religious and ethnic lines. The young woman from Ghana who sat in the office last week sounded amazingly like the one from Oklahoma who had been in earlier. The scholarly doctoral candidate from Pakistan would have been surprised if he could have met his counterpart from Idaho or California. They (and we) have in common basic anxiety about human sexuality, whether they seek factual information about birth control methods or assistance with a personal problem of an emotional nature.

Discomfort with sexual topics has been uniformly evident throughout this career; in light of the widespread publicity about a sexual revolution and major changes in values, this universal uneasiness seems remarkable. We are still secretive (as distinguished from private), ashamed, guilty and confused.

Informally and briefly discussed below are some of the concerns and questions most frequently heard over these twenty years. The comments are intended as stimulation for further questioning rather than as comprehensive treatments of the issues raised. One consistent theme has been evident throughout: the preoccupation with what is normal and what is natural. Perhaps the greatest contribution to be made by professionals and paraprofessionals in family planning and sexuality is in the area of reassurance regarding this preoccupation.

I know about birth control methods, but can you tell me which one is best for me?

The lack of a medically safe, effective and acceptable contraceptive has represented a considerable dilemma for family planning professionals. No method or combination of methods can be recommended wholeheartedly and we need to spend much time assessing the particular circumstances of a woman or couple at risk of pregnancy, while consistently giving the message that no matter how imperfect present techniques might be, they are preferable to undesired pregnancy. We speak of "choice" but the range is quite limited and we're often on the spot, apologizing for the lack of progress in contraceptive research. The most positive aspect of this dilemma might well turn out to be the opportunity of encouraging students to enter the field of research and ultimately to come up with the perfect method; or to go into politics and lobby for appropriations for such research.

Do you think it's normal to wait until marriage?

We must ask the question: Wait with what? The reply will invariably be: sexual intercourse, i.e., vaginal penetration. It is common to hear such statements as: "We've done everything else. . . ."; "I want to save something for marriage. . . ." Fortunately we are able to assure people that it is normal to wait and normal not to wait.

This glib pronouncement serves to encourage further investigation by the questioner: What does penetration mean to me? If intercourse means total commitment or involvement, am I ready for that? Is my partner? If my lover expects virginity, is he relating to me or to my hymenal membrane? Do I expect him to be virginal and if not, why not?

The intromission mystique leads to further questioning. Is a person who has experienced all manner of sexual activity, including orgasm, a virgin if coitus has not taken place?

My parents would be terribly hurt if they found out I wasn't a virgin.
It is interesting to note how differently we regard sexuality, as compared with other aspects of ourselves. In any other area, experience is appreciated, lauded, required. But we are expected to fall in love, get married and have babies, hopefully in that order, without preparation, training or experience. How to have the perfect love life, home life, sex life without knowing imperfection? Women say: I lost my virginity. How about: I gained experience?

I didn't think it would happen—I was unprepared.
What is "it"? Usually this means sexual intercourse; occasionally pregnancy is meant by this statement. The evil of preparation, of "premeditated sex," has given spontaneity a good name and now it is up to us to reverse the trend. In our society sex is, quite simply, not O.K. If it were, planning for sexual expression of any kind, but particularly for the kind that leads to pregnancy, would also be O.K. How can young people be expected to plan responsibly when they have been taught all along that they must be overwhelmed, out of control, overcome by passion? The degree of surprise displayed when pregnancy test results are given is indicative of the self-deception in this so-called enlightened age. What is so surprising? What should intercourse cause if not pregnancy, especially in healthy young persons? Is it necessary to take chances?

The contraceptive age, with all its limitations, does offer options. One of these is to change from gambling to planning. Yes, please is O.K.; no, thank you is O.K.; both involve responsibilities.

My doctor has never mentioned anything about sexuality.
It is remarkable how many annual physical examinations are performed without the slightest allusion to matters sexual, often without pelvic examinations. The sanctity of the genitals is perpetuated in good measure by the medical profession. We see female students well into their twenties who have never had an internal checkup; obviously this particularly applies to women using nonprescription contraceptives or none at all. It would appear that questions about sexual health such as menstruation, contraceptive use, libido, gratification and emotional well-being are seldom asked by physicians. Yet society expects these very professionals to be infinitely knowledgeable in this realm.

There must be something wrong with me—my periods are irregular.
Many women show great concern in this area and consider themselves abnormal and unhealthy. The word "regular" is poorly understood; to most people it means that menses occur every twenty-eight days and that everything else is not all right. Women need to know that there is great variation in menstrual cycles; that menstrual unevenness may be inconvenient, but not a

sign of danger or disease; that they may or may not be fertile, with or without regularity; that they must use birth control every single time; that ovulation can occur any time; that oral contraceptives should not be prescribed solely for menstrual irregularity.

I didn't learn anything at home about sex.

Everyone learns about sexuality at home. Positive and negative messages are received from infancy on; few of us get accurate information. All parents are sex educators, whether they do it well or poorly. Parents have traditionally feared that knowledge causes irresponsible behavior; that they need to be experts before talking about sex. Thus they have kept silent and perpetuated ignorance, anxiety, premature experimentation and much fear.

Sex is unmentionable; it assumes exaggerated proportions. Communication between parents and children is limited unnecessarily. Even today some young women are completely unprepared for their first menses and certainly the majority of adolescents have no idea what their parents use for birth control. In fact, most teenagers don't even consider that their parents are sexually active.

I didn't learn anything in school about erotic feelings and intimacy.

Quite a few school programs cover such subjects as menstruation and reproduction; the functioning of the various organs is adequately enough explained by physical education or home economics teachers in what appears to be a relentless pursuit of the Fallopian tubes and seminal vesicles. Lacking, however, is an atmosphere in which feelings, fears, relationships, standards and options may be explored. The school joins the home in depriving young people of a forum for value clarification. They remain victims of moralizing, instead of being encouraged to develop a personal morality.

How can I tell my family that I'm gay?

Even though homosexuality is increasingly viewed as a sexual variation rather than a sickness or emotional disturbance in and of itself, being open about same-sex proclivities is still very difficult for a great majority of gay women and men. Friends and counselors can do little more than encourage risk assessment and be supportive of either choice: to tell or not to tell. Is it preferable to live a secret life? To smile evasively when the expectation of marriage and parenthood is brought up? When derogatory remarks or silly jokes are made? People have to decide for themselves which way hurts less; neither will be easy as sexual variation has by no means achieved comfort status. (We are aware of an organization named Parents of Gays which has been helpful to a number of families.)

I worry about my fantasies—are they normal?

Fortunately we are able to reassure everyone that all thoughts are normal, while stressing that not everything in our fertile minds has to be translated into action. An amazing number of those concerned with fantasies have not considered the difference between thoughts and behavior. The mature, healthy person evaluates the appropriateness of the transition from fantasy to reality, a daily task not only in relation to sexuality but also to food, work, money and other aspects. Fantasy can enhance routine, can be creatively and constructively used; excessive preoccupation and compulsiveness can, of course, signal a need for help.

Is it normal to love more than one person?

Most of us have loved several people since we were born, such as parents, siblings, friends. The question, though not always clearly stated, implies romantic love and had best be rephrased: Is it normal to want to have sexual relations with more than one person in a given period of time? It is, for some people; and it is a matter of choice. Quite often these preferences are inadequately checked out among partners. To many women and men being "special" means being "only."

I don't believe in abortion but there's no other alternative in this case.

How rapidly both women and men discard yesterday's prohibitions when undesired pregnancy threatens to interfere with their lives. As parenthood assumes ever more special meaning and it is no longer automatic that everyone will or should be a parent, abortion often becomes the most responsible choice. Many women express how good it feels to be pregnant, how reassuring to learn that they are fertile (i.e., normal), but how poorly equipped they are for taking care of a child at the time. One bright young woman comes to mind especially. She had been raped by a fellow student after a drinking party, was pregnant and totally unwilling to discuss the alternatives as routinely outlined in a pregnancy counseling session. Abortion referral in hand, she turned around at the door as she was leaving, smiled kindly and said, "Well, I guess there goes my Right-to-Life League membership. . . ."

Is it normal just to want to be held?

Loneliness, the public health problem of major proportions, may be blamed for a good deal of genital involvement not based on erotic feelings, but rather on the need for warmth, affection, closeness and affirmation. This is complicated by the foreplay mentality which dictates that all activities lead, or should lead, to intromission. One wonders why *fore*—why not just play?

How do we let each other know what sort of contact we desire at a particular time? How do we acquire the courage to be honest in this regard?

I guess I need a referral to a sex therapist.

A great majority of students who make this request need everything but a costly treatment program. They are aware of inadequacies and dissatisfactions in their sex lives, but often don't know exactly what to ask for. In many instances they may be helped by a combination of sex information, permission to experiment (with masturbation and with their partners), communication skills, risk assessment, support and reassurance. A comparison may be made to music appreciation classes: Most people listen to music routinely; a special course will sharpen their awareness and thus their enjoyment. The need was for enhancement, not for cure.

Can you recommend some books on sex?

The current information explosion may be celebrated on one hand and treated judiciously on the other. We might cause more anxiety than we alleviate by creating spectators of their sexual behavior rather than participants in the new sensual awareness. It's a fine line.

One student comes to mind. She had been referred by her partner for not enjoying their sexual relations to the fullest. His diagnosis was based on her not having sex flush. He had read somewhere that this is a natural phenomenon of the erotically excited woman and then proceded to convince her that her orgasms were lacking in intensity. By the time the young woman reached my office, she was practically in hysterics. These two were clearly victims of the performance trap.

Other examples include the preoccupation with breast size, penis size (the magician, not the wand, works the magic!), technique and frequency.

Is it normal to have just one orgasm and not to have one every time?

Now that women have been given society's permission to enjoy their sexuality and participate equally, we have managed, in many instances, to exchange passive tolerance for athletic fetes. The great search is on for multiple or simultaneous orgasms. Partners ask for every slightest detail of the particular experience and response. Whereas we certainly encourage talking with one another, this quiver-for-quiver accounting can well be carried to extremes and can lead to intolerable pressures resulting in "faking it." We risk creating a new phenomenon, the tyranny of the perfect sexual response. Information yes, olympic events no.

How can we keep sex interesting after being together for years?

The best way to avoid dull routine is to introduce new material. We have surely learned that boredom and hurry are among the major deterrents to a creative sex life. In most situations the erotic aspect is a reflection of the rest of the relationship. If new and excitingly different activities are shared, most likely the sexual component will correspond. Some suggestions: take a trip, listen to a new piano concerto, meet some new people, redecorate a room, read *Alice in Wonderland* together.

How do you know when you're in love?

It's quite impossible to answer this most personal question adequately. But it does raise a number of other interesting ones. Is it necessary to be in love in order for marriage to work? Is there only one right person for everyone? Can we love someone a great deal and still not get along in close proximity? Do we break up a marraige when we're no longer in love?

It can be readily seen that there are very few simple answers; that even the instant society, replete with solutions to many technological problems, has merely managed to extend the list of questions. A few personal ones that remain puzzling: Does early sexual experience invariably lead to tragedy? How young is too young if responsibility is taken and neither unwanted pregnancy nor sexually transmitted disease occur? In view of the enormous teen-age pregnancy rate in our country, do we have the right to withhold positive sex and birth control information from anyone? When our children don't listen to our warnings and make serious mistakes, why do we withhold love instead of giving support as we wish our parents had? What about the double standard still so evident in the age of the women's movement? (Men are strong, women are aggressive. . . .) Why do we thoughtlessly use words like promiscuous, frigid, puppy love and the like? Why do we label and diagnose?

The best I've been able to do so far is encourage students, clients, children and friends to keep in mind a basic checklist for sexual health and well-being. These are the primary questions on this list: Does my behavior enhance the self-esteem of those involved? Is it entirely voluntary? Does it provide pleasure and gratification? Does it prevent unwanted pregnancy? Does it prevent the spreading of disease?

Much work needs to be done before we can move from anxiety, sexual ignorance, and exploitation to a comfortable integration of sexuality with the totality of our personhood.

References

Advincula, Fe et al. *A Survey of Student Concerns and Utilization of Birth Control Services.* Unpublished report prepared by and for the staff of the Student Health and Counseling Services. University of Southern California, 1976.

Calderone, Mary. *Sexuality and Human Values.* Boston: Beacon Press, 1968.

Canfield, Elizabeth. "Pregnancy and Birth Control Counseling." *Journal of Social Issues* 30, 1 (1974).

————. "Toward a Manifesto of Rights and Responsibilities for the Sexual Adolescent." In *Let's Make Sex a Household Word,* ed. Sol Gordon. New York: John Day, 1975.

Goldman, Carole. "Am I Parent Material?" Brochure published by N.A.O.P. (The National Alliance for Optional Parenthood, 3 No. Liberty, Baltimore, Md. 21201), 1976.

Gordon, Sol. *The Sexual Adolescent.* North Scituate, MA: Duxbury Press, 1973.

Hettlinger, Richard. *Sex Isn't That Simple.* New York: Seabury Press, 1974.

Mazur, Ronald. *Commonsense Sex.* Boston: Beacon Press, 1968.

National Liaison Committee of the American College Health Association; Planned Parenthood Federation of America; and Sex Information and Education Council of the U.S. *Sexual Health Services for Academic Communities.* Philadelphia: George F. Stickley, 1976.

Oswalt, Robert. "Sexual and Contraceptive Behavior of College Females." *Journal of the American College Health Association* 22, 5 (June 1974).

Pleck, Joseph, and Sawyer, Jack. *Men and Masculinity.* Englewood Cliffs, NJ: Prentice-Hall, 1974.

Weinberg, George. *Society and the Healthy Homosexual.* New York: St. Martin's, 1972.

12

Who Are All Those Sex Counselors?

Bonnie Bullough

Elizabeth Canfield's article emphasized the importance of good counseling, of imparting the results of the ongoing research, as an important aspect of the eductional process. This leads to the question of who is to do the sex counseling and sex therapy. So far there is no licensure in the field although institutions such as California State University, Northridge, do offer certificates in sex therapy for those already in the helping professions or for those who are acquiring expertise in counseling. The difficulty with counseling in the field of human sexuality is that it cuts across a lot of different disciplines. Physicians, nurses, psychiatric social workers, and others rightfully can claim some expertise in the field. Bonnie Bullough, a professor of nursing at California State University, Long Beach, and with a Ph.D. in sociology, raises some important questions. Several of the people who contributed to this volume such as Elizabeth Canfield and Marilyn Fithian lack some of the degree requirements that some would require for future entry into the field. The essential question is, can one do research and counseling or therapy without special degrees in sexology?

One of the most obvious consequences of the current sexual revolution is the proliferation of sex therapists and counselors. Included in this category are professionals who have added sex counseling to an already existing counseling role as well as several new types of counselors who are now making sex therapy their full time occupation. Although many observers feel the growth of this new class of specialists is long overdue, some, concerned over the rapid expansion of the field, argue for licensure, certification, or some other type of control. We belong to the group that believes that licensure and certification as sex therapists or counselors are not necessarily desirable goals since the field is so varied that licensing would either be unnecessarily restrictive or so broad as to be meaningless. Let us explain.

Throughout much of history there were at least two major sources of expert opinion on sexual matters, the midwife and the medicine man. While the midwife tended to have a monopoly on the delivery of babies, both she and the medicine man were more or less equally involved in giving advice related to fertility. Women tended to look to her while men relied on the medicine man for sex advice. A wide variety of charms, herbs, prayers and ceremonies were developed in various parts of the world to make men more potent and women more fertile. Children, however, were not always desired in unlimited numbers nor were they desired at particular times. Inevitably there were also charms and incantations to avoid pregnancy. Among the most effective approaches were sponges inserted into the vagina although some of the suppositories that changed the ph content of the vagina might also have proven somewhat effective. Some societies resorted to surgical procedures such as cutting a hole in the male uretha which resulted in the discharge of the sperm outside of the vaginal canal. Various abortifacients were also used.

Though the medicine man and the midwife never fully abdicated their role as sex educators or counselors, increasingly the ethics of the sex act came to be of concern to religion, and in western culture at least, the clergy became a major disseminator of sexual advice as well as the chief arbitrators of desirable sexual practice. In the Christian West, sex acts increasingly tended to be measured against the standards of their potential for procreation. Acts that did not fulfill this need were defined as sin. To inculcate these sins into public consciousness, a significant body of penitential literature developed which catalogued the possible sexual sins to be avoided. Essentially the purpose of the literature was to help the priest counsel his parishioners to avoid all nonprocreative activities. Avoiding sin by encouraging procreation (although within the marriage bond) remained the dominant sexual advice until the medical model of sexuality emerged.

It was not until the nineteenth century that physicians began to replace clergymen as the dispensers of sexual advice, taking back the functions once held by the midwife and the medicine man. The changeover marked the growth in the science of medicine as well as an expansion in the medical role beyond that of delivering babies or in treating venereal disease and urinary tract infections. Unfortunately medicine found itself in a new position of dominance without enough theoretical understanding of the sexual processes. This meant that physicians for the most part were content to describe as pathological what the clergyman had described as sin. The high point of this trend was reached in the works of Richard von Kraft-Ebbing who managed to define more than 300 sexual activities as pathological including all forms of nonprocreative sex as well as those aspects of procreative sex not performed in the proper position, i.e., with the woman on her back.

Medicine, however, had the advantage over religion in that research was possible in order to update or change outmoded concepts. Within medicine, the role of sexual expert was quickly claimed by the psychiatrist. In a sense, Sigmund Freud was instrumental in securing the dominance of psychiatrists, at least within the American setting, since he had emphasized the importance of sexual factors in the lives of the patients he treated. Increasingly under psychiatric influence, all sexual problems came to be conceptualized as part of larger psychoneurotic illnesses with the clear implication that such behavior could be cured if enough time could be set aside on a one-to-one basis. Sometimes such treatment was successful, more often it was not. Unfortunately this treatment was unavailable to most people with sex problems because they could not afford psychotherapy. Even more serious, however, was the fact that the medical psychiatric model led to people being labeled as sick or deviant regardless of how they regarded themselves or regardless of how they functioned in society. Psychiatrists claimed, or at least were popularly believed, to have the answers.

As psychiatrists temporarily became the dominant voice in evaluating sex behavior, clergy had to reassess their role. In the process, many changed from being arbiters of sexual conduct to counseling and advising their parishioners about sexual problems, in the process becoming sex counselors. In recent years more and more clergymen have moved in this direction giving impetus to a growing demand for churches to reexamine and reinterpret the alleged scriptural justification for restricting sex solely to procreation. Encouraging even such conservative denominations as Catholicism and Eastern Orthodox Christianity to seek reinterpretations are the growing fears of a world population crisis. Once they overcame their theological hangups about sexuality, clergy for the most part proved natural sex counselors since they could incorporate it into their general pastoral function and put the sexual problems of their parishioners in perspective. Many of them either have educational backgrounds which include psychology, sociology, or counseling techniques, or else they have learned these techniques on the job. Increasingly, also, clergymen are attending courses and workshops to increase their knowledge of the physiological and psychological processes related to sexuality.

Clergymen, however, are not the only group that have had to reassess their roles in the sex field. In the last three decades the expertise of psychiatry has begun to be challenged by both the rising behavioral sciences and by physiological advances. In order to meet the challenge, psychiatrists have begun to do some research of their own instead of going on untested assumptions or basing whole theories on a few case studies. Some of the psychiatrists have begun to take new approaches to sex counseling and therapy; evidence of this is the ferment within the psychiatric profession which has challenged traditional labeling of certain sexual behaviors as pathological.

Physicians, outside of the psychiatric specialty, have always given some advice relative to sexuality and they probably remain the best source of advice for problems that have a physiological basis including those caused by the disease process itself as well as iatrogenic problems (such as the loss of libido which sometimes follows the use of antihypertensive drugs). Since much of research into sex in the last decade has had a physiological basis, physicians have more to offer than they ever did in the past to help their patients. In general, however, physicians are probably less competent than clergymen as generalized sex counselors if only because their educational background seldom includes courses in counseling or sexuality. While physicians have ability to acquire knowledge in both of these areas, their time is usually much too expensive and their overhead too high to spend the time necessary to carefully assess the human problems associated with sexuality. Much better qualified in a sense are the nurse practitioners who are entering the field of primary care in increasing numbers. They may well fill an important intermediate position between that of the clergyman and the physician. They have the basic medical knowledge, the necessary coursework in counseling, and their salaries are low enough to spend the time necessary for effective counseling. Until about five years ago, their background in sexuality was little better than that of the physician, but most of the basic nursing curriculums have added sexuality courses, and nurse practitioner programs include sexual counseling as part of the course content.

Increasingly, however, these "traditional" counselors are being overshadowed by the new therapists who have adopted the techniques pioneered by Masters and Johnson and by Hartman and Fithian. Although the physiological data accumulated by Masters and Johnson has been the starting point for this group of therapists, and this has been supplemented by the behavioral science techniques of Hartman and Fithian, the basic approach of both teams is an educational one. It is built upon the assumption that sexual intercourse and other pleasurable sexual activities can be learned if the right teaching techniques are used. This approach defines the client as a student rather than a patient, and his or her problem is conceptualized as a need for new knowledge and skills rather than as an illness or aberrant behavior. These new sex therapists tend to start their program with a diagnostic work up in order to rule out any medical problems, and to better focus on the physiological or psychological problems involved. Common sexual problems include impotence and premature ejaculation for men and anorgasmia for women. In dealing with these problems the successful therapists have found that a relaxed atmosphere and course work emphasizing improved communication between partners as well as nongenital stimuli are important, although eventually the sessions include genital activity of some sort, usually culminating in intercourse. Because of this, most therapists deal only with couples, although a few are willing to consider the use of surrogates in selected cases.

Surrogates, working alone or with sex therapists, are the most controversial of the new type of sex therapists. They work on a one-to-one basis with their clients teaching them to overcome fears and participate fully in sexual activities. Surrogates are controversial not only because their use seems to violate traditional moral standards but also because some authorities feel that their clients suffer severe pangs of loneliness and rejection at the end of the therapeutic relationship. Surrogates, recognizing these psychological implications, argued that with good preparation the problem of separation can be handled, and that they are then able to help people who are either too shy or too disabled to be helped in any other way.

Another approach to sex problems that seems to be very successful, at least in some cases, is group counseling. It is used by a wide variety of professionals including psychologists, social workers, marriage counselors as well as a rather amorphous group that can only be called sex therapists. The therapy groups ordinarily specialize, i.e., in anorgasmic women, gay men, parents of homosexuals, or any other subgroup. Traditional techniques for encouraging group interaction are used to help group members air their feelings. Sometimes simply knowing that other people share the same life situation makes a problem a nonproblem. The feeling of being alone, of being stigmatized, turns out to be the real problem rather than any particular malady or behavior.

The group approach to anorgasmia (or preorgasmia) as it is hopefully termed has some special features. Many women have been socialized to believe that they should not or could not enjoy sex since if they did they would not remain "good" women. Others believe they are unworthy of enjoying sex. A significant part of their therapy involves consciousness raising so they can realize they are worthy and entitled to sexual pleasures. This process works particularly well in a group where members can reinforce each other.

There are many other approaches, and every kind of therapy from est to rolfing has been put into a sexual therapy situation by some counselor. Since there is no effective means of certifying sex counselors, all one needs to be a sex counselor is to proclaim himself or herself one and wait for clients. With all of these various counselors on the horizon is regulation needed? Though organizations such as the American Association of Sex Counselors and the Society for the Scientific Study of Sex have been making yeomen efforts to secure some sort of either national or state certification and regulation, it is still not clear that it is needed. Each approach seems useful for certain clients. If there was a certification procedure who would it rule out? Would the psychologists, the medical practitioners, the educators, the clergy, or the surrogates be eliminated? If the certification move had taken place a decade ago it would have cut out most of the new approaches to therapy. This is important to emphasize since the "new" therapists have a much higher success rate than that associated with traditional psychotherapy which until recently dominated the field.

Undoubtedly it is true that there are a number of "hustlers" working the sex vinyards of today. Eliminating them, however, could stifle innovation in the field. Undoubtedly one of the reasons for the great increase in sex therapists and counselors is that we are caught in a period of changing standards and we need to update our thinking. How much certification, however, do we need to do this? One of the most effective woman therapists I know is a retreaded English teacher; another male therapists who seems fairly effective once taught mechanical drawing in junior high school. Hopefully the sex counseling or therapy business is one that will work itself out of business except for a few hard core cases that really need expert help. Once we begin to put out more accurate information, and include aspects of sexual behavior in our educational programs, we will need fewer sex counselors. In the meantime there are a lot of people out there with some expertise about sex and we would prefer to avoid the grim professionalization of a new field that would cut out many of the groups which we believe offer effective sex, therapy. Sex is much too personal, and far too pleasurable, to leave in the hands of a few authorities. Hopefully all of the helping professions can be regarded as legitimate sex counselors once they acquire the necessary information and extend their expertise to include the sex field. Obviously it takes particular expertise to deal with the more troublesome cases, but these can be referred on to those counselors or therapists who specialize in that area without the necessary process of having a government license to authenticate such a specialty.

13

Aims and Objectives in Sexual Research and Theory

Lester A. Kirkendall

Lester Kirkendall, professor emeritus of family life at Oregon State University, is one of the surviving pioneers in American sex research and education today. Since his retirement he has given a great deal of attention to the aims and objectives of sexual research and theory. In the process of stating his aims Kirkendall summarizes much of the past research.

Certain features should characterize humanistic sex research. The same features should be found in research involving any aspect of human behavior. A grave mistake has been made in setting sexuality apart from the rest of life and assuming, as we do, that sex functions in a different way and for different purposes than the rest of our human capacities.

I have two purposes in mind as I write this chapter. First, in a highly generalized way I want to explore what should be the objectives underlying research on human sexual behavior and on other aspects of human behavior as well. Second, I will call attention to a trend found in authoritative statements concerning sex as they appeared some hundred or so years ago. These will be traced and linked with current sex research.

What position should we take toward sex research? Broadly speaking the research should be directed toward providing the individual a greater measure of freedom, tempered by the need for responsible consideration of others. The individual should also be encouraged to experience more joy in living—joy from being associated with those about him, joy from his own perception of himself, joy and pleasure from his body.

Beyond that, sex research should be directed toward developing a rationalistic and logical approach to understanding in this field. We should seek to expand and verify knowledge, whether or not it fits our previous concepts. Currently, for example, there is a great deal of interest in bisexuality, or preferably ambisexuality. Research on this is at this time minimal, though the presently existing knowledge makes it appear that for some it is a satisfying expression that brings into harmony more aspects of their nature than either heterosexuality or homosexuality. Would research verify this feeling? If it does, can we then accept ambisexuality as a legitimate and acceptable part of sexual expression for more and more persons?

Sex research should help dispel taboos that stand in the way of fact-finding and the utilization of knowledge. To do this, however, those conducting research must ally themselves with other responsible professionals who can help disseminate the knowledge gained through research and answer questions raised by it. The end objective would be to establish an affirmative and positive attitude toward sexuality so that it is accepted as an integral part of joyful human existence.

Whether or not we recognize it, sexuality is tied with all asepcts of life and should not therefore be divorced from research on other aspects of human behavior and social adjustments. If a more positive, affirmative attitude toward sexuality does develop, we will have to understand better than we now do how to deal with guilt and shame. Should these feelings as they relate to sex be erased? Or are they still important but now need to be seen in a different context? Certainly the knowledge of those professionals who deal with human feelings and emotions will be needed. This means that humanistic sex research must be multidisciplinary; it should be broad enough to include various fields concerned with human behavior as professionals attempt to understand the individual, human experience in small groups, and sexual conduct in a broad social context.

Sexual research, I think, needs to be conducted within a holistic framework. In advocating this approach I assume several things about humankind. For one thing, human beings function as a unit. Perhaps the physical, the mental, the emotional, the mystical features can be arbitrarily separated for the purpose of research, but the research has lost much of its value if it is not recombined and synthesized so that the person becomes once again a total being. I assume, too, that joyful associations of various sorts, when responsibly experienced, result in growth and development, not only for the individual but for society as well. This assumption runs counter to the belief that any experiencing of sexual pleasure will result in mindless hedonism, exploitation of others and ultimately to disastrous consequences of one kind or another.

I make an assumption that is even more positive. I assume that humans are social beings and that unless their needs for sociality are recognized they will not prosper or be happy. If the situation is too negative they will not even survive. In this matter I agree with Ashley Montagu (1970) and others.

An affirmative position on sexual expression will undoubtedly mean that sexuality will be incorporated into many diverse patterns of living. Therefore sex research needs to be concerned with a value system that enables one to express himself sexually, but with a concern and a responsible regard for others. Here the researcher and the philosopher become allies (Baker and Ellison, 1975). Other allies must be the sociologist, the psychologist, anyone who can help in appraising the advantages and disadvantages of diversity and pluralism.

My second purpose is to examine the trend that is revealed as both authoritative statements and the basic assumptions and presuppositions used in sexual research are analyzed. This analysis indicates a definite movement toward various of the qualities which should be embodied in humanistic sex research. The earlier "authoritative" statements were not research in the sense that we now understand it; some are better described as diatribes. The persons making them, however, were considered authorities because they came from disciplines commanding a high degree of respect. There were no facts to support a different view so these disciplines could maintain their authoritative stance.

One of the most respected of all disciplines was theology, and with its antisex bias it set the tone for both theological pronouncements and for the statements of others outside the theological framework. As theology was gradually superseded the medical field took over so far as being the authoritarian discipline was concerned. Medical writers took their cues from theology and, rather than establishing their position through scientific research, they accepted the same dour and hostile attitudes toward sex that had been expressed through theology, though now couched in medical terms. Vern Bullough (1974) wrote that

> . . . medical concepts about sexual deviation came to enforce tradi-
> tional religious concepts which were under attack. These ideas were
> amplified in the nineteenth century until all nonprocreative forms of
> sexuality were looked upon as pathological.

To go any further back than the last hundred years is impossible in such a short chapter. Even then only a few statements that illustrate the trend I have in mind can be included.

One of the most influential of medical men was William Acton (1871) who regarded almost any use of the sexual capacity as exceedingly damaging. Acton was particularly concerned with masturbation. For him masturbation (and this term covered all nonprocreative sex) was a "foul blot" which caused "many wrecks of high intellectual attainments." Acton derived his ideas form a Swiss physician, Tissot (1728-1797), and he in turn from Hermann Boerhaave who wrote *Institutiones Medicae* in 1728. Bullough (1974) quotes Boerhaave a saying that the

> . . . rash expenditure of semen brings on a lassitude, a feebleness, a
> weakening of motion, fits, wasting, dryness, fevers, aching of the
> cerebral membranes, obscuring of the senses and above all the eyes,
> a decay of the spinal chord, a fatuity, and other like evils.

This concern went beyond masturbation as we define it, however, and much concern was expressed for the terrifying consequences of nocturnal emissions or "wet dreams." Some physicians believed them to be normal if they occurred infrequently, but those who believed otherwise defined it as a disease, in medical terminology, spermatorrhea. One physician, Drysdale, had this to say:

> By spermatorrhea, or involuntary seminal discharges, is meant the loss of seminal fluid without the will of the patient, which when it occurs frequently, constitutes . . . a most dreadful disease. These discharges may be divided into the nocturnal and the diurnal. In the *nocturnal* ones, the patient has generally a dream on some venereal subject, an erection of the penis, and a discharge of semen, and wakes just as the discharge is taking place. . . .
>
> [The disease gets progressively worse, and] the emissions begin to increase in frequency, and the patient begins to feel his health declining. The emissions may now take place nightly, or even three or four times in the night in bad cases, and this soon brings on a state of great exhaustion. . . . As the disease progresses, discharges take place without a venereal dream or erection. . . . The patient wakes suddenly from a stupor, just as the discharge is pouring out, which he will try in vain to check; or perhaps, he does not wake till it is over, and then, as a lethargic consciousness, which of itself tells him what has taken place, slowly awakens, he puts down his hand and sickens with despair, as he perceives the fatal drain, and thinks on the gloomy morrow which will follow. . . .
>
> . . . [the nervous system is affected by] a feeling of weakness on rising in the morning, especially after a nocturnal emission, and even more after two or three in the same night; a sort of mistiness or haze in the thoughts, and dimness in the sight, while the eye loses its luster; enfeeblement of muscular power, with irritability of its fibre, often shown by palpitation of the heart. . . .
>
> As for the termination of the disease: if left to itself, it has a constant tendency to increase. The patient may, after years of suffering, sink into the lowest stage of weakness, and die . . . [death may be] by a kind of apoplexy, characteristic of this disease, and induced by the exhausted state of the brain. The disease has in many cases progressed to insanity, and idiocy; in one case . . . the patient had lost the knowledge of his friends, and the power of speech. (Brecher, 1969, pages 18-19)

By 1900 physicians, in order to avoid the severe consequences thought to result from the loss of semen, were advocating castration, cauterization of the genitals and prostate, the severing of nerves leading to the penis, and the use of various mechanical devices to obstruct access to the genitalia or to make sexual arousal extremely painful (Sadock et al., 1976).

This was particularly a male problem since women had been ordained by God to be indifferent to sex. This feminine indifference helped men to conserve their vital sexual energy. While the gravest danger was for males, women were not to escape scot-free, however. According to Tissot:

> Females who engaged in nonprocreative sex were affected in much the same way as males, but in addition would be subject to hysterical fits, incurable jaundice, violent cramps in the stomach, pains in the nose, ulceration of the cervix, and to the uterine tremors that deprived them of decency and reason, lowered them to the level of the most lascivious brutes, and caused them to love women more than men. (Bullough, 1974, page 101)

Acton

> . . . also maintained that sexual intercourse during pregnancy produced depravity, epilepsy, and sexual precocity in the child. Any prolonged or intense activity by any part of the mother's body, be it her brain or her vagina . . . would result in a disproportionate growth of that area in the developing fetus. (Sadock et al. 1976, page 59)

Richard von Krafft-Ebing, a famous professor of psychiatry at the University of Strassburg in Germany, was another highly influential person. His book, *Psychopathia Sexualis*, was published in 1886. As a youth he

> . . . developed an intense interest in the criminal cases involving deviant sexual behavior with which his maternal grandfather was concerned. This interest led him to study medicine and to qualify as a neurologist and psychiatrist. For the rest of his life he served as "alienist"—psychiatric consultant—to the courts of Germany and Austria; on many occasions he was also called as an expert witness on sexual crimes by the courts of other countries. (Brecher, 1969, page 55)

Brecher regards Krafft-Ebing's book as a "powerful and terrifying masterpiece," for he "portrayed sex in almost all of its manifestations as a collection of loathsome diseases." In his publication he used numerous lurid case histories to arouse horror and disgust. They featured lust-crazed rapists, sadistic and masochistic manifestations, and torture murders of innocent children and women. The following history will illustrate those used by Krafft-Ebing.

A certain Gruyo, aged forty-one, with a blameless past life, having been three times married, strangled six women in the course of ten years. They were almost all public prostitutes and quite old. After the strangling he tore out the intestines and kidneys *per vaginam*. Some of his victims he violated before killing; others, on account of the occurrence of impotence, he did not. He set about his horrible deeds with such care that he remained undetected for ten years. (Bracher, 1969, page 58)

The kind of authoritative statements coming from Acton and Krafft-Ebing would work directly against any of the humanistic objectives postulated in the beginning of this chapter. They do show the climate from which we have come, however, and the depth of the antihumanistic attitudes that prevailed a hundred years ago, or less. We can also see more clearly the source of certain attitudes that continue to plague us, even today.

We will turn now to two men who were contemporaries, Sigmund Freud (1856-1939) and Havelock Ellis (1859-1939) to examine their contributions. In contrast to the earlier "authoritative pronouncements" of Acton and Krafft-Ebing, their efforts over time moved the social milieu toward a humanistic outlook. Freud was an innovator in the sense that he both listened and talked to patients. This dialogue was therapeutic for the patients and helpful to Freud as he developed his theories for explaining human behavior. He was concerned with causation. Thus, he demonstrated the tremendous importance of the unconscious in human behavior, the significance both of the first few years of a child's life in molding later behavior and of parent-child interaction. Family relations have been greatly altered as a consequence of Freudian concepts.

Ellis's interest knew no racial or national boundaries; the whole world and all humankind were subjects of his inquiry to the extent that he could obtain information. His cross-cultural concern is particularly evident in the first chapter of the first volume of his *Studies in the Psychology of Sex*. He was concerned that each of his readers might vastly enlarge his perspective by knowing of the innumerable attitudes worldwide toward modesty regarding sexual expressions and practices.

Furthermore Ellis's concern was for normal sexuality. He was broad in his definition and various sexual activities which writers before him had called perversions he saw as enriching experiences. He noted that the "range of variations within fairly normal limits is immense." Ellis in many of his conclusions anticipated views that are accepted today as established. For example, he pointed out that masturbation is common to both sexes and used throughout life. For both males and females sexual acitivities and responses are experienced long before puberty. Both homosexuality and heterosexuality can be found in the life histories of many individuals; these expressions may be present in varying degrees.

[Ellis] urged, for example, that sexual manifestations during infancy and childhood be accepted casually, as a routine matter of course. He argued for the frank sexual education of both sexes. He favored greater freedom of sexual experimentation during adolescence and trial marriage as a prelude to actual marriage. He demanded equal rights—including equal sexual rights—for women, greater ease of divorce, and a repeal of the laws against contraception. And he stated with clarity the legal principle governing "consenting adults in private" that is only today beginning to reach the statute books: "If two persons of either or both sexes, having reached years of discretion, privately consent to practice some perverted mode of sexual relationship, the law cannot be called upon to interfere. It should be the function of the law in this matter to prevent violence, to protect the young, and to preserve public order and decency." (Brecher in Sadock, et al. page 78)

Thus we have in Ellis a person who made long strides toward a human-istic concept of sexuality. In our current sophisticated definition of research his contributions are mainly personal observations and reports of incidents and circumstances brought to his attention, yet they are releasing and freeing. Ellis himself supported movements that sought sexual reforms as he worked for a more relaxed and accepting attitude toward sexuality.

Following Ellis, other authors wrote treatises on sexuality utilizing a cross-cultural context. Some writers view these expressions as uncommon and unusual. For example, I have a book, *Curious Customs of Sex and Marriage: An Inquiry Relating to all Races and Nations from Antiquity to the Present Day* by George Ridley Scott (1953). It clearly lives up to its title. Others such as Bronislaw Malinowsky who wrote *The Sexual Life of Savages in North-Western Melanesia* (1929) and *Sex and Repression in Savage Society* (1927), and Ford and Beach who wrote *Patterns of Sexual Behavior* (1951) seek, as did Havelock Ellis, to make sexual expression, even when viewed as a cross-cultural experience, a human experience. *Patterns of Sexual Behavior* is especially effective in achieving this outcome.

Soon after the beginning of this century research in its more sophisticated sense began to appear. Questions of sampling and whether the sample is representative, techniques of analyzing data, the extent to which conclusions can be generalized, research design, and the possibilities of replication became issues that concerned researchers. The number of studies that raised such issues were not numerous, however. In 1948 when *Sexual Behavior in the Human Male* was published, Kinsey noted the then-existing American studies which were: "(1) scientific, (2) based on more or less complete case histories, (3) based on series of at least some size, (4) involving a systematic coverge of approximately the same items on each subject, and (5) statistical in treatment" (Kinsey et. al., 1948). The Kinsey research group found only nineteen studies of sex behavior (twenty-three titles) which displayed these qualities and were in any sense taxonomic. Publication dates ranged from 1915 to 1947. Kinsey found these studies lacking in certain respects. These were deficiencies that limited their value as humanistic research. A major complaint was that the research population was not representative, either geographically or otherwise. Ten of the nineteen studies were based wholly or primarily on college level individuals. The samples were small and lacking in the necessary homogeneity which would make statistical generalization possible. Nevertheless these research studies are the beginning of a more sophisticated approach to humanistic and humane understanding than were the authoritative statements appearing some hundred years ago.

The two studies by Kinsey and his associates (Kinsey et al., 1948, 1952) were definitely breakthroughs in that they enabled the field of sexual research to expand greatly. People were clearly willing to disclose and talk about their sexual experiences. As a consequence of these surveys it was now possible to study various aspects of sexuality which formerly had not been thought about, or were tabooed.

The sex research done by Masters and Johnson destroyed a number of taboos. They observed and filmed couples as they experienced intercourse with the intent of both treating sexual dysfunctions and enhancing the sexual pleasure of the participants. It is interesting, in view of our concern for highlighting the humanistic aspects of sexual research, to note four things that have evolved for Masters and Johnson out of their initial research. First is the direction in which the researchers have moved following the completion of their research. Not content simply with amassing information, even though it broke fresh sod, Masters and Johnson decided to apply their new-found knowledge in assisting couples. With the establishment of a counseling service they set up a situtation which had two purposes. They counseled couples directly and also trained others to be counselors. Second, they put sexuality into a more affirmative context. They hoped to enlarge the typical concepts of sexuality and so emphasized that they could not deal with a single individual alone; a relationship was always involved and they must deal with a relationship, not an isolated person. Furthermore, they spoke of sexual relating in terms of the total body and in pleasurable terms. For example, a couple reporting sexual dysfunctioning were asked to avoid intercourse for a time, and "pleasure" each other through touch, body contact, and loving closeness. Finally, they have been concerned with permanence in the relationship, feeling that short-term associations have less chance of bringing satisfaction to the participants than do long-term relationships. This provides a good illustration not only of humanistic sexual research, but of the researchers putting these humanistic principles into action.

At one time it was felt that research on human behavior should be conducted in a setting free from value considerations. Humanistically, this seems inappropriate; to speak of humanistic principles in itself implies a value orientation. But in terms of a continuing breakdown of restrictions and a movement toward a more humane and humanistic orientation, ways have been found of breaching this barrier. Both theories and studies have been made which are definitely concerned with values and a value framework.

Several authorities have concerned themselves with ways in which values are developed, though not indicating that they are specifically concerned with promoting a specific set of values. They approach the issue as theoreticians and discuss various stages in moral development as they relate to healthy maturation. Two persons immediately come to mind, Erik H. Erikson (1902-) and Jean Piaget (1896-).

Erikson has developed a theory of human development that portrays eight steps an individual takes as he moves toward maturity. They represent tasks that the individual must master if he is to have a satisfying experience in moving from one developmental stage to the next. The eight tasks are to develop (1) a basic trust; (2) autonomy; (3) initiative; (4) industry; (5) indentity; (6) intimacy; (7) generativity; (8) ego identity.

Piaget observed children's thinking about moral circumstances as they played at marbles and discussed the need for rules, their readiness and willingness to change rules and the extent to which they respect imposition of rules. This experience propelled him into a study of moral development. Here Piaget's subjects, children from ages two to fourteen or fifteen, compared motives and consequences as against acts, adult injunction against their own sense of fairness, their own personal desires against social needs. Clearly, aging made a difference in these matters. As Osborn (1959) writes, "Piaget's work has shown the growth of moral consciousness to be correlated with the growth of co-operative tendencies; the replacement of egocentricity by sociality."

Kohlberg is a recent investigator. He has been concerned with the stages in moral development from childhood through adolescence. He isolated six stages, which freely translated, are (1) obey rules to avoid punishment; (2) conform to obtain rewards, to have favors returned; (3) conform to avoid disapproval, to fend off possible dislike of others; (4) conform to avoid censure by legitimate authority and resulting guilt; (5) conform to maintain the respect of others, with community welfare as a central concern; and (6) conformity geared to one's conscience and universal principles as the bases for moral judgments. He postulates that as people mature more and more adults will move into stages five and six; though this postulation has yet to be adequately verified.

Kirkendall in 1961 published *Premarital Intercourse and Interpersonal Relationships,* a study based on findings coming from interviews with 200 college-level males with experience in intercourse outside marriage. The value framework used focused upon a desire to know those qualities in a sexual relationship that promoted or detracted from the ability to set up a relationship. Developing relationships in which there is affection and motivation is each-other centered, where protections of various kinds are offered a partner, and communication is open and honest—these are important in satisfying associations. Short-term relationships for the most part lacked these qualities.

Over the last sixty or seventy years much more information about ways in which moral growth occurs, and something of its nature, has been revealed. This knowledge is directly useful to those interested in advancing humanistic principles in various aspects of life's activities.

Humanistically the findings of Erikson, Piaget, and Kohlberg should be linked with the observations of Abraham Maslow as he speaks of love and sex in self-actualizing people.

> . . . it seems clear that healthy people fall in love the way one reacts to one's first appreciated perception of great music—one is awed and overwhelmed by it and loves it. . . . St. Bernard said it very aptly: "Love seeks no cause beyond itself and no limit; it is its own fruit, its own enjoyment. I love because I love; I love in order that I may love. . . ." (Maslow, 1955, page 255)

He further comments:

> In self-actualizing people the orgasm is simultaneously more important and less important than in average people. [Sex] is often a profound and almost mystical experience, and yet the absence of sexuality is more easily tolerated by these people . . . [the self-actualizing person] simultaneously [enjoys sex] . . . much more intensely than the average person, yet at the same time [considers it] . . . much less important in the total frame of reference. . . .
>
> An excellent parallel may be made between this and the attitude of these people toward food. Food is simultaneously enjoyed and yet regarded as relatively unimportant in the total scheme of life by self-actualizing people. When they do enjoy it, they can enjoy it whole-heartedly and without the slightest tainting with bad attitudes toward animality and the like. And yet ordinarily feeding oneself takes a relatively unimportant place in the total picture. These people do not *need* sensuality; they simply enjoy it when it occurs. (Maslow, 1955, pages 242–43)

The research and theory noted thus far have been concerned mainly with sexual expression as manifested in personal circumstances or in situations where the individual is somehow associated with others in nonpolitical ways. Humanistically, it is important to keep in mind that people function in a social context and that this context can help to stimulate growth and development, or it can be repressive. Some attempts have been made to study those social situations in which sexuality is exercised either to understand sexuality better, or perhaps to alter and improve the social situation. Three illustrations will be noted.

In 1957 a *Report of the Committee on Homosexual Offenses and Prostitution* (generally known as the Wolfenden report) was published in England. It may be questionable to call the *Report* a research publication in the more elaborate and sophisticated sense, but certainly it is a compilation of the testimony of witnesses and of statistical materials showing the status of homosexuality and prostitution in England at that time. Some attention is also given to the way in which homosexual offenses are treated in other European countries. The purpose of the *Report* was to make recommendations to the English Parliament for changes in the laws of England and Wales as they regulated homosexuality and prostitution. So far as homosexuality was concerned the Commission recommended

   (i) That homosexual behavior between consenting adults in private be no longer a criminal offense.
  (ii) That questions relating to "consent" and "in private" be decided by the same criteria as apply in the case of heterosexual acts between adults.

The recommendations for changes in laws about prostitution were few and in the direction of penalizing those who used prostitution for their own personal gain, i.e., pimps and procurers.

The United States Congress created two commissions—one to study homosexuality, and one for pornography and obscenity. The Task Force on Homosexuality was established under the auspices of the National Institute of Mental Health. This report recognized the importance of research but did no research of its own. It did recommend the establishment of a Center for the Study of Sex Behavior. The thought was that the Center would be concerned with research, training and education, prevention and treatment, and questions of social policy with respect to sexual behavior. The Center has not been created.

An act of Congress passed in 1967 created a Commission on Obscenity and Pornography. The Commission composed of eighteen members prepared a report which was published in 1970. This Commission relied on research conducted and collated by the Effects Panel of the Commission. The areas of concern to which this research "was addressed included sexual arousal, emotions, attitudes, overt sexual behavior, moral character, and criminal and other antisocial behavior related to sex." [The Report, page 23.] The Commission felt that where explicit sexual materials are sold freely seemingly "exposure to erotica had no impact upon moral character [of youth] over and above that of a generally deviant background." [page 27]

The Commission concluded (though there was some dissent on certain points)

. . . that, for America, the relationship between the availability of erotica and changes in sex crime rates neither proves nor disproves the possibility that availability of erotica leads to crime, but the massive overall increases in sex crimes that have been alleged do not seem to have occurred. . . .

In sum, empirical research designed to clarify the question has found no evidence to date that exposure to explicit sexual materials plays a significant role in the causation of delinquent or criminal behavior among youth or adults. The Commission cannot conclude that exposure to erotic materials is a factor in the causation of sex crime or sex delinquency. (page 27)

The Report of the Task Force on Homosexuality was never published officially. *The Report of the Commission on Obscenity and Pornography* is available through the Superintendent of Documents. The latter *Report* was rejected by President Nixon prior to its publication.

These *Reports,* while not fully accepted, do indicate two important developments. In the first place they represent an interest on the part of all American citizens, collectively speaking, in deciding how to deal with certain controversial aspects of sexual expression. In the second place, they recognize that sexual problems are not purely personal. They exist in a social context and it therefore behooves all responsible persons to be concerned with their resolution.

This is an abbreviated review of trends in the field of sex research and theory. But it shows that over the years humanistic principles have been embodied more and more in our efforts to deal with sexual problems. The concern to capture and express affirmatively the growing acceptance, worldwide, of the humanist point of view led to the publication of *A New Bill of Sexual Rights and Responsibilities.* This statement which sets forth humanistic principles as they relate to sexuality has been endorsed by signers, a few from foreign countries. The statement closes with this paragraph:

We believe that freeing our sexual selves is vital if we are to reach the heights of our full humanity. But at the same time, we believe that we need to activate and nourish a sense of our responsibilities to others.

References

Acton, William. *The Functions and Disorders of the Reproductive Organs in Childhood, Youth, Adult Age, and Advanced Life Considered in Their Physiological, Social, and Moral Relations.* 5th ed. London: J. & A. Churchill, 1871.

Baker, Robert, and Elliston, Frederick. *Philosophy and Sex*. Buffalo, NY: Prometheus, 1975.

Brecher, Edwin. *The Sex Researchers*. Boston: Little, Brown, 1969.

Bullough, Vern L. "Homosexuality and the Medical Model." *Journal of Homosexuality* 1 (Fall 1974): 99-110.

_____. *Sexual Variance in Society and History*. New York: Wiley, 1976.

Calderone, Mary S. *Sexuality and Human Values*. New York: Association Press, 1974. (Piaget's and Kohlberg's studies.)

Ellis, Havelock. *Studies in the Psychology of Sex*. Philadelphia: A. Davis, 1906.

Erikson, Erik H. *Childhood and Society*. New York: Norton, 1963.

Final Report of the Task Force on Homosexuality. *ONE Institute Quarterly* 8, 22.

Freud, Sigmund. *An Autobiographic Study*. Translated by James Strachey. New York: Norton, 1935. (Copyright renewed 1963 by James Strachey.)

Kinsey, Alfred C. et al. *Sexual Behavior in the Human Female*. Philadelphia: W. B. Saunders, 1953.

_____. *Sexual Behavior in the Human Male*. Philadelphia: W. B. Saunders, 1948.

Kirkendall, Lester A. *A New Bill of Sexual Rights and Responsibilities*. Buffalo, NY: Prometheus, 1976.

Kohlberg, Lawrence. "Stage and Sequence: The Developmental Approach to Socialization." In *Handbook of Socialization*, ed. D. Goslin. Chicago: Rand McNally, 1968.

Kurtz, Paul. *The Humanist Alternative: Some Definitions of Humanism*. Buffalo, NY: Prometheus, 1973.

Lamont, Corliss. *The Philosophy of Humanism*. New York: F. Ungar, 1965.

Lewinsohn, Richard. *A History of Sexual Customs*. New York, 1958.

Maslow, Abraham H. *Motivation and Personality*. New York: Harper, 1955, 1970.

Montagu, Ashley. *The Direction of Human Development*. New York: Hawthorn, 1970.

Nagel, Ernest. "The Enforcement of Morals." In *Moral Problems in Contemporary Society*, ed. Paul Kurtz. Englewood Cliffs, NJ: Prentice-Hall, 1969, pp. 137–60.

Osborn, Reuben. *Humanism and Moral Theory*. Buffalo, NY: Prometheus, 1970. First issued, 1959.

Report of the Commission on Obscenity and Pornography. Washington, D.C.: U.S. Government Printing Office, 1970.

Report of the Committee on Homosexual Offences and Prostitution. London: Her Majesty's Stationery Office, 1957.

Sadock, Benjamin; Kaplan, Harold; and Freedman, Alfred M. *The Sexual Experience*. Baltimore: Williams & Wilkins, 1976.

Taylor, G. Rattray. *Sex in History*. New York: Vanguard, 1954.

14

Sex and the Law

Thomas F. Coleman

Law in a sense is practical social science, just as medicine in a similar sense is practical biology. American law as far as sex is concerned took over many of its concepts from religion, labeling almost everything as a crime that religion had designated as sin. One of the results of the ongoing sex research is to challenge the assumptions behind many of the laws. Some of the changes in the laws are summarized by Thomas F. Coleman, a Los Angeles attorney specializing in sex law. Coleman is publisher of the *Sexual Law Reporter,* a national periodical that reviews court cases and legislation relating to sexual matters.

During the past decade, our legal system has been confronted with a revolution. The sexual mores and behavior of Americans have changed drastically, but the body of sex law, both legislative and judicial, is based on the politics and attitudes of another era. Judges, legislators, and administrators have been faced with the task of closing the gap between "what is" and "what should be." They have also reevaluated the fundamental principles upon which many laws regulating sexual behavior have been based. Some of the areas undergoing reanalysis in legal circles are rape, transsexualism, abortion, contraception, homosexuality, alternative love relationships, and prostitution.

Sexual law seems to be a narrow speciality. But a closer look shows that it is an area so broad that it will be impossible to discuss fully all the major developments over the past ten years. An overview of certain areas will be given, spotlighting major court cases or legislative development. However, consensual sexual behavior and homosexual civil rights have created the most controversy and initiated the most change and will be discussed in detail.

Rape, Prostitution, and Transsexualism

The traditional rape case usually involves two witnesses, the male defendant and the female victim. While there have been some homosexual cases, the overwhelming majority have been heterosexual in nature. In most cases the only prosecution witness to the crime is the female victim. The trial becomes a credibility battle between the female victim and the male defendant. The jury usually has two issues to decide: (1) whether sexual intercourse has occurred, and (2) whether the sex act was committed against the will of the victim. Since the trial was a credibility contest the defense attorney uses every lawful tactic to discredit the female victim. The two most often used devices are (1) to introduce evidence about the past sexual history of the victim to show that she is immoral or promiscuous, and (2) to have the judge instruct the jury with the "cautionary instruction." The law in most states required the judge to instruct the jury at the close of the case to "examine the testimony of the complaining witness with caution." However, the testimony of other witnesses was not to be viewed with caution. The law also allowed the defense attorney to ask the female victim about her past sexual life. Questions were asked concerning the number of sexual experiences she had, with whom she had them, and other such details. The law assumed that if she was of previous unchaste character that it was likely that she consented on this particular occasion.

Feminists developed an organized effort to change the law with respect to the cautionary instruction and cross-examination of the rape victim about her past sexual history. Legislation has been introduced in many states to shift the focus of rape cases from the victim to the defendant. Challenges have been made in court as well. After legislative debates for the past four to five years, over one third of the states have enacted laws prohibiting use of the cautionary instruction and cross-examination of the rape victim about her past sexual conduct.

Efforts to decriminalize prostitution have met with little or no success, although many civil libertarians have been working to achieve that result. Some state bar associations have adopted resolutions calling for decriminalization of prostitution. This has been done year after year by the California Bar Association. The American Bar Association, however, narrowly defeated a resolution on such decriminalization. The ABA did urge the states to repeal laws prohibiting noncommercial private sexual behavior among consenting adults. Every state in the country has laws regulating prostitution, soliciting for prostitution, or loitering for the purpose of prostitution. Nevada is the only state in which municipalities are given the option to allow prostitution. Numerous court challenges have been made attacking either the prostitution laws themselves or the methods of police enforcement. So far the existing laws and police procedures have survived most attacks.

With the refinement of surgical techniques, more persons are undergoing sex reassignment surgery than ever before. The courts and legislatures have not been prepared for the legal implications of male to female or female to male changes in sex. Transsexuals have demanded the right to change the gender indication on their birth certificates, to be free from employment discrimination, to be entitled to a name change, and have called for an end to police harassment. In the case of *M.T. v. J.T.*[1] the New Jersey Supreme Court was faced with the question of determining a person's gender identity for purposes of marriage. A postoperative male to female transsexual married the male defendant. Although he knew of the change of gender prior to the marriage, the defendant attempted to avoid support when the couple separated. He alleged that the marriage was void because the plaintiff was "really a man." In upholding the validity of the marriage, the Court held that "for marital purposes if the anatomical or genital features of a genuine transsexual are made to conform to the person's gender, psyche, or psychological sex, then identity by sex must be governed by the congruence of these standards."

In recent federal cases, however, transsexuals have not received judicial recognition of their civil rights. In two such cases, federal judges have held that discrimination against transsexuals in private employment is not a violation of the federal civil rights statute's prohibition against sex discrimination. The earliest reported appellate case dealing with transsexualism that could be found was decided by a New York court in 1966. That court upheld the City Board of Health refusal to change the sex designation on the transsexual's birth certificate. Since that decision, an additional fifteen appellate cases have discussed and often expanded the rights of transsexuals.[2]

Private Sexual Behavior

Most of the laws regulating sexual behavior in existence in the mid-1960s had been enacted at the turn of the century or in the early 1900s. The criminal codes of most states had not been revised, as a package, for fifty to one hundred years. While these codes were probably reflective of societal attitudes when they were adopted, there can be no doubt that attitudes, especially in the area of sexual behavior, have drastically changed over the years.

In the late 1950s the American Law Institute, with the assistance of judges, lawyers, and legal scholars, drafted a "Model Penal Code" as a guide to the various state legislatures which were about to embark upon a wholesale revision of their penal codes. One of the most controversial recommendations of the ALI was the decriminalization of private sexual acts between consenting adults.

In 1960 Illinois became the first state to adopt this ALI recommendation. The age of sexual consent was set at eighteen years. In addition, Illinois decriminalized noncommercial sexual solicitations between adults.

Although many states were studying possible penal code revision in the early and mid-1960s, there were no further major legislative advances with respect to consensual sex until Connecticut revised its penal code in 1969. Since the decriminalization in Illinois and Connecticut, an additional twenty-one legislatures have voted to decriminalize private sexual acts between consenting adults: Alaska, Arkansas, California, Colorado, Delaware, Hawaii, Idaho, Indiana, Iowa, Maine, Nebraska, New Hampshire, New Jersey, New Mexico, North Dakota, Ohio, Oregon, South Dakota, Washington, West Virginia, and Wyoming. In Idaho the decriminalization never took effect because the legislature repealed this sexual provision before the effective date of the new code. In Arkansas, this sexual reform was operative for one year, and then its legislature reenacted criminal provisions for private homosexual behavior, retaining decriminalization for heterosexuals. The Arkansas legislature took this action in the same session it adopted a resolution commending Anita Bryant for her campaign against homosexuals in Dade County, Florida. As of this writing the reforms in Iowa, Indiana, Nebraska, Alaska, and New Jersey have not gone into effect although passed by their legislatures. So we presently have sixteen states that have completely decriminalized private sexual behavior among consenting adults, and five states in which such reform will be effective soon.

At first glance one might interpret these legislative changes as being reflective of drastic changes in popular attitudes. However, this is not necessarily so. The methods by which these changes occurred must be examined before passing judgment as to how reflective they are of popular attitudes.

In only one of these states was there a special bill specifically designed to decriminalize private sex for adults. In two states decriminalization was accomplished in a legislative reform of rape laws. In the remaining states the decriminalization was hidden in the general penal code reform package. Usually the chances for passage of sexual law reform are greatly enhanced when the method for such reform is through a bill containing hundreds of other statutory changes. The chances of public, church, or conservative legislators opposing the bill are thereby diminished greatly.

California was the only state in the country that decriminalized by way of a special bill. Although proponents of the reform worked for several years, in 1975 there was a tie vote in the state Senate on the bill. When conservative senators threatened to leave the Senate floor to break the quorum, they were locked in the room for several hours until the Lieutenant Governor was flown back to Sacramento from Denver to cast the deciding vote in favor of decriminalization.

In the mid-1960s the New York legislature passed a general penal code revision. The proposed decriminalization of private sex was strongly opposed by the Catholic Church. As a result, the legislature compromised and decriminalized for married couples only. Acts of oral copulation or sodomy between consenting single persons are criminal to this day in New York. Special bills to further reform the law have met with defeat each year in Albany.

The Texas legislature reformed its sex laws when it revised its entire penal code in the early 1970s. It went further than New York and decriminalized for all consenting heterosexuals, but retained homosexual conduct as an infraction.

In order to get a proper perspective on attitudes within the legal system toward sex, we should also examine developments within the courts, administrative agencies, and the executive branch of government.

Ever since its landmark decision of *Griswold* v. *Connecticut*[3] in 1965, the United States Supreme Court has been developing the constitutional right of sexual privacy. In *Griswold* the Court voided a law which infringed on the rights of married couples to use contraceptives. The Court acknowledged that a right of marital privacy existed and told the government to stay out of the marital bedroom. A few years later the Court expanded this "marital right of privacy" in the case of *Eisenstadt* v. *Baird*.[4] In that case the Court said that single persons also have a right of privacy and that the state could not forbid their use of contraceptives. In the early 1970s the Court again expanded the right of privacy in the series of abortion cases beginning with *Roe* v. *Wade*.[5] The right of privacy was held to be so fundamental that the state could not prohibit abortions during the first trimester.

Sexual civil libertarians were hoping that someday this sexual right of privacy might actually be extended by the Court to include the right to engage in private sexual behavior by consenting adults without inteference by state regulations. Relying on the *Griswold, Eisenstadt,* and *Roe* cases, several appellate courts and federal courts indicated that statutes prohibiting such private behavior were unconstitutional. Proponents of decriminalization seemed to be gaining momentum in the courts—and then came *Doe* v. *Commonwealth's Attorney*.[6] Two anonymous homosexuals filed suit in federal district court in Virginia attacking that state's sodomy law. The Virginia law made it criminal for all persons to engage in oral or anal sex, whether married, single, heterosexual, or homosexual. The federal court, in a two-to-one decision upheld the state law. The anonymous homosexuals appealed to the U.S. Supreme Court. Without even granting hearing or permitting oral arguments, the Supreme Court summarily affirmed the lower federal court. Justices Brennan, Marshall, and Stevens were of the opinion that the Supreme Court should have granted a hearing. This decision made headlines in newspapers across the country and was considered a serious setback to sexual civil libertarians.

In the areas of contraception and abortion the U.S. Supreme Court has extended the right of privacy to juveniles. In *Planned Parenthood of Central Missouri* v. *Danforth*,[7] the Court declared as unconstitutional laws that required parental consent prior to an abortion for a minor. On June 9, 1977, in the case of *Carey* v. *Population Services International*,[8] the Court declared as unconstitutional, laws that made it a crime to distribute contraceptives to minors under sixteen. Arguments were made to the Court that this prohibition was necessary in order to discourage premarital sex among teenagers. The Court held that it would not allow this type of indirect approach to curb teenage promiscuity. Noting that it had not yet definitively decided whether and to what extent states may regulate private sexual behavior among adults, it declined to decide which constitutional rights minors may have to engage in such sexual behavior.

Although legislative and judicial development of sexual privacy has been somewhat slow, proponents gained considerable leverage when the American Bar Association adopted a resolution in 1973 which urged all state legislatures to decriminalize such conduct.

Until the courts and legislatures spell out the right of sexual privacy with respect to contraception, abortion, and sexual conduct, the debate and controversy will continue. The legal implications of the *Griswold* case, decided some fourteen years ago, are not likely to culminate into a full-blown right of sexual privacy for at least another decade.

Homosexual Civil Rights

During the past ten years we have seen the development of comprehensive legislation prohibiting discrimination in housing, employment, public accommodations, credit, and insurance, on the basis of race, creed, color, and national origin. More recently we have seen such legislation with repsect to age, sex, marital status, and physical handicap. Such antidiscrimination legislation has been passed by Congress, almost every state, and many municipalities. It seems that the majority now feels that it is immoral and illegal to discriminate against all but the homosexual minority.

Discrimination against the homosexual minority has been an acceptable, if not mandatory, tradition in our country. Many of the reasons for this discrimination are popular beliefs that homosexuals are sick, sinful, criminals, and child molesters. After homosexuality was declassified as an illness by the American Psychiatric Association and the American Psychological Association in recent years, the sickness theory has been rapidly crumbling. Now that twenty-one states have decriminalized private sexual acts, it is difficult to stereotype homosexuals as criminals. Recent studies in major cities such as Los Angeles and San Francisco show that the overwhelming number of child molestation cases are heterosexual in nature.

Currently there are no state or federal laws prohibiting discrimination against homosexuals in housing, employment, or other business transactions. Only about forty municipalities have legislation protecting gays in any of these areas.

The law is quite complicated with respect to employment discrimination against gay people. First, we must distinguish between public and private employment. Absent protective legislation, voluntary nondiscrimination, or union contracts, private employers are free to discriminate against homosexuals.

Public employment is governed by a different set of rules. Any public employer is bound to obey the constitutional mandates of *due process* and *equal protection* of the laws. This means that a government employer may not discriminate against any employee or prospective employee for *arbitrary* reasons.

Is discrimination against homosexuals in public employment a violation of the guarantees of due process or of equal protection? Might an inquiry into an employee's sexual orientation violate his or her right of privacy? Is discrimination against a gay rights activist by a public employer a violation of that employee's freedoms of speech, press, and association? Ultimately, the extent of constitutional protection afforded gay people will be decided by the courts.

Gay people have been denied many jobs because of the refusal of the federal government to grant security clearances to homosexuals. Today, after several years of litigation and lobbying, many clearances have been granted.

Until recently the federal Civil Service Commission considered homosexuality a disqualifying factor in federal employment. But again, after years of litigation and several important victories in federal court, the Civil Service Commission has changed its position. Homosexuality will no longer be an automatic bar to federal employment.

Gay teachers have had the most difficult time achieving employment protection. In California in the late 1960s a teacher was fired because of noncriminal private sexual acts with another consenting teacher. The sexual activity occurred in the privacy of a bedroom. The California Board of Education revoked his teaching credential on the ground of immorality and moral turpitude. In *Morrison* v. *Board of Education*,[9] a sharply-divided California Supreme Court held that this action by the Board was illegal because it had failed to show that the teacher was unfit.

In the early 1970s Joe Acanfora was involved in a gay student organization in Pennsylvania. After moving to Maryland, he applied for a teaching position. He failed to mention his connection with the gay organization when he filled out the job application. After working successfully as a teacher in the Maryland schools, he was fired because the school board discovered Acanfora was gay. He sought relief in the federal courts, but with no avail.[10]

Peggy Burton taught school in Oregon. Although she was a "model teacher," she was fired when the school district was informed by someone that she was a lesbian. Ms. Burton filed suit in federal court. The United States Court of Appeals for the Ninth Circuit held that her termination was illegal and ordered that she be paid back wages. However, they would not order her reinstated.[11]

John Gish taught school in New Jersey. Gish was a gay activist and was involved in demonstrations and gay political organizations. Gish was taken out of the classroom when the school discovered his gay rights involvement. The school board demanded that he submit to a psychiatric examination. The only grounds for this request was the fact that Gish was gay and involved in gay rights. John refused to submit to an exam and sought protection in the state courts. The New Jersey appellate court held that he must submit to the examination.[12]

The latest setback for gay teachers was delivered by the state of Washington Supreme Court in *Gaylord* v. *Tacoma School District*.[13] Gaylord was a teacher of longstanding in the Tacoma area. He was not openly gay and certainly not involved in gay rights. When a former student told an administrator that Gaylord might be a homosexual, the administrator confronted Gaylord with this accusation. Gaylord admitted he was a homosexual. Subsequently Gaylord was fired and appealed the decision. Although he never admitted to having engaged in illegal sexual activity, and although private sex is no longer criminal in Washington, the Washington Supreme Court upheld his dismissal. Referring to the Catholic dictionary, the Court held that although not illegal, homosexuality is immoral and therefore grounds for dismissal.

The battle for civil rights for homosexuals also continues in the areas of immigration, naturalization, military service, child custody, and marriage.

Several court cases in Washington, Minnesota, and Kentucky have held that two persons of the same sex have no right to enter into a civil marriage contract, absent specific legislation providing for such contracts. The law in many states has been vague on this point, but any ambiguity has usually been removed by opinions of attorneys general or by specific legislation prohibiting marriage between persons of the same sex.

Administrative and court battles are currently being waged against the Immigration and Naturalization Service ban on gay immigrants. After a recent federal court decision on the subject, the INS has removed homosexuality as a disqualifying factor for naturalization.

National attention was drawn to the military's discrimination against homosexuals in the case of Air Force Sergeant Leonard Matlovich. Matlovich was involuntarily discharged by the military because of his homosexuality. The federal district court judge who heard the case sustained the discharge, but begged the military to reconsider its position on homosexuality. In a more recent case, a federal judge in California has declared that the military must prove, in each case, that the person's homosexuality makes him or her unfit for service.[14] The judge declared as unconstitutional the automatic ban of all homosexuals from military service.

Many gay people have had their children taken away from them in child custody proceedings. Some judges feel that homosexuality automatically makes a parent unfit. The case law in this area is slowly developing; there are only a few reported appellate decisions. The American Psychological Association has taken the position that homosexuality should not be the sole or even primary consideration in child custody proceedings. Whether this recommendation will be followed by the courts is yet to be seen.

The body of American law, whether administrative legislative, or judicial, with respect to gay civil rights, is in a very confused state. Whereas twenty years ago homosexuals had no civil rights, today they have some. The turbulence within the legal system during the last decade is bound to continue for at least another. Just as the issue of black civil rights gained national attention, gay civil rights seems to be one of the major issues of the coming decade.

15

A Personal View of the Sex Revolution

Helen Colton

What has the ongoing research into human
sexuality meant to me as a person? This is the
question asked of several different individuals
and their responses are included in the last
part of this book. Leading off is Helen Colton,
the founder and director of Family Forum, a
counseling agency. She is a Humanist
Counselor, the West Coast editor of *Forum*
magazine, and the author of several books.

We are a culture conditioned to accentuate the negative. How much more
easily we reel off a litany of things we *don't* like about a person, about an
experience, about social change, than the things we *do* like. Frequently I hear
negative evaluations of the Sexual Revolution. We talk about its excesses, its
vulgarities, its dehumanization. And so I, the perennial optimist and idealist—
(we need more of this ilk)—want to report on some positive things I see
happening as a result of the Sexual Revolution and their meaning to my own
sexuality.

First I'd like to tell you some reasons why I am in the sex education field at
all, what propels me to this platform and other platforms all over the country
talking about sex.

The day I first menstruated—some forty-seven years ago at the age of
twelve and one half—was deeply traumatic for me. When I showed my
mother my bloody panties, she slapped my face! She then explained she was
doing it for my own good. It was an old tradition, a superstition from our
Jewish heritage that if you slapped a girl the first time she menstruated, she'd
have rosy cheeks all her life. Years later a Hebrew scholar explained to me
that the face-slapping custom began, upon a girl's first menses, to warn her
that now that she was capable of bearing a child, she had better be a good girl
and not engage in that nasty and verboten behavior—sex. As I like to tell my

audiences, I have joked with my mother, whose name is Rose: "Mom, I have rosy cheeks all right, not by courtesy of Rose but by courtesy of Revlon."

Another reason I am impelled to talk about human sexuality, especially as it relates to family life, is the traumatic experience our family underwent, when I was about fourteen or fifteen, when my mother found out my father was having an affair with another woman. A family council was held, in which collateral relatives were called in to hear about my mother's pain and my father's heinous straying from rectitude. While I was scared by the whole experience and empathetic to my mother's intense sorrow and rage, the humanistic nurturing part of me also felt pity for my father—which I dared not express. This experience, too, became part of my stored-up confusion and psychic pain around the subject of sex.

Still another reason for my interest in sex as a proper subject for scholarly pursuit was my own incredible ignorance. I was angry because I was permitted to go through the early part of my life—a lover of knowledge, a constant reader, a devotee of libraries, valedictorian of my high school class—without ever being taught, or without my ever coming across in my wide reading, the proper names for the parts of my own body. It was with great shock in my early twenties that I heard someone at a family party use the words "penis" and "vagina." Some instinct told me those were the proper words for male and female sex organs and not the scatological ones I had known until then. It is still unbelievable to me that I did not even know that sexual relations customarily began on the wedding night!

All of these amorphous feelings suddenly became crystallized for me on Sunday morning, January 26, 1964 when I was attending a weekend program on *Man and Civilization: The Family's Search for Survival* at the University of California Medical Center in San Francisco. There, I heard Dr. Lester A. Kirkendall give a talk on sex education and family stability. It was a talk which opened up whole new horizons for me and which has led, in the years since then, to my writing, lecturing, teaching, and counseling about sex. I have an intense desire to keep other young people like the young person I once was—boys as well as girls—and families from experiencing the needless pain inflicted on us by a prurient, inhibited, and hypocritical society that has taken the ecstatic pleasure of sexual experience and tarnished it for so many of us. "My goal," I once wrote, "is to save others the heartaches and trauma I experienced through lack of up-to-date information and attitudes."

And now a positive report on the Sexual Revolution. First, the state of sex education. Many of you remember the attack on sex education by Robert Welch of the John Birch Society who, in January 1969, wrote that our nation's most urgent requirement was for "organized nationwide, intensive, and angry determined opposition" to sex education in public schools. Sex education, he believed, was a Communist-inspired plot to destroy American youth. By so doing, the Communists would have a weakened, busily fornicating populace which cared more about pleasure than patriotism.

Taking up the cudgels of morality, the Reverend Billy James Hargis of the Christian Crusade declared that he, too, believed that sex education was "part of a gigantic conspiracy to bring down America from within." The Communist Manifesto apparently included a hitherto secret section known only to Robert Welch and Reverend Hargis—"Overthrow by Orgasm." The latter told a rally of conservative Americans in Boston: "I don't want any kid under twelve to hear about lesbians, homosexuals, and sexual intercourse. They should be concerned with tops, yo-yos and hide-and-seek." Neither of these two sages bothered to learn that the Soviet society, even more prurient than ours, has practically no sex education at any level. (Hargis is less vocal since four of his male students and one female student accused him of having sexual relations with them. It seems he performed a wedding service for a young couple who, exchanging confidences in their nuptial bed that night, revealed they had both had sex with Hargis.)

In the years since then, despite these widely publicized attacks, sex education has proliferated in the American educational system. Every state now has a variety of sex education courses at various levels and more communities introduce programs all the time. There are many fine courses, textbooks, sex education films, open discussions between parents and children, between teachers and students. Colleges offer M.A.'s and doctoral theses are being written and published, all in the field of human sexuality. What we have is of varying quality. Much of it is good. We need more of it and will be achieving more. But the important point is that despite attacks against it, sex education continues to grow. It has achieved a permanent place in our educational system.

Another positive result of the Sexual Revolution is the status of sex counseling as part of marital counseling. Fifteen years ago, my first husband and I went for marital counseling. We saw a counselor weekly for about three months. If you can believe it, during that period *not one word* was ever said about sex being among the possible causes of marital disharmony. Counselors and clients, as recently as fifteen years ago, were so uninformed as to what might be said about sex, so unaware of the physiology of sex and the dynamics of the act, that it is unlikely we would even have known *what* to say, even if we had been comfortable talking about it. Who knew about clitoral stimulation? How many women had psychological and societal permissions to make overtures to their husbands? Who knew how to tell a husband about your sexual frustration without fearing you were impairing his masculinity?

Contrast this with today. We have many fine sex counselors with marvelous training. I am constantly impressed by the quality of the training I see at professional conferences, the constant reach for higher standards, for new insights. Of course there are some negatives. Some therapists are incompetent charlatans, out for the fast buck. But as a result of the Sexual Revolution, huge numbers of human beings are learning, for the first time, to express their sexuality to the fullest with joy, rapture, ecstasy, undiminished by guilt and old mental tapes. A study a few years ago found that many couples report better sex lives than ever before. Many longer-lived citizens are enjoying sex, no longer afraid of being labeled "dirty old men" and women.

Among other positive results of the Sexual Revolution is that traditional taboos, among them the Masturbation Taboo, the Touch Taboo, the Word Taboo, are in various stages of being toppled.

Masturbation is as natural a function as eating, sleeping, and elimination. It is the major way we human beings express our sexuality during our early years. Anthropologists who have studied sexual behavior in many societies report that from infancy onward, as soon as they have muscular ability to do so, "most boys and girls progress from fingering of their genitals in the early years to systematic masturbation by the age of six to eight." Sex researcher Alfred Kinsey reported orgasm-like responses in babies of both sexes at four to five months of age.

How sad I find it, that throughout history, billions upon billions of human beings have engaged in self-stimulation with much guilt and terror as a result of warnings of dire consequences they'd have to pay because they activated the pleasure center in their brains through stimulation of their genitals. "Don't have pleasure," civilization has said so far, "It'll cost you."

And yet the origin of this masturbation taboo is incredibly simple. It began because early rulers and religions, seeking to increase their numbers and thus their power, declared, often under penalty of death or ostracism, that any sexual expression that did not lead to procreation was perforce illegal, perverted, and immoral. Quite simply, the act of masturbation did not make babies and the human race was constantly exhorted to "be fruitful and multiply." (There is a common misimpression that the biblical reference to Onan "spilling his seed upon the ground" was about masturbation. Actually it was about *coitus interruptus* or withdrawal. Onan preferred to spill his seed rather than impregnate his brother's widow.)

Civilization's philosophy about masturbation is now happily changing, largely as a result of our need for population control. Acts of sexual pleasure that do not lead to making babies are now laudable. I sum up this changing philosophy this way: Up until recently, masturbation was something you did under threat of extreme penalty. A while back, the philosophy began to say it was okay to masturbate as a reluctant recourse only if you didn't have a partner with whom to engage in intercourse. Now the growing philosophy is saying that masturbation is something you do *not instead of* but *in addition to* having sex with a partner. It is life-enhancing, one additonal form of sexual gratification.

I have no recollection of ever masturbating while I was growing up. I scarcely have any recollection of touching myself genitally although I am sure I must have done so. My first masturbatory experience did not occur until I was in my middle forties and newly divorced. I had not yet met a man with whom I wanted to have a physical relationship and so, for the first time, I masturbated, thinking all the while about a scene in a novel I had recently read in which masturbation was presented as a shocking act on the part of the sexually frustrated heroine. That experience was one of the most profound and freeing of my life. I felt such power about being in charge of my own life, of owning my own body.

I consider it a wonderous part of the Sexual Revolution that we cannot only talk about masturbation and even admit to doing it but that we can advocate it, teach people how to do it, sell vibrators to make it better, encourage nubile young people to engage in it as an alternative to inter-course, and even publish books, such as Lonnie Barbach's *For Yourself*, which describes how women learn to masturbate in what are called pre-orgasmic groups, and have it become a Book-of-the-Month alternate selec-tion! A long way indeed from what we were secretly saying and doing about masturbation a dozen years ago.

Even television, that cultural lagger, now permits the word. And that has changed in less than five years. At that time I appeared on the Dinah Shore Show, answering questions of a panel of women. The show was taped and as fate would have it, was scheduled to be shown Wednesday morning, January 24, 1973 when Henry Kissinger was negotiating the Vietnam peace settle-ment. The program was on the TV equipment but the network decided instead to show the negotiations live from Paris. However, the translation was so garbled that the network returned to the scheduled programming.

At that instant there suddenly appeared on screens across America the face of Dinah Shore saying in girlish innocence, in response to advice I had just given a lonely widow about how to handle her sex need: "Oh, so then masturbation is really okay." Coffee cups dropped throughout the land as shocked housewives called their local stations to protest.

Recently I appeared for forty minutes on a Los Angeles station answering call-in questions about female orgasm. The words "masturbation," "orgasm," "climax," "penis," and "vagina" were used frequently. And while there was some mild protest from a few little old dinosaurs in tennis shoes, the majority approved.

The ending of the Touch Taboo among us Americans, albeit still in its early stages, is another example of what the Sexual Revolution will come to mean to us. As a counselor I have come to know the importance of touch to the human organism. We are all born with intense skin hunger and have a deep need essential to our mental and physical well-being to be stroked and touched. Even when we are not feeling any sex urge, we still want to be held close and cuddled. I call this *sensual* need as differentiated from *sexual* need—the need for orgasm. Studies show that the touching sets up electrical impulses which travel along our neural pathways and stimulate the brain.

One of the famous early studies was done by Dr. Rene Spitz in the 1920s. He found that infants at a New York hospital, who were well fed and kept in sterile conditions, suffered a higher death rate than infants kept in less sanitary conditions at a Mexican orphanage. The difference lay in the fact that the New York infants were left alone a great deal; the Mexican infants were fondled, caressed, and played with by women from the village.

I am very empathetic to people who live alone and do not have someone around on a steady basis with whom to meet their touch needs. When I counsel such people I take a moment when they arrive at my office to hold them close and give them some of my body warmth. I can often feel the tension ooze out of their bodies at this closeness. I have long gotten over any feeling that this may be misinterpreted as being sexy. There is nothing sexy about it. My holding them close is a loving, caring, nurturing, maternal act, comforting their bodies as I would comfort their psyches.

I care, too, about families being comfortable with physical touch of each other without being embarrassed or up-tight that they might experience erotic feelings. I think it is normal for parents and children to experience such feelings about each other. Most of us choose never to *act out* those feelings; we do not, in fact, have sex with our children. But it is okay to acknowledge without guilt the pleasure we may get from holding them close.

A more recent study, "Body Pleasure and the Origins of Violence," is by Dr. James Prescott of the National Institute of Health. It appeared in the April 1975 issue of *The Futurist* magazine. I consider this one of the most important articles of the last decade. Prescott documents that the societies that are most inhibited about touching are the societies that are most capable of acts of war, violence, brutality, cruelty. In brief, where human beings are tender and physically affectionate, they are less willing to be cruel to fellow and sister human beings.

The final taboo I want to talk about is the Word Taboo. As a writer, I am in love with words, their sounds, syllables, vowels, consonants. How marvelous that we human beings can create sounds in our voice boxes and give them so many meanings! Words are fun to be around, to mouth, to weave and reweave into patterns so as to achieve an exact, precise meaning.

Every culture and period has had its taboo and verboten words, deriving most often from those areas of human experience about which societies have been prurient and secretive—the body processes, our digestive, eliminative, and procreative functioning. In England, not long ago, the word "bloody" was so taboo that a book of etiquette warned hosts not to serve guests meat that was too "ensanguined." In fourteenth century Italy the contemptuous expression "I suck my thumb at you" was about on a par with the expressions "Fuck you" or "Up yours" today. In Chaucerian poetry, the word for "fuck" was "swyve."

I think it is fun and societally healthy that today we can read heretofore forbidden language right out loud in print, not just in the underground or college press but in mass circulation newspapers and magazines, to wit: The *Los Angeles Times,* quoting John Kenneth Galbraith on a politician "who had all the mobility of a man who was up to his ass in pre-stressed concrete." The *National Observer,* writing about Governor Jerry Brown: "When he first was governor, Brown said, 'I don't even want to think about the presidency . . . just being governor is a pain in the ass'." *Newsweek* magazine, saying about Senator Barry Goldwater: "To Goldwater this was, in one of his favorite expressions, 'a bucket of shit'." The *Los Angeles Times,* quoting Lyndon B. Johnson on J. Edgar Hoover: "I would rather have him inside the tent pissing out than outside the tent pissing in."

It is ironic indeed that perhaps the greatest influence in freeing up language may be the pious and proper Richard M. Nixon. The biggest leap forward in printing heretofore repressed language has come out since the publishing of the raunchy language on the Watergate Tapes.

Be that as it may, some of our taboo language is slowly in the process of becoming obsolete, as the word "swyve" has become obsolete. As it is increasingly spoken in films and plays and printed in mass publications, our national nervous system is being desensitized to the shock effect of words. As has happened before and will happen again, new words will come along. One can see an entry in some dictionary of the future:

Fuck—an archaic slang word originally derived from the German verb, *ficken,* to plant seeds in the ground to grow crops. This came to be the word *fuck,* meaning to plant seeds in a human to grow a baby. Unacceptable in public speech and print until popularized by an American president in the latter third of the twentieth century. The word has now fallen into disuse through overuse.

Before long we may be a culture in search of new verboten words. Candidates that this optimistic reporter recommends for the future include "war," "gun," "bomb," "kill."

And so what does all of this say? Certainly there are excesses in the Sexual Revolution. Certainly there are negatives. But overall it is a positive experience. We are en route from being a pleasure- and sex-negative society to becoming a pleasure- and sex-positive society. We Humanists are important and necessary to that evolution. We are enduring. We will prevail.

At this point in evolution, no species kills its own kind in such great numbers as does the human species. We are capable of such behavior because in the words of my beloved friend and teacher, the late Dr. Charles L. Conrad, "We are not down out of the trees long enough yet to have become human." We are human *becomers,* engaged in the long slow evolutionary process of *becoming* civilized.

Freeing our sexual selves is one of the obligatory steps humankind must take in order to move closer to a civilized state. The Sexual Revolution can help us move closer to that civilized state. The Sexual Revolution and its excesses may be likened to a child that is a burden and a nuisance because it soils itself but then grows up to be a beautiful human being. The Sexual

Revolution can ultimately give each of us individually more joyful sex lives and all of us collectively more humane beings with whom to share the planet.

This poem, adapted from a 2000-year-old poem by Lao Tze, sums it up for me:

If there is right in the soul, there will be beauty in the person
If there is beauty in the person, there will be harmony in the home
If there is harmony in the home, there will be order in the nation
If there is order in the nation, there will be peace in the world.

16

We Were There at the Beginning

W. Dorr Legg

W. Dorr Legg was one of the founders of
ONE, Inc., the oldest continuing
organization in the United States devoted to
educating the public about homosexuality.
Though the term "Gay Liberation" is now in
common usage, and many people have
come out of the closet and proclaimed
themselves as homosexual, this has not
always been so. Mr. Legg states, in a highly
personal way, how the movement was
established.

In 1950 a movement was founded in Los Angeles which later came to be
known by various names: Homophile, Homosexual Rights, Gay Liberation
and some others. Records exist of earlier attempts to establish such a
movement but up to that time none of them had survived for very long. My
own association with this mid-century development known as ONE, Inc.
dates from 1952, and as a full-time occupation since 1953.

The quality of research into male and female homosexuality at that time
was a mixture of facts and fantasy, the latter having pretty much the upper
hand. *Sexual Behavior in the Human Male,* by Kinsey and his associates,
had already been stirring up scientific and religious circles and commanding
much space in the media with an impact equal perhaps only to the uproar
over Darwin in the mid-nineteenth century.

In my opinion, it was Kinsey's data on male homosexuality which had
especially agitated scientific and popular views on the subject. Such controversy and discussion undoubtedly prepared the way for the newly
founded Homophile Movement to turn a critical eye on whatever had been
said or written on the subject.

Fortunately, there were a number of people with a wide range of
background and training who had been drawn into ONE, Inc. They met
together, night after night, month after month, to argue and discuss the
whole field of what at the time had been considered to be authoritative

information about homosexuality. These deliberations reminded some of the participants of the larger-scale fermentations among the American colonists which led eventually to the founding of this country. Some said that their feelings of outrage and rebellion had greater justification than those of the Founding Fathers who fought against political oppression whereas this new movement was a struggle for personal identity and selfhood which touched the very deepest feelings in millions of homosexual men and women in the United States.

Those who had enlisted in this new movement soon discovered that "the enemy" lurked mainly in four principal directions: Religion, Science, Law, and Society; that its favorite weapons were "The Conspiracy of Silence" and "The Heterosexual Assumption." Having thus identified the trouble spots the Movement's brash investigators lost no time in appointing themselves to be a Grand Jury of sorts to bring in indictments wherever justified and demand corrections and reformation of the culprits. They began to investigate anthropology, biology, history, law, literature, philosophy, religion, sociology, and psychology regarding homosexuality.

In the early 1950s harassment of homosexuals by the police with subsequent arrests were occurrences of such almost daily crisis that the whole question of human rights and law almost inevitably took precedence over anything else. We found ourselves asking why laws which could be used so savagely against homosexuals existed. How did they happen to be enacted? Were there constitutional or other premises which validated them? On these and other questions the textbooks were virtually silent and even the friendliest attorneys seemed to find such questions either obscure or without much point. We were forced, therefore, to start doing our own legal research.

It was not long before we discovered that a great deal of legal terminology concerning sexual behavior and many of the statutes which were having such ruinously damaging effects upon the lives of homosexuals who fell afoul of them contained the exact, or only slightly altered, wording of sixth century law written under the direction of the Christian Roman Emperor Justinian. The American legal system professed to be founded upon the separation of Church and State, yet where homosexuality was concerned the Church was still sovereign. I vividly recall attending a public forum on homosexuality held in San Francisco in the fifties and listening to a bright young ACLU attorney discuss questions of law and homosexuality. When he was asked about the relationship of the First Amendment and the civil rights of homosexuals his face went blank. Later, a letter received at ONE from the then national director of the ACLU stated that there was no connection between homosexuality and civil liberties!

Is it any wonder that our "Grand Jury" brought in a damaging list of indictments against the legal profession for its neglect of what seemed the most simple levels of research? Legal scholars could hardly be accused of a

"Conspiracy of Silence" when they apparently were not even aware that there was anything to be silent about. In an unflattering reading of the phrase it was concluded that it was all too true that "justice is blind."

The field of anthropology presented an encouraging contrast to the status of legal philosophy at the time. Anthropologists had long been faithfully reporting a picturesque catalog of homosexual behavior among societies past and present around the world. Their bibliographies were one of the most useful starting points available to us during the early fifties. The book *Patterns of Sexual Behavior,* Ford and Beach (1951) at once became a foundation text to set beside the Kinsey book as a model for pointing the ways in which proper research into homosexuality should be conducted. While anthropology most certainly was not silent about the topic neither was it drawing many conclusions from its findings. Its preoccupation with kinship and clans, endogamy and exogamy, positioned the field far too securely within the framework of "The Heterosexual Assumption" for it to have indulged in much reasoning along deviant lines.

No one could have accused religion of being party to any "Conspiracy of Silence" at the time. Indeed, religion seemed to find homosexuality one of the topics it most wished to discuss. Sermons denouncing it were a dime a dozen, whether Catholic or Protestant. Articles on the topic in denominational journals were pretty sure to guarantee a sell-out of all copies, for homosexuality was sin as all agreed and sin has always been a popular theme in theological circles.

Unfortunately, we soon found that few of the clergy had the slightest awareness that their oft-quoted proof texts might be highly suspect on linguistic, textual and other grounds. Nor had the theologians themselves felt called upon to deal in theological terms with such matters as "Nature," "Natural Law," "Morals," "Marriage," or, most embarrassingly of all, "Man," when it came to thinking about a population of millions, as Kinsey had then shown to be the case. The earliest issues of *ONE Magazine* began raising such questions but it was only after many years of such prodding that various denominations began to pay some attention to homosexuality. Even today most major denominations are still struggling to come to theological and moral terms with the topic.

Philosophy, though it might claim all knowledge as its purview, was silent on the issue. True, Plato had been notable for seeing that there was indeed something to discuss, but since then philosophers (some of them homosexual themselves) had almost uniformly supported the "Conspiracy of Silence" about the topic as loyally as if in obedience to Mafia enforcers in the halls of academia.

When it came to literary studies it was discovered that most of them were the very models of how to conduct a "conspiracy of silence." To most researchers in such fields the thought of associating homosexuality as an aspect of the life of some great writer appeared to be quite unthinkable. The proposition ran something like: A Great Writer Could Not be Homosexual: Homosexuality Is A Defect: Therefore, The Two Statuses Are Incompatible. Then, why waste time on giving attention to records that would only raise confusion or undermine well-established "knowledge"? The policy seemed to have been thoroughly established at the time, one not to be lightly challenged. When, in 1954 an article in *ONE Magazine* rather decorously dealt with the evidences of Whitman's homosexuality, one of his lesser biographers came storming into *ONE*'s offices to protest such an outrage against a great American monument.

Homosexuals found themselves wholly mystified as to why the entire framework, setting and circumstances of a writer's life and works should be judged relevant in some respects but irrelevant insofar as their homosexual aspects might be concerned. To our unenlightened thinking it seemed possible that a factor such a homosexuality could well have played a very central role in a writer's life and *oeuvre*; that neither of these could be said to be adequately evaluated without considering the implications of so major an aspect of both. Literary research instead, was all too often so absorbed in arcane little private observances as to have drifted quite away from the real writer and the real world. However, despite such cavils it was admitted that the writers themselves often came closer to throwing light upon complex human situations than did any of the more scientific forms of description.

The field of history asked to be believed as telling the story of Man— when and how and why we got into the situations in which we found ourselves. History's elaborate apparatus of political, economic, military and other approaches explained all things, it was said, but could this be true when little or no mention ever was made about a great social "underground" population which must assuredly have had some effects upon the course of human events?

Not only was history discreetly saying little about the homosexuality of England's Edward II, but who was paying any attention to the very real homosexual intrigues surrounding Kaiser Wilhelm prior to the outbreak of World War I? Those on the "Jury" knew enough history to be well aware that historians as a profession seemed to think that the tides of social change took place quite apart from any possible connection to the inner life of human beings, at least if that inner life happened to be homosexually oriented. Awkwardly enough, the inner lives of a great many men and women, pivotal influences in the story of history, were in fact homosexually oriented. Why was it that historians were reluctant to report the records and examine their meanings? A few of them did indeed give some notice to the homosexual aspects of their studies, notably the Durants. Four of the volumes of their *Story of Civilization* had been published by 1950 and contained numerous helpful index references to the presence of homosexuality throughout all historical periods, even though not all historians thought highly of the work of the Durants.

The "Conspiracy of Silence" was in virtually complete control of the field of biology. So also was "The Heterosexual Assumption." Did not everyone know, for instance, that the predestined role of "all" organisms was to exist and then, to reproduce? Biology with great confidence talked of meiosis, mitosis, genes (the helix came a bit after 1950) and achieved high levels of accuracy in reporting but without asking some of the questions which could be asked. As, for instance, did biology have a social obligation to study the genetic implications of the doctrine that reproduction is a law of nature (i.e., a physiological potential) and therefore a value not to be questioned? While such questions were commonplace in the development of agriculture and animal husbandry and had led to many useful developments, there was a mystique which held that it would be inappropriate to apply them to humans.

We found this type of censorship inexcusable. Where more than with humans should serious questions be asked? Biology could be very helpful, it was felt, were it to explore the possibility that there might be positive genetic advantages in encouraging substantial numbers of homosexuals not to reproduce, a consideration quite separate from anything Malthusian. It also seemed not unreasonable to hope that biology could be investigating whole areas of questions concerning human development which had at the time been largely abandoned to the bizarre speculations of medical writers who began with Freud and then soared on and on.

When it came to psychology and psychiatry, what could one say? There certainly was no "Conspiracy of Silence" concerning homsexuality. Psychology and psychiatry already had all the answers, or so it was believed. Whether Bloch, Fenichel, Stekel and other early sexologists or the more contemporary behavioralist and other schools, there seemed to be little agreement between their positions other than that "The Heterosexual Assumption" was an axiom which reigned supreme. Man was by "nature" heterosexual, hence homosexual behavior by definition was unnatural. How, then, can it be explained? The struggles of the psychologists and psychiatrists were instructive regarding the etiology of their theories but, for the most part, of little else.

Why could not all these earnest people just open their eyes to look at homosexuals by the thousands, as Kinsey had done? Instead, like Freud, who with his Dora case had structured towering theories, or others with their handsful of disturbed patients, who had for the most part done no better or worse, homosexuals were often tempted to cry a plague on them all. They found Kinsey a refreshing antidote for too steady a diet of what was predominantly in print at the time. Incurable optimists as the Jury were, they felt sure that one day psychological research would be able to deal comfortably with homosexual behavior minus such labels as deviant, an immature developmental stage, or other phrases from the catechisms of the 1950s. Those of us who were trained in statistical methods took unkind pleasure in pointing out at the time, and for many of the following years, that many a prestigious name in psychology and psychiatry was not above a bit of rearrangement of the data to suit his particular theory.

Fortunately for all concerned, Dr. Evelyn Hooker began her trailblazing studies in the early 1950s. So skeptical was this writer and others whom she approached asking for cooperation with her project, that our attitude was pretty much "just one more of those psychologists." In due time, however, it became clear that she was not going to be afraid to work first with data and then go to theory, instead of the other way around, as had seemed all too customary among psychologists. We soon saw that her work was going to mark the beginning of the end for the "medical model" for viewing homosexuality which had for far too long been saying: homosexuals do not fit our picture of human development; therefore, they must be sick; being sick we will be glad to accept payment for trying to "cure" them.

In the early 1950s sociologists gave homosexuality a sentence, or a paragraph or two, in their works. An exception notable for its being virtually unique at the time was "Sociologic and Legal Aspects of Sexual Deviation," by A. B. Mangus, in *Special Report on California Sexual Deviation Research*, State of California (1954). While scarcely earthshaking in its analysis, these dozen pages did serve to suggest ways of approaching questions about homosexuality in terms radically different from those of the exponents of the "medical model."

Homosexuals found it both incomprehensible and unacceptable that a field which purported to be studying social groups in our culture should have apparently quite overlooked a population of millions of men and women whose patterns of behavior were being given no study or analysis. How could the Grand Designs of so careless a discipline be taken seriously? It seemed fairly obvious that social description must begin by observing all of the numerically major groups found within a population, and especially, those having notably atypical value systems. Despite their failure to have done so, it was hoped that sociologists might still prove to have one of the most helpful methods for arriving at realistic views of homosexuality in our society.

Its indictments against standards of research at the time concerning homosexuality among "experts" and in the universities having been presented, the "Grand Jury" then retired from the field to let others continue. ONE, Inc. thereupon appointed a what-to-do-about-it-all committee to outline the next steps. After several months of further study the committee said in effect "if 'they' will not do the necessary work we must do it ourselves." This led to the formal organization within ONE, Inc. of "ONE Institute of Homophile Studies."

Since 1956, around forty courses have been offered on dealing with such subjects as psychological theories of homosexuality; the sociology of homosexuality; homophile literature; a four-semester survey of homosexuality in history; homophile ethics and many others. *ONE Institute Quarterly of Homophile Studies* began publication in 1958 to provide a forum for such discussions. The twenty-two issues of the journal stand as a remarkable attempt to treat a human phenomenon as a field for serious study rather than as some exotic and curious aberration. Classes and lectures continue at the Institute, expanding and developing information and theory as rapidly as personnel and resources have permitted.

A very valuable resource in this work has been the growth of the Baker Memorial Library (after Blanche M. Baker, M.D., Ph.D., a psychiatrist who worked closely with the Institute during her lifetime), a research collection. The growth and richness of this collection have been very gratifying, particularly so in regard to the number of young doctoral and master's candidates who have come to use it in their work. To summarize, research changes since 1950 have indeed been cause for considerable encouragement. Psychoanalytic dogma has either retreated or drastically revised its anal-oral-Oedipal clichés. Literary journals today can discuss homosexual influences on a writer's work with quite a degree of comfort and freedom. Quite as importantly, university and other presses are starting to issue honest translations of many of the classics. Historians are now beginning to find that social attitudes and sexual behavior are as valid aspects of historical interpretation as is economic theory.

Progress in sociology has been remarkable. Courses in homosexuality in American society are now taught in a number of universities. Law reforms have been made or are under way all across the States and in many cities. Homosexuality is now freely discussed in print and over the air to a degree quite unthinkable in 1950. Here a cautionary note needs to be put forward lest the public discussions be found just one more passing fad and the topic become only another rather arcane topic for the scholars to play around with.

The research decision today, as it has been in the past, is whether homosexuality is something that certain individuals "have" as they might have smallpox or is it a basic phenomenon which is characteristic of a minority population group not yet well understood? It is with such questions and the exploration of their ramifications that the future of research into homosexuality must be sought. Good data-collecting is a must, of course, but the harder part comes in the task of interpretation untainted by a *priori* conclusions and sets of values not relevant to a population so unfamiliar to many of those who undertake such research. While the research goals lie out there for all to see, no claim can be made that the path will be easy.

References

Bloch, Iwan. *Strange Sexual Practices,* trans. Keene Wallis. New York: Anthropological Press, 1933.

————. *Strangest Sex Acts in Modes of Love of All Races.* New York: Falstaff Press, 1935.

Bullough, Vern L. *Sexual Variance in Society and History.* New York: Wiley Interscience, 1976.

Caprio, Frank S. *The Adequate Male*. New York: Medical Research Press, 1962.

Durant, Will, and Durant, Ariel. Various volumes on history of western civilization published by Simon and Schuster.

Fenichel, Otto. *Perversionen, Psychosen, Chakaterstorungen*. Vienna, 1931.

_____. "Uber Homosexualitat." *Psychoan Beweg* (1931): 511–26.

Ford, Clellan S., and Beach, Frank A. *Patterns of Sexual Behavior*. New York: Harper, 1951.

Henry, George W. *Sex Variants*. New York: Paul B. Hoeber, 1948.

Hooker, Evelyn. "The Adjustment of the Male Overt Homosexual." *Journal of Projective Techniques* (1957): 18–31.

_____. "An Empirical Study of Some Relations Between Sexual Patterns and Gender Identity in Male Homosexuals." In *Sex Research: New Developments*, ed. John Money. New York: Holt, Rinehart & Winston, 1965.

_____. "The Homosexual Community." In *Sexual Deviance*, ed. John A. Gagnon and William Simon. New York: Harper & Row, 1967.

_____. "A Preliminary Analysis of Group Behavior of Homosexuals." *Journal of Psychology* 43 (1956): 217–25.

Kinsey, Alfred C.; Pomeroy, W. B.; and Martin, C. *Sexual Behavior in the Human Male*. Philadelphia: W. B. Saunders, 1948.

London, Louis S. and Caprio, Frank S. *Sexual Deviations*. Washington: Linacre Press, 1950.

Stekel, Wilhelm. *Onanisme et homosexualite*. Paris: Gallimard, 1951.

_____. *Bi-Sexual Love*. trans. James Vanteslaar. Brooklyn: Physicians and Surgeons Book, 1934.

17

Charles to Virginia: Sex Research as a Personal Experience

Virginia Prince

Charles Prince and Virginia Prince are the same person. Charles is a transvestite who dresses up as and assumes the role of a woman, and for the last ten years has lived full time as a woman.

About twenty years ago she began publishing a magazine, *Transvestia*, devoted to the subject of transvestism, and in the process has met with and counseled with hundreds of transvestites all around the world. She explains what the recent research has meant both to her and to other transvestites.

There I was walking down the street in the small town. As I walked toward the hotel which was the headquarters of the gathering I had come to attend, I passed many townspeople along the way. Since it was a summer resort town people wore extremely casual and careless clothing. The women were in blue jeans, shirts, boots, etc., without makeup or much jewelry and with short and windblown hairdos. They were quite unremarkable. But here and there would be a woman in a dress, nylons and moderate-to-high heels with well styled hair. They really stood out and they were indeed remarkable. Because all such well turned-out ladies were, in fact, males. The occasion was the third annual Fantasia Fair and it was held in the picturesque resort town of Provincetown, Massachusetts, at the tip end of Cape Cod. This once-a-year gathering attracted males from all over the country who enjoy wearing women's clothing and, if possible, "passing" as women in public.

Such people are called "transvestites" from the latin roots of "trans" (across) and "vesta" (clothing)—as in vest and vestments. The term was coined in the early part of this century by Magnus Hirschfeld, a famous

167

German sexologist. Although he understood homosexuals very well, being one himself, he began to see a lot of German business, professional, and military men who were successful in their careers, married and fathers, yet having one unusual facet in common—they all enjoyed dressing up in women's clothing. This was something new under the psychiatric sun and in the good medical tradition of naming conditions he named this behavioral pattern "transvestism" meaning cross-dressing. This name was coined specifically for heterosexual persons but, unfortunately, of recent years it has come to be used by many people to refer to anyone who cross-dresses for whatever reason. Since the principle motivations of homosexual cross-dressers is generally different from that of heterosexuals who cross-dress, it is not helpful to have a term which does not differentiate between them. Thus I have coined the word "femmiphilia" for the condition and "femmi-phile" for the individual. It means "lover of the feminine" and thus properly describes the heterosexual cross-dresser. The convenient abbreviation "FP" will be used in the balance of this chapter.

The gathering of FPs referred to above was a very interesting experience for all those who attended, and provided a lot of insight into both the participants and to the society in which they were immersed. Attending the fair provided the participants with a very rare opportunity to be their "girl" selves and to be out in the world as "women." Since the town had been posted with invitations to a symposia that would be given for the enlightenment of the townspeople, none of the locals were surprised to see our "women" on the streets and in the hotels, restaurants and shops. As a matter of fact we were the best dressed "women" in town. Perhaps because there are a lot of gay people among the year–round residents, the town was very accepting and open–minded. We were welcomed in restaurants and shops and treated like anyone else. This was a very surprising experience for many of the FPs on their first day. Many had never been out in public dressed before, and even those who had experienced this thrill were accustomed to surreptitiously watching those around them to see whether they were being "read" which is to say, had anyone penetrated their appearance and detected that they were really males in the guise of women. Here in Provincetown that feeling lasted only a few minutes. When they stepped outside, the local people only gave them a passing look as they would anyone and went on their way. After this had happened several times it was obvious that the FPs simply forgot what they were wearing at least insofar as it was something to feel guilty or concerned about. They just walked the streets, went into the curio and other shops, had breakfast and lunch in the restaurants and found that they could really be just "people" like everyone else. It was a very liberating experience for most of them.

The reason for relating this experience is to illustrate how much society has changed in the last twenty years. In 1958 or 68 (and, to be honest, even in 1978 in many parts of the country) a public gathering of men dressed as women could not have taken place anywhere with the exception of the occasional "drag" balls held in various large cities. But these are dress-up evening clothes occasions, not just ordinary people-out-on-the-street affairs. In many parts of the country twenty years ago there were laws which, although worded in various ways, all said the same thing; namely, that while nobody cared if women wore men's clothes, a man could not wear women's clothes without being fined or jailed if caught. This restriction was finally lifted when some attorneys applied the argument of unequal application of the law and unconstitutionally restricting personal freedom. Some places still have such laws but most of them have been challenged and removed from the books. In those days women were not liberated as they are today, gays were still in the closet and sex was pretty much locked up. So progress has been made—and that is encouraging. Now the task is to see that the gains that have been made are not lost.

But what about such people? Why should men want to traipse around in lingerie, dresses and high heels? To risk public censure, possible legal problems, embarrassment and family disruption? Naturally none of them want any of these things to happen and they take great precautions to avoid them. But sometimes they are discovered, parents punish them, wives divorce them, newspapers write about them, friends drop them and they are exposed not as practitioners of a strange but harmless habit, but as degenerate, perverted people. They are then fired from jobs, deserted by friends and in many cases have their lives ruined. Why is it that women can seek their liberation but men cannot?

Past psychiatric wisdom blamed the pattern on dominant and overprotecting mothers, on genetic causes, hormonal imbalance and a lot of other things. While there may be individual FPs who cross-dress for one or another of these reasons, in my opinion none of the explanations get to the root of the matter. Women, on their way to liberation, are well aware of the dividing influences of our society as mediated by parents, schools and peers so that they grow up indoctrinated with femininity and with limited goals. But how many men stop to consider that they too have been indoctrinated with masculinity by the same system? But more than that, they have been indoctrinated *against* femininity. They spend their youth (and their manhood) trying to be sure that no one sees *any* femininity in them. They are oppressed into that form of bisected humanity in precisely the same way as women are pushed into the other half of their bisected humanity.

Curiosity is a basic human characteristic. What happens then, when such a bisected human (young boy or man) walks down the hall in his empty house (the rest of the family having gone away for several hours) and sees his sister's lacy panties thrown carelessly on her bed? Or, when drying off after a shower he picks up the lid to the clothes hamper to throw the towel in it and notices his mother's pink, lace trimmed slip at the bottom? In either case simple curiosity might lead him to pick up the dainty garment, feel its softness and note its lacy trimming. He might well be further motivated to wonder what it might be like to wear garments like that, and if he was he would remove his own clothes to find out. When he puts the garment on he will likely get an erection because that intimate a relationship with a fe-male—even by proxy as it were—would be too much for him. But the experience would be not only erotically exciting, but strangely fulfilling in some other intangible and unexplainable way. But when the orgasm is over he would, if experience is any guide, tear the clothes off, go back into his own, and feel terribly stupid and guilty, unable to understand why he would have done such a thing, swearing he never would do it again. But many would do it again and again.

Whatever the circumstances that originally get a young male (or an older one) into feminine attire, it is likely to stir some depths of awareness that cannot be stirred in any other way. If it does he will repeat the perfor-mance and improve on it as occasion presents itself for many years to come. Every time he indulges he will feel guilty and many times he will swear off, but he will keep it up. Why? Because when "he" is in feminine clothing he finds himself able to make contact with that suppressed part of himself, his own original femininity that he has had to suppress every day. It is the only way that a man can have access to this part of his total self. While young men today *are* making very slow progress in escaping from the rigid limitations of masculinity it is nothing like the progress the women are making.

The experience of Fantasia Fair was not a particularly liberating one for me personally but it was interesting to watch the others adjusting to their new freedom. I knew what they were going through because I had been there and back myself in all the good and bad meanings of the expression. I've seen a lot of changes in society and myself in the last twenty years. Let me share it with you.

Starting at the age of about twelve I found myself fascinated with wearing my mother's clothes on all occasions when the family would be out. It was sexually exciting and thrilling but it was also frightening and it gave rise to a tremendous load of guilt and shame. With that kind of pressure I should have quit—and I did—many times. I felt terrible about it, guilt-ridden and wondering what was wrong with me—an otherwise normal, functional boy. For a while I supposed that I must be a homosexual—though I had no interest in other boys sexually. When I got that straightened out in my head I decided that I must be psychopathic. But on the other hand, I was an intelligent, above-average student, an athlete, member of clubs, etc. But even if I was not either of those two things surely I must be the only otherwise normal boy who was so weird as to want to wear girl's clothes.

I went through adolescence with those worries, and I kept on dressing on every occasion when I thought I could do so safely. While it started out as an erotic experience each time, there came a time when, after eroticism had run its course, I discovered that there was still a very special pleasure in "being" a "girl." Instead of just being an erotically aroused male in a dress, I found that I was somehow different. I did not know for years what was going on—or more properly what was coming out. It was that part of myself that had been hidden and suppressed in all my growing years—just as it is in all men. It was my own other half, that half that when openly expressed is termed feminine. "She," Virginia, was born a long time ago, not as long ago as my legal masculine self, but she first began to work her way out into the light of day the first time I put on something feminine. But I did not know it then. I did not know that in me (as in all other males brought up as boys taught to deny any gentleness, tenderness, grace, beauty, emotion, etc.) there was a "girl within" just biding "her" time. When I, as a boy, put on girl's clothes they were "her" clothes and she knew it and let me know it by the enjoyment I experienced in wearing them.

Now to some people I may sound like someone with a multiple personality or a schizophrenic. I am neither one. In multiple personalities one of the "selves" does not know of the existence of the other. In schizophrenia the personality is not split—the individual is split away from reality. I knew both sides of myself and I lived in a world of intense reality. What I want to emphasize is that all newly born babies, whether male or female, possess all the potentials for human expression that distinguish us from chimpanzees. I am not, of course, referring to those genetic and hormonal programs that distinguish one individual from another, and that develop babies into sexually mature and reproductively functional adults. No, I am referring to the culturally determined behavioral patterns, interests and activities that can be expressed by an individual during his or her life. We all come into life with all of them, but almost immediately we begin to be divided into two parts: that part which is supposedly appropriate to persons of one genital construction and that which is reserved for people of the opposite anatomy. Boys are restricted to those potentials regarded as appropriately "masculine" and are dissuaded from or punished for exhibiting those qualities deemed "feminine." Few if any of these have any biological connection with sex and could as well be expressed by males as by females, and in other cultures many of them are.

But as a boy grows up, any accidental or intentional expression of any so-called "feminine" characteristics brings down parental displeasure and great peer pressure to desist and switch back to appropriate boy-type behavior. Such behavior is naturally associated with one's feeling about one's boyness, a part of which is the kind of clothes boys wear, and, in earlier times, how they wore their hair and dressed with no makeup and little jewelry. Dressed this way a boy tends to act this way and would feel very out of place to be acting in a way that characterizes how a girl might act. But in a dress, regardless of the reason or occasion for getting into it, these feelings can more properly be expressed, and that part of one's total humanity which he has learned to suppress and deny seems to coalesce into an incipient personality as a "she," and she in effect peeps out at the world doubtfully and fearfully. But each time that he dresses after that she steps a little further out into reality. As I have said, I did not realize this in my youth, but as I became more knowledgeable and had more experiences as I got older, I came to realize that that is precisely what happened, and other FPs have repeatedly verified it.

As I grew older I married, had a son and lost both wife and child in a divorce after the former learned of my FP interests. But I also found that there were a few others like myself in the world. Eventually I began to publish a magazine for them called *Transvestia* and then wrote books about the subject such as *Understanding Cross-dressing* and *The Transvestite and His Wife* trying to help them and their wives to understanding, acceptance and peace of mind about the whole thing. (All these items may be obtained from Chevalier Publications, Box 36091, Los Angeles, CA 90036.)

In 1968 after my second marriage ended in divorce, I sold my business. I was then free to live my life as I wanted having no more domestic or business responsibilities. I therefore crossed the gender line completely and I have lived as a woman full time ever since. I am therefore to be classified as a "transgenderist" now and no longer as an FP. But in so doing I did not forget what I learned as a boy and man. My masculine past is alive and well in the back of my head. I have my options back and the choice of what to experience or how to react to it is entirely up to me—I do not *have* to react in a masculine or in a feminine way nor do I have to be consistent between them.

I no longer regard the lingerie, dresses, makeup and jewelry that I wear as being properly the property of the other gender. I now feel after ten years as a woman that I *am* the "other" gender and that the clothing is not only mine legally since I bought them, but properly mine since I regard myself as a woman. This feeling has been fortified by the fact that I have had my beard removed by electrolysis and that as a result of a course of hormone therapy I now possess a nice pair of 38B breasts. Thus I come and go and do whatever I wish just like any other woman. I enjoy the company of men for dinner, dancing, talking, travel, etc. but only up to the point where they change from genderal beings to sexual beings and want to have a sexual experience with me. I am just not oriented that way. I have never had anal or oral copulation with a male and do not desire any. I do not put down those that do, that is their thing, but it is not mine. I did not change my life style for sexual reasons but in order to be able to experience and express the rest of my total humanity.

FPs (transvestites), TGs (transgenderists) and TSs (transsexuals) are often confused in the public mind but they are not the same even though they are all genetic males who wear dresses and appear as women. The FP lives, works and functions as a male and a man and is usually married and a father. He cross-dresses on an occasional basis when the situation permits. He is satisfied with being both a male and a man as long as he has an opportunity to express his "girl within" often enough to keep her pacified. The TG is one who has crossed the gender boundary on a full–time basis. That is, he dresses and lives as a woman twenty-four hours a day and works, travels or housekeeps like any other woman and is in fact a "she." She is not desirous of going through a sex change because she realizes that she is already doing everything that a TS could do after surgery—except copulate with a male and since that is not her orientation, there is no point in going through surgery to attain the possibility. She is content to be a male woman. The TS, on the other hand, wants the surgery, to be totally female or totally male as the case may be.

Although I personally try to dissuade people from having the surgery, except in special cases, it is interesting that three of my best girl friends are former men who have had the surgery. All three are intelligent types which, of course, appeals to me, but somehow I think we are closer and better friends now than we would have been if I had remained Charles and they had remained Tom, Dick, and Harry. Of course we never met as men so how can I make such a statement? Well, I can think of two important reasons. To begin with men are always busy consciously or unconsciously "being" men and proving their masculinity and their adequacy and competency. I know about that because "Charles" my former self, was a very competitive person—in athletics, in high school and college, academically and in social situations. This constant competition keeps a certain wall between men who are otherwise dear friends. Each has to live up to expectations in order to maintain the friendship. Each knows that if he were to slip a little and evince an interest in something feminine or were to dress a little too foppishly or take up some hobby or activity more usual for women, that he would lose face in the eyes of his friends. Thus he toes the mark. The four of us would have done that too—even unknowingly.

The second factor is positive and occurs after our conversion to womanhood rather than before. Women are not as competitive for one thing, so we do not have that to contend with. But more importantly, now we are all open, free to be whatever we are, and to act as seems appropriate at the moment. Being all androgenous individuals (though I prefer "gynandrous" as putting the more important feminine side first) we have access to all of our total selves. If a situation calls for activity we can take it even though natural born females might remain passive; we are all assertive having learned our aggressiveness on the masculine side; we are all physically able to handle ourselves and our bodies somewhat better than most women of our ages are; we know where men are coming from, having been there ourselves, and this makes us better able to deal with them in a straightforward manner, though I must say this sometimes upsets them since they aren't expecting it. We each know where each other has been in our private lives before (as men) so no secrecy is necessary and we can be open about things. But most of all, we are all four "whole" people to a much greater degree than any of us were before, or than other people are now. This gives us a kind of camaraderie and understanding that is very special. We all recognize that we are different and greatly in the minority but out greater knowledge and awareness makes us more than a match for the rest of the world. We all happen to be creative people too, which is another bond between us. It is my firm belief that the greater happiness and peace that TGs and TSs claim is not due to any bodily alteration but simply to the fact that we have all escaped from the bondage of gender role expectations and requirements and are free agents to use everything we learned in the past as one gender as well as what we have learned since the switchover to the new gender.

One remarkable by-product of this is our personal sufficiency. This may not be the best way to put it but it is somewhat indefinable. All four of us live alone, all four of us are perfectly comfortable in doing so. We enjoy our own company when that is appropriate but we all like to go out both together and with other people to dinner, theater or whatever. But the significant thing is that while we are alone we are not lonely. This is an important observation and difference. Most people, except for really reclusive types, are incomplete by themselves and feel more comfortable and happy when living with someone of the opposite sex. Obviously this opens the possibility of sexual relations but I am not talking about that aspect of life. Most marriages serve the purpose of bringing together two persons in a mutual dependency in which the missing (meaning suppressed) parts of one are more or less supplied by the manifest parts of the other so that between the two of them they have at least one complete human being in the house.

When one person is androgenous (gynandrous) and has access to both the masculine and feminine parts of one total person, he or she is not so in need of another person to fulfill life. This unification of the duality of masculine and feminine in one person is what makes people like the four of us so self-sufficient. We enjoy other people but they are not necessary to our happiness and survival. We are good company each for our own private selves.

Having experienced ten years of womanhood now after fifty-five years of masculinity, I have learned a lot of things and experienced a lot of things that had not been part of my life before. Accustomed to being assertive, it was a novel experience for me when I went to dancing school to have to wait until some man asked me to dance—and to see a suitably tall man walking down the line of women and pass me by to ask some other woman while I had to just stand there meekly and take it. That was new. To have a man make a number of individually harmless but collectively direct remarks which were calculated to lead me to bed if I had been so minded, was also new to me. I have learned what all women already know, that is that most of the time men do only have one thing on their minds—sex (as if you did not know!). I have had the experience of losing the friendship of a man when I was foolish enough to beat him in a couple of games of chess. I have become aware that if I should unthinkingly ask a stupid question or do a foolish thing that I *do* not have to feel self-conscious or awkward because men do not see it that way. To them I am a woman and women are unpredictable and do silly things because "she's only a woman." But all of this just adds to one's understanding of what women have been up against since primitive times. My respect for men has been severely shaken and I am a strong supporter of Women's Liberation and of the ERA.

I look to the day when men can come to understand that they are as much in need of liberation as the women, and maybe then we can get on with a rational sort of society that will be better for everyone because *all* the potentials of *all* the citizens will be available to improve human conditions. I think it would be fitting to close with a quotation from Theodore Roszak in an essay titled "The Hard and the Soft" in the book *Masculine-Feminine*. He says . . . "The woman most desperately in need of liberation is the woman every man has locked up in the dungeons of his own psyche. THAT is the basic act of oppression that still waits to be undone, though the undoing might well produce the most cataclysmic reinterpretation of the sexual roles and of sexual normalcy in all human history."

18

Why Did I Do It, or What the Surgery Has Meant to Me

Jude Patton

Earlier in this book Julius Winer explained
some of the procedures involved in
transsexual surgery. Why would anyone want
to have such surgery? This is the question that
Jude Patton addresses himself to in his article.
Born a female, Jude is now a male, and his
account is a very personal one of the meaning
and implications of the past few decades of
sex research and a fitting conclusion to this
book.

"Why did you do it?" "How did you feel when you were a child?" "What was
your life like when you were a female?" "What is your life like now as a
male?" I must have answered these questions and many like them hundreds of
times in the past six years—the years since I underwent sex reassignment
surgery from female to male at Stanford University in 1972.

In 1940, when I was born, "the pill" had not been invented, abortions
were still done in out of the way places by furtive abortionists, and unwed
mothers were still ostracized. It's no small wonder that my biological mother,
a twenty-six year old registered nurse who had conceived me during a
relationship with a married man, gave me up for adoption. I was in a foster
home for just two months before being adopted by a couple who'd been
childless during their first ten years of marriage. As it turned out, I could not
have asked for a better mom and dad than the ones who chose me as their
child.

It's funny, and I've heard this happens quite often, but within a short time
my mom became pregnant and my brother was born within a year of my
adoption. We were very close growing up. From the beginning my parents
placed us in stereotyped "little girl" and "little boy" roles. I wore my long
dark hair in "banana curls" and nearly always was dressed in frilly dresses.
Mom tells me she polished six pairs of white shoes a day, so I'd always be neat
and clean. It probably took six pairs of shoes and then some to keep me clean

177

because I was forever exploring and playing rough games with the boys in the neighborhood. I was often the only girl on the baseball team, or basketball team, or football team and was treated like one of "the guys." I was proud of the fact that I was better at sports than most boys my age and soon was a walking encyclopedia of rules from the basic rulebooks. Also I had an easy time as a student and gained some sense of superior achievement from earning good grades, as well as recognition from peers and teachers.

I think it's much, much easier for girls who are tomboys than it is for boys who are sissies. My tomboy activities really earned me a form of praise or recognition, rather than teasing or harassment. The few girls I chose as friends were also tomboys, though not so entrenched in the whole attitude as I was. I honestly cannot remember any peer pressure—not in grade school or junior high, nor even in high school. I had grown up in a small midwestern town and had gone through all schooling with the same kids, so they just accepted me for whatever I was. Also, knowledge about sexuality or "alternative lifestyles" was practically nil. It was just assumed by everyone that I was a tomboy and would eventually "grow out of it."

Until seven or eight years of age I firmly believed all little girls wanted to grow up to be men. I did not know I had different ideas than my friends. Also, as a child, I could *not* explain the "difference" I felt in myself in the terms that are used by most transsexuals today. I had not *learned* to say that I felt "like a male trapped in a female body structure." But I *was* different and I was constantly aware of that feeling of somehow being in a "different space" than other people—not above, or below, but somehow off to one side—alone.

When I was twelve years old I heard about Christine Jorgensen and read newspaper articles about her. I knew then that I wanted sex reassignment surgery, but I was not sure surgery was available for females. Also I wondered how I would ever get to Denmark and where all the money would come from. So I filed away the information in my mind for something to fantasize about. Fantasy in play, especially in quiet "dreamy" times played a big part in my life from early childhood. I always saw myself as a male—as an adult male, usually as a hero figure of some sort—most fantasies dealt with my rescuing a female or saving the day with my quick wit or physical prowess.

My mom has a photograph of my brother and me, taken when I was six years old, and he was five. We are dressed in identical Roy Rogers cowboy suits and my cowboy hat is cocked down over one eye. I can remember exactly how I felt in that cowboy suit—the image I had of myself as the male hero. I would never have associated the *true* image—a very feminine–appearing little girl with large dark eyes and long dark hair—with the fantasy image.

I must have first heard the words "queer" and "morphadite" (hermaphrodite) when I was about ten years old—epithets hurled at each other, girls and boys alike, during tense play or competition. I don't even think most of us knew what the terms stood for. We just knew they were words of mockery—used to put someone down. When I *did* discover the meanings I began to hunt for books that dealt with sexuality. I can remember sneaking into my mother's bedroom and searching for the marriage manual she kept hidden under clothing in a dresser drawer. Like most kids at that time, what little sex (mis)information I got was generally learned on the streets—from older kids.

Eventually I found books that dealt with homosexuality and something called "Eonism" (named for the Chevalier d'Eon, a famous transvestite). Without exception, these books referred to homosexuality as a mental illness or a criminal activity. By that time I had identified myself as being a lesbian, based on my limited knowledge of a few lesbians who were very mannish-appearing women. Most people were into stereotyped roles in the late forties and fifties, and gays were no exception. One partner in a couple was usually masculine in appearance, the other took a more feminine role. Can you imagine what a terrible burden it is for anyone, especially a child, who has identified himself as being "different at best—a mental case or criminal at worst" and having to struggle with it all on his own because he knows that he cannot discuss his "terrible secret" with anyone, not even with people he loves and trusts. That was my experience, an experience shared by most transsexuals whom I have since met.

To the struggle of dealing with new found self-knowledge, however incorrect, add the struggle of dealing with puberty—something that is difficult for most people, and absolutely devastating for a transsexual. For some time, after reading a particular story in a sex book about a pseudohermaphrodite whose male genitalia dropped down from within his body after a fall over a fence (after having been raised as a girl for twelve years), I fantasized that this could happen to me. I wished on falling stars and four leaf clovers to become a boy; I prayed every night that magically I'd somehow be transformed. Instead, I found my body changing, developing breasts and curves and female body hair distribution. The more my body changed, the more I tried to hide the changes, and the more I became ashamed of my appearance. I cried and stormed out of the room if my mom mentioned buying me a bra. I cried for days after my first menstrual period, because I knew it meant the end of my fantasy of magically changing into a boy. Again, there was no one I felt I could discuss all my feelings with, so I just kept them inside.

At ten years old I had never had my hair cut—it was so long that I could sit on it. But that summer, when school was out, my mom bribed me with a five dollar bill to get it cut. I kept getting it cut shorter and shorter until, at fourteen, I wore a crew cut about an inch long all over my head. I was also wearing boy's clothing at every opportunity. The unisex look was *not* "in" and I still had to wear girl's clothing to school, but every other minute I insisted on wearing a pair of Levi's and shirt. I got to the point that just to gain an additional half hour of being comfortable, I would carry Levi's and a shirt to school with me and then change clothes as soon as the bell rang at 3:30. In girl's clothing I felt so uncomfortable and unnatural that I took great pains to hide myself as much as possible. I'd sit in the back of the room, I'd never walk in front of a crowd of people, never join school social activities. But, in boy's clothes, I felt natural and was comfortable, just being "myself."

By the age of fourteen I began having crushes on girls. Boys had been attracted to me when I had long hair, but when I became so boyish looking in my crewcut and masculine attire, none bothered with me. I was glad not to have to deal with them anyway. My first recognition of being *sexually* interested in females came one morning, after wakening from a dream. I realized I had dreamed of making love to my best friend. I was surprised by the dream, since I had not consciously thought of that kind of feeling. And I was so naive about sex that I did not even know what I wanted from "making love" except physical closeness and kissing. I was painfully shy and completely nonassertive or aggressive, so I was sixteen years old before my first overt experience with a girl. She initiated the friendship and, later, the physical intimacies. I can remember clearly one particular incident after I had spent the night with her. Her mother observed what we *thought* was a secretive kiss—a kiss that obviously was not a "sisterly" one. I was sure we would be punished, that we would never be allowed to see each other again. Instead, her mother told her that she hoped that she did not become too close to me—that she had a girlfriend once whom she had loved very much and had gotten hurt when the relationship ended. Our relationship ended too, after almost a year. For her it had been only an adolescent phase, an experience that I doubt was ever repeated. For me, it was the "real thing." I was hurt and "carried a torch" for a long time. I lost weight, was generally depressed, and convinced I was somehow unworthy of love.

During that period I managed to finish high school. I began having problems with teachers and counselors—but *not* because I was a poor student or one who was a troublemaker. I am sure my mandatory visits to a school counselor were the result of my "difference" and my masculine appearance and behavior, but it was never discussed openly—except for such questions as, "Why don't you let your hair grow and try to look more feminine?" Other adults began suggesting to my parents that there must be something wrong with me and that perhaps they should take me to a psychiatrist. Thank God they never did. Instead, they defended me, saying, "She's our daughter and, if wearing men's clothing and having short hair makes her happy, that's what we want for her." I can only imagine what might have happened if a psychiatrist had attempted to "cure" me.

My dad had been sick almost constantly with one physical complaint or another from the time I was about fourteen. His most severe problem was his heart. His usual occupation was as a pipefitter, though he hardly ever managed to work more than a few months at a stretch because of either illness or bad weather. At the time I graduated from high school, both he and my mom were in the hospital. I used that as an excuse not to attend my high school graduation. The real reason is that everyone dressed formally and I was horrified at the thought of wearing a dress and hose and high heels. From the time I left high school I have never worn female attire again, except on one occasion—when my dad died, just before my twenty-first birthday. I did it out of respect for him and I was so uncomfortable that I could not even think about his death, just how unnatural I felt. I was tearing the clothes off on the ride back home from the funeral, anxious to get back to my masculine clothing. Being forced to wear feminine attire was also the major factor in my refusal to attend college. In those days, women could *not* attend school wearing shorts or slacks. I turned down a four-year full scholarship because I knew I could not subject myself to four more years of *skirts!*

During the first couple of years after leaving high school, I discovered that I was not very employable. Employment was at a low anyway, but employers generally took one look at me and never hired me, because of my appearance. I could *not* pass as a man, I looked like a young boy instead. (I got into movies for fifty cents when I was twenty-six years old because they thought I was under twelve.) Actually, I could not sustain the charade of "boy" for any prolonged period of time. Most of the time I left people wondering what "it" was. In no time at all, I learned what prejudice was. I was the butt of cruel jokes, aware of snickering and stares and remarks following me everywhere. But I had dealt with *feeling* different and I learned to deal with others' hostility; I could turn it around in my mind so that *they* were the ones who were wrong, not I! Instead of feeling miserable about being different, I was proud of my difference. I even began to *work* at being different. In the days when few were "out of the closet," there I was "letting it all hang out." I actually found some sort of perverse pleasure, knowing that my masculine appearance caused some people discomfort.

Most of my leisure moments were spent in sports activities—but no longer on neighborhood boys' teams. Instead, I bowled nearly every evening, becoming good enough to win several trophies and prizes. I also liked solitary activities, particularly horseback riding. The lack of a job and income left me feeling pretty low. I scrounged for money to go out—taking any kind of odd job, from delivering flowers for a florist (at ninety-three cents an hour) to digging ditches for a neighbor to babysitting or taking in ironing. My dad's major illnesses had put our family on a financial roller coaster, and his death was the final stop.

Finally, I found semisteady employment in factory work—first at a glass container manufacturer and later at a large company as an ammunition and explosives inspector. From the first night on the job, I was thrown in among women who were lesbians. In fact, I was sought out *because* of my boyish appearance.

Being boyish looking, I was later to learn, had certain advantages in attracting women and certain disadvantages in maintaining relationships, once begun. It seems to me that for the most part, the women who were attracted to me were attracted by the masculinity. And yet they could not deal with being labeled "gay." I also seemed to attract women who had had little or no prior experience with lesbian relationships. It was almost like being a stepping stone. I was the step between being attracted to males and being attracted to females. Of course, it was not so obvious to me at the time—but after reflecting on past relationships, the theory seems to hold some truth.

I also was to learn that being "obvious" and "out of the closet" at a time when few dared to be meant that it was not only difficult for straight people to deal with me, but for gays too. I was an embarrassment to them. If seen with me, others might point an accusing finger at them. Sometimes I was asked not to attend certain functions or not to come into gay bars. From the beginning of my association with the gay lifestyle, I recognized that I still felt "different" and the lesbians I became friends with were also aware of the difference. Yet none of us knew how to describe the difference. Just as I had been surprised as a child to learn that all little girls did not want to grow up to be men, I was surprised—and disappointed—to learn that masculine lesbians did not want to be men either. Many hours were spent philosophizing—trying to explain my thoughts to my friends without the knowledge of the correct terms to describe my feelings. Finally, I was acknowledged as being O.K.—kind of like being a tomboy was O.K. After all, *maybe* I'd grow out of these feelings, too.

My early shyness continued even after meeting several women and being involved in short-term relationships with them. But I gained a reputation, of sorts, as being very intelligent and another reputation as a good lover. I soon found myself in demand—with women pursuing *me*. I went from one relationship to another, sometimes dating three women in one day. I was flattered by the attention—really needed it to counteract my failures in gaining employment and the ever-present prejudice. During this same period I met a woman that I fell very much in love with. I was attracted to Janet from our first meeting. She was in a gay bar for the very first time in her life at the invitation of a woman she worked with. What was amusing was that I was pointed out as an example of being "too far out" to be acceptable. Perhaps that was what interested her. In the next seven months we spent more and more time together. We could talk for hours on end and I like to believe that we found each other fascinating. I deliberately adopted a "hands off" attitude, though I was sure Janet knew of my feelings for her. What I did not know is that she was hoping that I'd make the first move. Finally, we both made the move at the same time. What a marvelous period of my life—being in love with someone who was in love with me. There was more than that for me in the relationship. I also felt our involvement was symbolic somehow of an elevated status for me. After all, I had won her love in competition with all the others who had tried. And, believe me, they tried. Janet was attractive, intelligent, and *new* to the gay scene. That last qualification probably was first in importance for some.

After the first months of love went by, I became gradually aware that the woman I loved was ashamed of my appearance. Janet was afraid that people would label her a gay if she were seen with me. Soon she would only accompany me to drive-in movies or to gay bars. She would not be seen with me in other public places. When her friends or relatives visited her, I was asked to hide—to *literally* get in a closet, or a bedroom, or the bathroom. When problems in our relationship had begun to occur, I had, on the spur of the moment, hitchhiked to California. With the difficulties in our relationship and employment problems, and the continual harassment because of my adopted lifestyle, I had gotten to the point of wanting to run away and start anew. California had always been a dream for me. We laughed and called it "the land of fruits and nuts." I was positive that I would find more acceptance in the liberal atmosphere I'd heard about.

I stayed with friends for the first couple of months. I had gotten a job the day after my arrival in Los Angeles, doing work that I had always wanted to do, as a veterinary assistant. So it seemed as if the decision to come to California had been the correct one. The initial year saw many changes. I learned that within two weeks of the time I had left home, my grandmother was placed in a nursing home and my mother was placed in a state mental institution by "well-meaning relatives." Janet had promised to join me in California as soon as possible. Instead, she did not correspond for over six months. I phoned her long distance two and three times a week. Finally she told me that she was not sure that she cared for me any longer and suggested that our relationship would never be resumed. I began to develop new friendships and eventually began dating other women. Within a year I had established a steady relationship with another woman and we planned to move in together. About the same time I received a phone call from Janet saying she had decided to come to California after all and expected me to put her up. Our relationship was established again, and my other relationship ended. I learned that Janet was dependent on pills. She needed dexadrine just to be able to get through the day. She developed her dependence when a physician prescribed dexadrine for her chronic lack of energy and fatigue. Years later she learned that hypoglycemia was the cause of her fatigue. But meanwhile she began with one pill per day and by the time she kicked the habit (after the end of our relationship) she was up to eight or ten 15 mg. dexadrine spansules per day. Living with her became almost a nightmare. With pills she just barely managed, without them she slept for twenty hours at a time, could not or would not hold a job. I desperately wanted her love and for the relationship to return to the way it had been in the beginning. I lived for a way to make her happy even when it meant buying pills on the street or during a trip to Tijuana.

It was during this period, about the age of thirty, that I first learned that sex reassignment surgery had been performed on females. I began searching for more information, not really knowing where to look. Fate stepped in; within a relatively short time span I met two persons who were preoperative female to male transsexuals. In fact, one of them was hired at the same place that I worked. Through them I learned what books and other sources of information were available. I also learned where to go for psychiatric evaluation, and once approved, where to receive hormone therapy. I was excited and elated at finally beginning on the road to my true identity. Not having any guidelines, I hardly knew what to expect. The physical changes were much more rapid than I anticipated. Within two weeks after beginning hormone therapy my voice changed from a soprano to a lower tone. By the end of six weeks I was shaving my face every day. The hair growth began under my chin and gradually developed into a full beard. Since I had remained on my old job, and wanted to continue there until I had surgery, I opted for wearing long sideburns, but no beard. I still cannot believe that the customers were so unaware of the physical changes. They saw only what they expected to see. Some other physical changes were also rapid—menstrual periods stopped immediately, I grew hair on my chest, abdomen, and back and the hair on my arms and legs increased. It was like going through puberty a second time, only this time loving every change.

For most transsexuals the initial period of transition may present an array of problems. Many have attempted to conform to society's expectations of their biological sex and have tried desperately to present the image/role presumed to be their destiny. Since I had *not* conformed to the feminine role expected of me and had lived at an "in-between" stage for over fifteen years, the transition went smoothly. As I became more masculine in physical appearance, the questioning looks and remarks ended. It was not long before I was presumed to be male.

Just after beginning hormone therapy I met Marilyn in a gay bar. She had been curious about the possibilities of a relationship with a female, since she had been unhappy in her marriage and in other relationships with males. She approached things head on, by going to a place where she was most likely to encounter a number of lesbians. She was attracted to very masculine-appearing females, which was the primary reason she became involved with me. I've always valued honesty, so I told her at the time we met that I was not a lesbian, but a transsexual, and of my plans for sex reassignment. I thought that she might choose not to continue seeing me, but instead she was fascinated by the whole idea. We began seeing each other on a regular basis. I wasn't really ready to begin another committed relationship, because I was still dealing with the feelings I had for Janet and the pain of losing her. So I encouraged Marilyn to see other people and not become too involved with me. I felt I could not give her the kind of complete love and devotion she was so willing to give me and so desperately wanted for herself. For a time she did see other people, while I continued to go out, but usually did not date. Eventually we drifted back together. Her help and support during the preoperative transition period was invaluable.

In 1970 my mom remarried and moved with her new husband, a seventy-eight year old widower, to California. After a few months they bought a house in Santa Ana. I visited them every weekend and sometimes once during the week. They had only been married six months when my stepfather suffered a stroke, which left him paralyzed on one side and unable to speak coherently. After a short period of hospitalization, he was sent home for my mother to care for. Because of his condition, he needed constant supervision. My visits increased until finally I gave up the small house I rented and moved in with them and began commuting to work to Los Angeles.

One of the many things to be dealt with once the decision for sex reassignment is made is how to tell relatives and friends. I waited until the last minute to tell my mom what I planned to do. Amazingly, she had not noticed the physical changes that were apparent to most others. I was worried that she might have too much to handle with my stepfather's recent stroke and now my sex reassignment. So I did not tell her of my plans until one night about two weeks before the first surgery was scheduled. Her immediate reaction was "Ho hum, I'm tired and I think I'll go to bed." The next morning her major worry was the fact that I would be undergoing major surgery and she had the usual concerns that most mothers have.

By the time my sex reassignment surgery was scheduled, I had been on hormone therapy for about a year and had been living in a male role. I had had one 1½ hour psychiatric evaluation to begin receiving hormones and another 1½ hour psychiatric evaluation at Stanford, during their screening process. I've never had any psychotherapy or counseling. The rest of the screening process included a complete physical examination, including a buccal smear to check my chromosomes, and a hormonal assay to check levels of hormones. The exam showed that my body was that of a normal female. I also was required to meet with a lawyer, a peer advisor, and the surgeon who would perform the operations.

In September of 1972 I underwent the initial stage of surgery, a reduction mammoplasty and the beginning of construction of a penis from tissue taken from the abdomen and skin grafts from my thigh. Again, I had no idea what to expect from the surgery—except the two photos of results from two other similar surgeries shown to me by the surgeon. The pain was not only bearable, it was far, far less than I had anticipated. I think the state of euphoria I experienced from finally having achieved my goal had much to do with the lack of pain. I can remember waking up and looking down and seeing that my chest was flat and touching my chest and genitals through the layers of bandages to see if it was really true. In December I underwent a second surgery. This time the construction of the penis was finished and I had a total hysterectomy. A few months later, in April, 1973, I had a third surgery to close the vagina and add (prosthetic) testicles. Unfortunately, I developed complications from that surgery and had to return in September to have one of the procedures repeated. So, it was almost exactly a year from the start to the finish of my surgical transition. The total cost amounted to about $6500.00. But I also lost approximately six months' income. Marilyn and I resorted to all sorts of tactics to raise money for the costs. We sold some of our possessions, borrowed money from small loan companies, invested in stock (and *doubled* the money in two months!). Several friends loaned me varying amounts of money. It took me *years* to repay the loans and I *still* owe Marilyn money.

I had no idea of what the final appearance and function of my "new" body would be. But I can comfortably go without a shirt even though there is minimal scarring on my chest. I am able to have intercourse, and both I and my partner can achieve orgasm. Of course there are limitations, particularly in urinary function. But doctors are working on new techniques and I am confident that, when improvements are offered in the existing methods of surgery, I can go back for revision.

Like most transsexuals, I expected that after surgery I would live my life in my new identity as a "normal" male and pursue ordinary interests. But I've always considered myself as outside the ordinary, and I think most people who know me agree. During the year of surgery I was asked by a friend to contact a college professor who was interested in having a transsexual share his experience with students in a human sexuality class. I was frightened at the prospect of being "on stage," but the experience was something I actually enjoyed. That one incident changed the course of my life. Through word of mouth, I began getting more and more invitations to speak at classes and seminars. Eventually professionals began referring people to me for information and peer counseling. My interest grew and I found that I devoted more and more time to these activities and less and less to others.

Meanwhile, I was determined to finally begin my formal college education. I had taken many kinds of classes before, but none for credit. However, I had *never* stopped self-education. I had always had a voracious appetite for books, and some time ago had ceased to read most fiction in favor of nonfiction books. My favorite reading was in human sexuality (particularly "deviant" sexuality), psychology, and biology. I managed to arrange working hours so that I had the majority of the day free and began going to college. I felt I had lost so much in time and opportunity that I wanted to do all I could to make up for it as fast as I could. By my third semester I was attending one school as a full-time student and three others as a part-time student. I was in school five days a week, four evenings, and watched televised courses on weekends, all the while working two part-time jobs and continuing my activities as a guest speaker and peer counselor. That semester I managed to take thirty-eight semester units—or more than double the normal academic load. I was *not* a 4.0 average student, but I did manage to earn three scholarships and a couple of grants, and transferred from a junior college to a four-year university. I graduated in June, 1978, from U.C., Irvine, with a B.A. in social ecology as well as a B.A. in psychology in an external degree program at another university. In addition, I have completed all the courses necessary for certification as a hospital pharmacy technician. Last year I took the state exam and became a registered animal health technician. Because my interests and activities have centered more and more around furthering education about minority lifestyles and counseling, I'm presently enrolled in a degree program leading to an M.A. in marriage, family and child counseling. I plan to work with persons who've lived in so-called "alternative lifestyles" or who exhibit "deviant behavior." I feel that I have a lot to offer in knowledge and empathy, as well as a constructive philosophy of coping with problems in these areas. I am very encouraged by the response I've received from educators and people in the helping professions.

Without the support of my girlfriend, Marilyn, and my mom, I know I could not possibly have accomplished everything I've done so far. I feel rich in the experiences I have had and continue to share with others. I feel confident that the future holds more of the same. I like and respect the person I've become and I hope to continue to grow. A few weeks ago a student asked me the question, "If you were just born today, would you choose to be born male and never have to *seek* sex reassignment, or to be born female and *never want* sex reassignment, or to be born female and have sex reassignment just as you've done?" I was prepared to answer immediately, because I'd asked that same question of myself, years ago. My answer to myself then, and my answer to the student's question is the same: If I had the choice, I would do it exactly *the same* way I did it. I could not be the kind of person I am today without the experiences I've had, and I value the person I have become. Marilyn puts it another way. She says that she has always related to what is between my ears, not what is between my legs. When a student asked her whether she would choose to date a male or a female if our relationship ended, her reply was that she would choose a transsexual. She was *not* implying that a transsexual was physically androgynous, but she feels that socially and emotionally she is relating to a person who embodies both masculine and feminine qualities — a *whole* person.

Occasionally a friend I haven't seen in years will exclaim, "But you haven't *really* changed, you're still the same person." They expect that a "sex change" would change not only physical appearance, but the entire personality. I try to explain to them that I am still the same person, looking *out* through the same eyes, but it is they who are looking *in* at me differently. Perhaps that is the reason I've chosen to try to promote understanding among people about others who are labeled as "different." For years I was treated as something less than human. Today, I have the same basic sense of values, etc., but because I've changed my exterior so that it truly reflects who I am inside, I am treated as worthwhile. I contend that I was "worthwhile" and "human" all along. I hope I can help others to experience their "differentness" with dignity and pride.

A Guide to
Further Reading

A good way to investigate further into the ongoing research in the sex field is to read some of the current research. Some of the monographic literature is available in the specialized journals dealing with sex, and these also include bibliographical listings of research published in other journals. See, for example, the *Journal of Sex Research, Archives of Sexual Behavior, Journal of Homosexuality, Journal of Sex Role Research, Journal of Marriage and the Family,* and the *SIECUS Report.* This last is a monthly publication of the Sex Information and Education Council of the United States, and it makes a special effort to summarize some of the current literature.

For earlier studies there are several bibliographic guides. A good overall bibliography is Flora C. Seruya, *Sex and Sex Education: A Bibliography* (New York: Bowker, 1972). More specialized is Vern Bullough, Dorr Legg, Barret Elcano, and James Kepner, *An Annotated Bibliography of Homosexuality* (2 vols., New York: Garland Publishers, 1976). More analytical and selective is Martin S. Weinberg and Alan P. Bell, *Homosexuality: An Annotated Bibliography* (New York: Harper & Row, 1972). For prostitution, see Vern Bullough, Barret Elcano, Bonnie Bullough, Margaret Deacon, *A Bibliography of Prostitution* (New York: Garland, 1977). Particularly helpful is the *Catalog of the Social and Behavioral Sciences, Monograph Section of the Library of the Institute for Sex Research, Indiana University* (4 vols., Boston: G. K. Hall, 1975). For an update on the status of the current laws, *The Sexual Law Reporter* is particularly helpful.

Offering a general overview of the field of sex research as of the 1960s is Albert Ellis and Maurice Abarbanel, eds., *The Encyclopedia of Sex Behavior* (2 vols., New York: Hawthorn, 1967). Several college level texts are also helpful, such as Erwin J. Haeberle, *The Sex Atlas* (New York: Seabury Press, 1978) and Herant A. Katchadourian and Donald T. Lunde, *Fundamentals of Human Sexuality* (2nd ed., New York: Holt, Rinehart and Winston, 1975). At a more popular level, but equally helpful, is Alex Comfort, *The Joy of Sex* (New York: Crown, 1972).

More specialized studies include John Money and Anke Ehhardt, *Man and Woman, Boy and Girl* (Baltimore: Johns Hopkins University Press, 1972); the two Kinsey studies, Alfred C. Kinsey, et al., *Sexual Behavior in the Human Male* (Philadelphia: Saunders, 1948), and *Sexual Behavior in the Human Female* (Philadelphia: Saunders, 1953). More recent, and plagued by a poor sampling technique but still helpful, is Shere Hite, *The Hite Report* (New York: Macmillan, 1976). For an historical viewpoint, see Vern L. Bullough, *Sexual Variance in Society and History* (New York: Wiley Interscience, 1976), and Vern L. Bullough and Bonnie Bullough, *Prostitution* (New York: Crown, 1978). See also Vern L. Bullough, *Sex, Society and History* (New York: Neale Watson, Science History, 1976). For a more popular study, see Vern L. Bullough and Bonnie Bullough, *Sin, Sickness and Sanity* (New York: Garland, 1978; New American Library, 1977). Also helpful is Norman Himes, *Medical History of Contraception* (New York: Schocken, 1970), and John T. Noonan, *Contraception* (New York: New American Library, 1967). For sexual problems and therapies, see William Masters and Virginia E. Johnson, *Human Sexual Response* (Boston: Little, Brown, 1966) and *Human Sexual Inadequacy* (Boston: Little, Brown, 1970); Helen S. Kaplan, *The New Sex Therapy* (New York: Bruner/Mazel, 1974); Richard Green, *Sexual Identity Conflict in Children and Adults* (New York: Basic Books, 1974), and John Money and Richard Green, eds., *Transsexualism and Sex Reassignment* (Baltimore: Johns Hopkins University Press, 1969); William Hartman and Marilyn Fithian, *Treatment of Sexual Dysfunction* (Long Beach, Calif.: Center for Marital and Sexual Studies, 1972). There are many others including the works listed in the bibliography of each article. The interested reader should simply begin, and by using this book as a kind of guideline he/she will soon be able to tell what is valid research and what is not.